MACEDONIA

HISTORY · MONUMENTS · MUSEUMS

Publishers:
George A. Christopoulos, John C. Bastias

Managing editor: Myrto Stavropoulou
Art director: Tonia Kotsoni
Translation: David Hardy
Secretariat: Anna Carapanou, Maria Leventopoulou
Photo research: Evi Atzemi, Anna Carapanou
Maps: Tonia Kotsoni (historical),
        "CHARTOGRAPHICA HELLENICA" G.D. Tsopelas (modern)
Topographical maps and archaeological plans: EIKONOTYPO S.A.
Photography: Sotiris Chaïdemenos, Dimitris Benetos, Yannis Krikis, Pantelis Magoulas
Colour separation: F. Sakellariou – P. Mougios Ltd.
Phototypesetting: G. Athanasiou
Printed and bound in Greece by EKDOTIKE HELLADOS S.A.

The section on the Macedonian dialect of the Greek language was
written by Mrs. Anna Panayotou, Professor of Linguistics
at the University of Cyprus.

MACEDONIA

HISTORY · MONUMENTS · MUSEUMS

IOANNIS TOURATSOGLOU

Ephor of Antiquities

EKDOTIKE ATHENON S.A.
Athens 1998

ISBN 960 - 213 - 330 - 9
Copyright © 1995
by EKDOTIKE ATHENON S.A.
1, Vissarionos St., Athens 106 72
Greece

CONTENTS

Prologue

The Guide to Macedonia by Dr. Ioannis Touratsoglou, Ephor of Antiquities, is an itinerary through the Greek land of Macedonia, its history and its monuments. Macedonia's natural beauty and its wealth of monuments make it a favoured land in which to wander, offering the visitor both emotional and intellectual stimulation. With all its diversity, Macedonia never disappoints.

Macedonia occupies a particularly important position in the general historical advance of Hellenism. According to a statement in the historian Polybius, this region was the "rampart" of Greece against the invaders from the north, thus enabling the Greeks of the south to develop their classical civilization. Ancient Macedonia, however, also brought about the political unification of ancient Hellenism under the leadership of its king Philip and this enabled his warrior son, Alexander, at the head of the Macedonians and other Greeks, to conquer almost the entire known world within the space of ten years, disseminating Greek culture and the Greek spirit to the ends of the inhabited world. Alexander and his Macedonians, finally, were the exponents of human values that had been born and developed in the Greek world, and the creators of a spirit of ecumenism and intellectual unity, preparing the ground in this way for the spread of Christianity. The new modes of thought, of life and of art, in the form in which they took root in the East, were encountered there by the Romans, who were already familiar with them from their contact with the Greek world of Southern Italy and Sicily.

The wealth of discoveries from excavations of recent years in Macedonia, moreover, has shown that in this northern part of the Greek world, there occurred during the 4th century B.C. a synthesis of the artistic currents of the different Greek workshops, and a crystallization of the forms of Greek art, particularly in painting and architecture. The artistic prestige and influence of Macedonia contributed to the formation of the nature of Roman art and Macedonian artistic achievements of the 4th century B.C. served as its models (in the sphere of painting: the similarity of the wall-paintings in the Macedonian tombs and on Macedonian painted stelai to Roman wall-paintings, and in the sphere of architecture: the parallels between the Macedonian house and the Pompeian style of house-villa). Thereafter, Rome brought the work of the Macedonians to completion, transmitting the Greek heritage to the West.

The modern visitor, browsing in the rooms of the Archaeological Museum of Thessalonike, and on archaeological sites such as Pella, Dion, Amphipolis, Olynthos, and above all Vergina with its brilliant royal tombs, can make contact with the impressive Greek civilization of ancient Macedonia.

Roman and Byzantine Macedonia have no cause to envy Ancient Macedonia. Thessalonike, co-capital of the Byzantine Empire and one of the largest Medieval European cities, is full of brilliant examples of Byzantine architecture and Byzantine art, which supplement the majestic public buildings of the Roman period that preceded it. Other cultural centres flourished, too - Kastoria, for example, or Beroia, culminating in the unique monastic state of Mount Athos which is still today a "living Byzantium".

The Macedonia of more recent times, too, can point to the brilliant *archontika* (mansions) owned by Macedonian merchants under the Ottoman Empire, at Siatista, Kozani, Kastoria, Beroia and elsewhere, and can offer to the visitor memories of the struggles of Macedonian Hellenism for national liberation.

We believe that this brief Guide will form an ideal introduction to this ancient Greek land and will help the visitor to comprehend its cultural message and accord to it the affection it deserves.

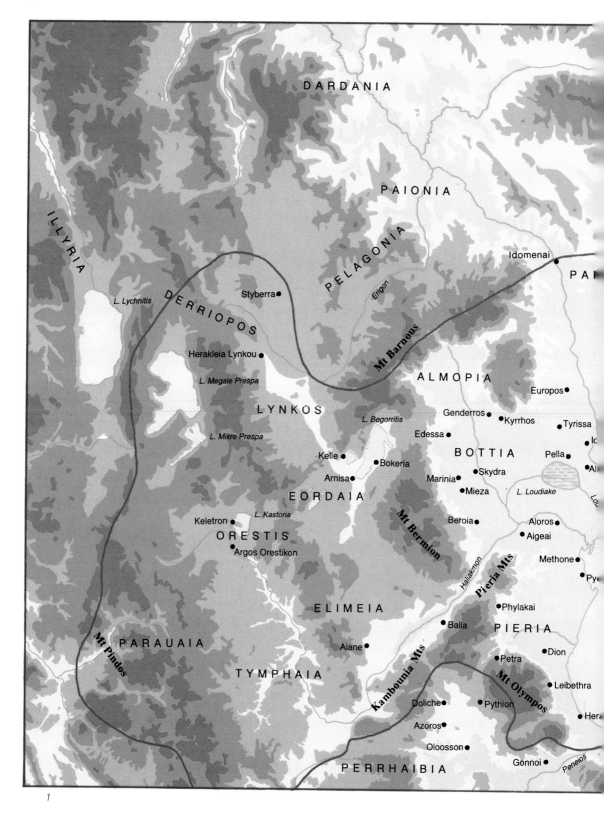

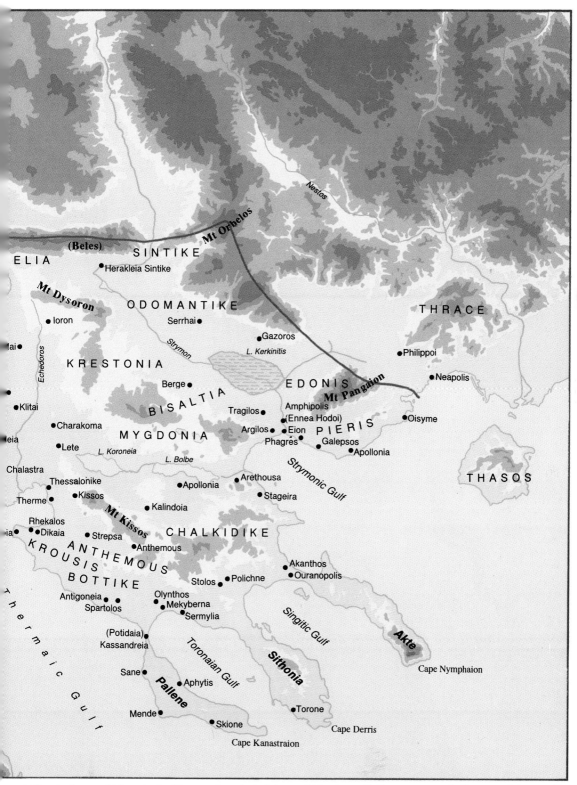

1. *Physical map of Macedonia. The great central plain of Bottiaia and the small plain of Pieria, can be seen, watered by the rivers Haliakmon, Loudias, Axios and Echedoros. Both are surrounded by mountain massifs. The boundary of Macedonia before the Roman conquest is indicated by a red line.*

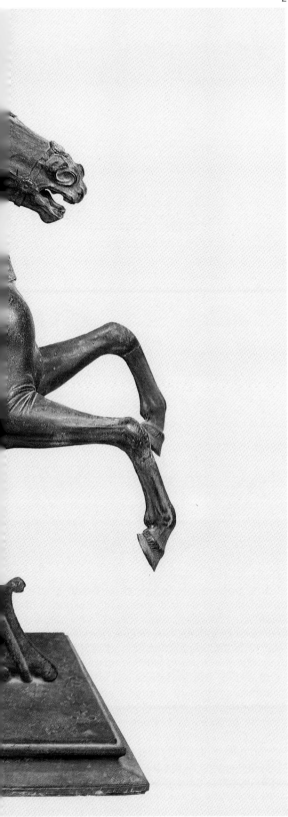

2

HISTORICAL REVIEW

Occupying the bigger part of northern Greece, Macedonia first appears on the historical scene as a geographical-political unit in the 5th century B.C., when it extended from the upper waters of the Haliakmon and Mount Olympos to the river Strymon. In the following century it reached the banks of the Nestos. The history of the Macedonians, however, may be said to commence somewhere around the beginning of the 7th century B.C.; at this time the Greek tribe of the *Makedones,* whose home was in Orestis, began to expand, driving out the Thracians and contending with the Illyrians, and gradually occupied Eordaia, Bottiaia, Pieria and Almopia, finally settling in the region called by Thucydides "Lower Macedonia, or Macedonia by the Sea".

Prehistoric period

This region of high mountains, large rivers, lakes and fertile plains makes its appearance on the stage of civilization as early as the Early Neolithic Period (Nea Nikomedeia, region of Yanitsa). The density of the settlements, however, shows a vertical increase at the end of the 5th millennium B.C. (Late Middle Neolithic) and attests, throughout the whole of the region though especially in central and east Macedonia, to significant mobility on the part of the population and to its characteristic dynamism. These same settlements prospered until the Early Bronze Age - that is, until the beginning of the 3rd millennium B.C. -most of them organized in the plains, with houses either square or rectangular in plan, sometimes with wooden

2. Alexander the Great buried those who died at the Granikos' battle with great honour. A special posthumous tribute was reserved for his 25 Companions who fell in the battle. Alexander commissioned 25 bronze equestrian statues from the great sculptor Lysippos and erected them alongside a statue of himself at the Macedonian sacred city of Dion. Pictured is a bronze statuette of Alexander astride Boukephalas, a copy of the statue by Lysippos (Florence, Archaeological Museum).

3

4

5

posts and sometimes with stone foundations for the walls.

Stock-breeding, based on the raising of goats and sheep, was one of the prime factors in Macedonia's development, in combination, of course, with other intra-community activities and occupations, such as hunting and fishing. An improvement in the quality of diet is indicated by the diversity of crops cultivated: grain, vines and olives. Exchanges of cultural goods (jewellery, quality pottery) now multiplied, clearly an example of prestige gifts rather than evidence of commercial contacts.

The Bronze Age finds Macedonia with fewer settlements, a circumstance that may be interpreted either as the result of the contraction of the population or as the result of the development of central cores at the expense of small-scale satellite settlements. The houses are now quite frequently two-roomed, with the areas relating to the preparation of food kept separate; they are constructed with wooden posts, and have one of the ends apsidal in form. A still primitive system of planned streets can be detected in some of the settlements.

Both bovines and sheep and goats, along with pulses and cereals (wheat and barley) formed part of the daily diet of the inhabitants of Macedonia, who at this period were serving their apprenticeship in the production of bronze tools, used alongside stone implements. The pottery, and especially the quality pottery, usually

3. Early Neolithic clay female figurine from Nea Nikomedeia, ca. 6000 B.C. Beroia, Archaeological Museum.

4. Middle Neolithic painted vase from Servia, ca. 4500 B.C. Florina, Archaeological Museum.

5. Late Bronze Age vase with incised decoration from Tsaousitsa. 1500-1050 B.C. Thessalonike, Archaeological Museum.

6. Gold funerary mask and bronze "illyrian" helmet from a tomb at Sindos, ca. 520 B.C. Thessalonike, Archaeological Museum.

monochrome, reveals relations with the Bronze Age pottery of central Europe, neighbouring Epirus and Thessaly, and also with that of the north-east Aegean. In time, it also acquired a certain independence, despite the fact that in the later centuries of this same period (Bronze Age), it was to be influenced by the outstanding achievements of the Mycenaean wheel.

Overworking of the land and the steady increase in the density of the settlements, which now show a preference for semi-mountainous sites, suggest the evolution, with the passage of time, of a certain hierarchy and a central authority. The articulation of society is indicated in a general way by the differentiation in burial customs.

The transition to the following period, the Early Iron Age, though not yet clearly demarcated, is distinguished by clear destruction levels or levels indicating the abandonment of settlements. The houses, with stone-built bases, now frequently have wattle-and-daub walls. The dead were generally buried in organized cemeteries with earth tumuli covering groups of cist graves, simple burials directly in the earth or in jars; this is one of the hallmarks of the period, which is defined by the appearance of protogeometric decorative elements on the local pottery (Vergina, West Macedonia), the lavish use of bronze objects, mainly jewellery, the founding of settlements on spacious sites, and the exploitation of iron deposits for the construction of weapons.

Geometric and Archaic periods

The relative isolation of the Macedonian region in the period from the 10th to the 8th centuries B.C. - an isolation due to the temporary unavailability of the commercial routes from south to north - was soon overcome, and Macedonia entered upon the Archaic period as the promised land for the hundreds of colonists who came to the coasts of the Aegean from many cities in southern Greece. It was during this period that colonists from southern Greece founded Methone, Sane, Skione, Potidaia, Akanthos and many other cities-ports on the coasts of Pieria and Chalkidike.

Bounded to the south by a long chain of mountain ranges -Ossa, Olympos and the Kambounian Mountains, to the west by the Pindos range, to the east by the river Strymon and then the Nestos, and to the north by Orbelos, Menoikion, Kerkine, Boras and Barnous, Macedonia was cut off from the main body of Greece, on the ramparts of Hellenism, and lived until the 6th century by the teachings of the Homeric epic.

The state-form was unusual: in one sense a federal state composed of autonomous Macedonian tribes subject to the central authority (Orestai, Elimeiotai, Lynkestai), yet also an ethnos with a strong, though democratic monarchy, and a society of farmers and stock-breeders capable of defending their land against all foreign designs, Macedonia evolved with the passage of the centuries into a power of world-wide (for the period) influence and prestige.

The country was self-sufficient in products to meet basic needs (timber, cereals, game, fish, livestock, minerals) and soon became the exclusive supplier of other Greek states less blessed by nature, though at the same time it came to be the target of expansionist schemes dictated largely by economic interests. A particularly "introspective" land, with conservative customs and way of life and a social structure and political organisation of a markedly archaic character, speaking a distinctive form of the Doric dialect, Macedonia took over the reigns of the Greek spirit in the 4th century B.C., when the city-state was entering on its decline; revealing admirable adaptability in the face of the demands of the present and the achievements of the past, and ingenuity and boldness when confronted with the problems of the future, the country was quickly transformed into a performer of new roles, opening up new roads towards the epoch of the Hellenism of three continents.

7-8. Macedonian bronze jewellery (pendants) dating from the Geometric period. Kilkis, Archaeological Museum.

7

8

Language

The Macedonians were a Dorian tribe, according to the testimony of Herodotus (I, 56): "(The Dorian ethnos) ... dwelt in Pindos, where it was called Makednon; from there ... it came to the Peloponnesos, where it took the name of Dorian". And elsewhere (VIII, 43): "these (that is, the Lacedaimonians, Corinthians, Sikyonians etc.), except the people of Hermione, were of the Dorian and Makednon ethnos, and had most recently come from Erineos and Pindos and Dryopis". A Dorian tribe, then, that expanded steadily to the east of Pindos and far beyond, conquering areas in which dwelt other tribes, both Greek and non-Greek.

For many centuries, Macedonia remained on the fringe of the Greek world. In the mountainous regions of Macedonia, at least, the way of life will have consisted predominantly of transhumant pasturage. Education will, at best, have been confined to aristocratic circles and those connected with them. We do not, therefore, expect to find any written texts of a private nature from the Archaic period. In the rest of the Greek world, writing is related to the structure and mechanisms of the city-state, and is used mainly for the recording of justice in the broadest sense of the word. Under a monarchical regime like that of Macedonia, however, and in a world of nomads, we would hardly expect to find public documents.

At about the end of the 6th century B.C., the changed socio-economic circumstances deriving from permanent settlement and the intensifica-

9

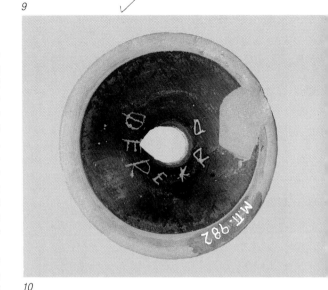

10

11

9. The underside of the base of a kylix dating from the Classical period with an incised name, probably that of its owner: ΦΕΡΕΚΡΑ(ΤΗΣ) - Pherekrates. From Polychrono in Chalkidike. Thessalonike, Archaeological Museum.

10. Base of a skyphos incised with the name ΠΥΡΟΣ - Pyros. Thessalonike, Archaeological Museum.

11. Black-glaze vase of the Classical period with the name ΙΠΠΟΜΑΧΑΣ-Hippomachas - incised on the base. From ancient Edessa. Edessa, Archaeological Museum.

12

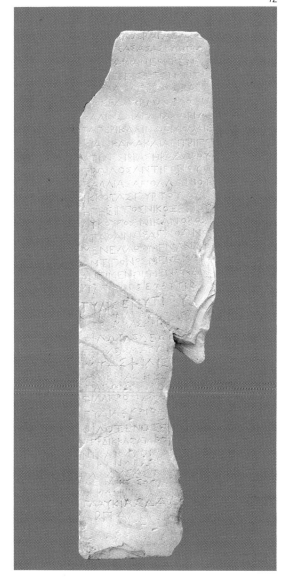

[Ἀγαθά]νωρ Ἀγάθων[ος]
[ἱερατε]ύσας<ας> Ἀσκληπιῶι,
[Ἀπόλλ]ωνι ἀνέθηκεν.
[Οἵδε] ἱερεῖς ἐγένοντο
[ἀφ' ο]ὗ βασιλεύς Ἀλέξαν-
δρος ἔδωκε Μακεδόσι
Καλίνδοια καὶ τὰ χωρία
τὰ περὶ Καλίνδοια Θαμισ-
κίαν, Καμακαίαν, Τριπο-
ᾶτιν· Σίβρας Ἡροδώρου,
Τρωΐλος Ἀντιγόνου,
Καλλίας Ἀπολλωνίου,
Ἱκκότας Γύρτου,
Ἡγήσιππος Νικοξένου,
Λυκοῦργος Νικάνορος,
Ἀγαθάνωρ Ἀγάθωνο[ς],
Μενέλαος Μενάνδ[ρου],
Ἀντίγονος Μενάνδρ[ου],
Ἀντιμένων Μενάνδρ[ου],
Κράτιππος Εὐρυτίο[υ],
Γῦλις Εὐ(ρ)υτίου,
Κανουν Ἀσσα[.]μίκου,
Κερτίμμας Κρίθωνο[ς],
Φιλώτας Λεων[ίδου],
Πτολέμμας Μ[.....],
Μύας Φιλίσ[κου νεl-του]],
Ἀμερίας Κυδ[ία],
Πάσων Σκύθ[ου],
Φίλαγρος Μενά[νδρου],
Γυδίας Κρίθων[ος],
Φιλόξενος Ε[- - -],
Περδίκκας Ἀμμα[- - -],
Νικάνωρ Νικά[νορος],
Νικάνωρ Κρ[ίθωνος?],
Γαδδῦς Ἀστί[ωνος?],
Ἀντιφάνης Σώσ[- - - -],
Παρμενίων Ἀ[- - - -],
Γλαυκίας Δαβρ[εία],
Ἅρπαλος Φα[- - -].

tion of economic and cultural relations with the rest of the Greek world led to the creation of the preconditions for the use of writing, mainly for the purposes of diplomatic relations. The local dialect a member, as far as we can judge, of the group known as the north-west Greek dialects, which included Phokian, the Lokrian dialects, etc., had no written tradition, whether literary or other. Consequently, the rise of education and culture was to the detriment of the Macedonian speech. Attic was selected as the language of education, and the local dialect was "smothered" by the written language, the koine, and was never, or hardly ever, written down, being restricted to oral communication between Macedonians.

From as early as the time of Alexander the Great, moreover, Macedonian lost ground to the koine in this sphere too, if we are to believe the historical sources, and there is certainly no evidence that it was spoken in the centuries after Christ. Only its memory was perpetuated through the use of personal names until the 4th century A.D.

Although very little of the Macedonian tongue has survived, there is no doubt that it was a Greek dialect. This is clear from a whole series of indications and linguistic phenomena by which the koine of the region is "coloured", which are not Attic but which can only have derived from a Greek dialect. For example:

The vast majority of even the earliest names,

13 ✓

12. Inscribed marble stele dating from the second half of the 4th century B.C., known as the "Inscription of Kalindoia". From Kalamoto near Zangliveri. It contains a list of the priests of Asklepios and Apollo (probably the officials of the city). The starting date of the series of names in the list is the re-foundation of the city of Kalindoia as a Macedonian city by Alexander the Great, who made grants of the royal land owned by him in the area to Macedonian settlers.

13. One of the funerary stelai found in the earth deposits of the Great Tumulus at Vergina, with the names of the deceased: Xenokrates son of Pierion and Drykalos son of Pierion. Drykalos and Pierion are typical Macedonian names. Thessalonike, Archaeological Museum.

whether dynastic names or not, are Greek, formed from Greek roots and according to Greek models: Hadista, Philista, Sostrata, Philotas, Perdikkas, Machatas and hundreds of others. In general, the remnants of the Macedonian dialect that have come down to us have a completely different character from Ionic. This circumstance is patent proof that there can be no question of the ancient Macedonians having been Hellenised, as has been asserted (Kärst), for such Hellenisation could have been only by the Greek colonies on the Macedonian coast, in which the Ionian element was predominant (Beloch).

The fact that Roman and Byzantine lexicographers and grammarians cited examples from Macedonian in order to interpret particular features of the Homeric epics must mean that Macedonian - or rather, what survived of Macedonian at the period in question - was a very archaic dialect, and preserved features that had disappeared from the other Greek dialects; it would be absurd to suggest that these scholars, in their commentaries on the Homeric poems, might have compared them with a non-Greek language. The name given to the Macedonian cavalry - hetairoi tou basileos - "the King's Companions" - is also indicative: this occurs only in Homer, and was preserved in the historical period only amongst the Macedonians.

The anonymous compiler of the Etymologi-

14

δ|≗8

15

14. Inscription from Chalkidike dating from the second half of the 4th century B.C. Thessalonike, Archaeological Museum. The text relates to the fixing of borders between the Ramaioi and the Paraipioi, who dwelt in the semi-mountainous hinterland of Chalkidike, in the area of mount Cholomon; the borders were determined on the basis of natural boundaries (rivers: the Ammites and the Manes; hills or mountains: mount Hermaion), place names (Heptadryon, Prinos, Lambyris, Makron Ergasimon, Leuke Petra), rural sanctuaries (the Hermaion, Dioskourion, sanctuary of Artemis), paths and roads, and even private farms (the farm of Eugeon).

15. Roof-tile with the stamp ΠΕΛΛΗΣ - "of Pella". Pella, Archaeological Museum.

cum Magnum notes in the entry on Aphrodite, probably adopting a comment by the earlier grammarian Didymos: "V is akin to F. This is clear from the fact that the Macedonians call Philip "Vilip", and pronounce falakros [bald] "valakros", the Phrygians "Vrygians", and the winds (fysitas) "vyktas". Homer refers to "vyktas anemous" (blowing winds). Observations of this type abound.

Male and female names occur in Macedonian ending in -as and -a, where in Attic we have -es and -e: Alketas, Amyntas, Hippotas, Glauka, Eurydika, Andromacha, and dozens more.

A feature bequeathed by Macedonian to the koine and also to Modern Greek is the genitive of so-called first declension masculine nouns in -a: Kallia, Teleutia, Pausanea (the Attic ending was -ou).

The long alpha is retained in the middle of words (as in all dialects other than Ionic-Attic dialects): Damostratos, Damon etc. and "laos" rather than the "leos" of Ionic Attic, is used to form compounds, occurring as both the first and the second element (Archelaos, Laodika).

The koine of Macedonia, for all its conservatism and dialect colouring, follows a parallel path to the koine of other regions, though not always at the same moment in time. Whatever the case, all the changes that marked the Greek language in general and the north Greek dialects in particular, can be followed in the inscriptions of Macedonia.

Classical period

Although Herodotus and Thucydides, both of whom were aware of the genealogy of the Macedonian Argead or Temenids dynasty, made Perdikkas I the head of the family, and moreover attributed to him the foundation of the state (first half of the 7th century B.C.), tradition records the names of kings earlier than Perdikkas (Karanos, Koinos, Tyrimmas). It was, however, only after protracted clashes with the Illyrians and the Thracians, and temporary subjection to Persian suzerainty (510-479 B.C.) - a period during which the Macedonians established themselves in "Lower Macedonia" - that the country acquired its definitive form and character. Through the organisational and administrative abilities of its first great leader, Alexander I, called the Philhellene, whose timely information to the southern Greeks contributed to the defeat of the Persian forces of Xerxes and Mardonios, the suzerainty of the Macedonian kingdom was extended both to the

16

west of the lower Strymon valley and to the region of Anthemous. This brought economic benefits, including the exploitation of a number of silver mines in the area of lake Prasias (the first Macedonian coins were struck at this time), and the independent Macedonian principalities of west and north Macedonia were united around the central authority, recognising the primacy of the Temenids king. The entry of the state into the history of southern Greece was sealed by the acceptance of Alexander I by the *hellanodikai* as a competitor in the Olympic games (probably those of 496 B.C.), in which, as we know, only Greeks were allowed to participate.

16. Silver octadrachm of Alexander I, 495-452 B.C. Paris, Bibliothèque Nationale.

17. The Argeads kingdom at the end of the 6th and the first half of the 5th centuries B.C.

17

GENEALOGICAL TREE OF THE ARGEAD OR TEMENID DYNASTY

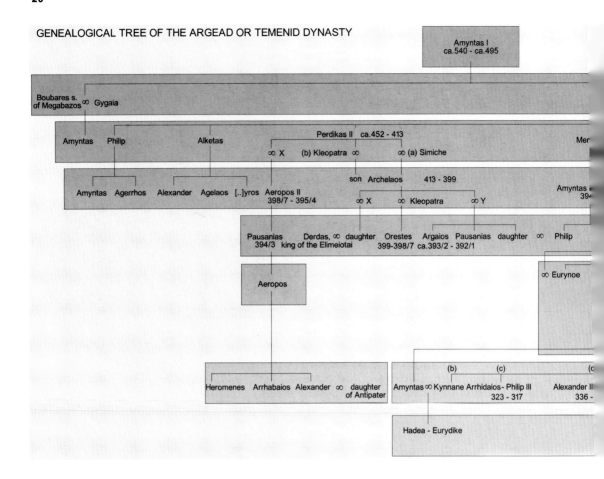

Perdikkas II, the first-born son of Alexander I, who ruled for forty years (454-412/13 B.C.), not only had to face dynastic strife, but also had to be continuously on the alert to deal with the problems created for him by the Thracian tribes and the Lynkestai and Elimeiotai on one hand, and on the other by the doubtful outcome of the Peloponnesian War, which threw the Greek world into turmoil in the 5th century B.C., bringing Athenian and Spartan armies, at various times, into the heart of Macedonia. Acting always according to the dictates of political advantage, Perdikkas II proved himself a skilful diplomat and a wily leader, astute in his decisions and flexible in his alliances, and set as the aim of his diplomacy the preservation of the territorial integrity of his kingdom.

The completion of the internal tasks that Perdikkas II was prevented from accomplishing by the external situation fell to his successor, Archelaos I; he is credited by the ancient sources and modern scholarship alike with great sagacity and with sweeping changes in state administration, the army and commerce. During his reign, the de-

fence of the country was organised, cultural and artistic contacts with southern Greece were extended, and the foundations were laid of a road network. A man of culture himself, the king entertained in his new palace at Pella, to where he had transferred the capital from Aigai, poets and tragedians, and even the great Euripides, who wrote his tragedies *Archelaos* and *The Bacchae* there; he invited brilliant painters - the name of Zeuxis is mentioned - and at Dion in Pieria, the Olympia of Macedonia, he founded the "Olympia", a religious festival with musical and athletic competitions in honour of Olympian Zeus and the Muses. By 399 B.C., the year in which he was murdered, Archelaos I had succeeded in converting Macedonia into one of the strongest Greek powers of his period.

In the forty years following the death of Archelaos I , Macedonia formed a field for all kinds of conflict and realignments, and was the object of competition between kings who reigned for very brief periods; the country was ravaged by the savage incursions of the Illyrians, captured by the Chalkidians, and obliged to yield to the de-

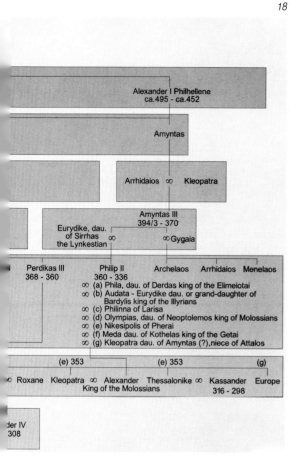

Alexander I Philhellene
ca.495 - ca.452

Amyntas

Arrhidaios ∞ Kleopatra

Amyntas III
394/3 - 370

Eurydike, dau.
of Sirrhas ∞   ∞ Gygaia
the Lynkestian

| Perdikas III | Philip II | Archelaos | Arrhidaios | Menelaos |
| 368 - 360 | 360 - 336 | | | |

∞ (a) Phila, dau. of Derdas king of the Elimeiotai
∞ (b) Audata - Eurydike dau. or grand-daughter of
　　　Bardylis king of the Illyrians
∞ (c) Philinna of Larisa
∞ (d) Olympias, dau. of Neoptolemos king of Molossians
∞ (e) Nikesipolis of Pherai
∞ (f) Meda dau. of Kothelas king of the Getai
∞ (g) Kleopatra dau. of Amyntas (?),niece of Attalos

| (e) 353 | (e) 353 | (g) |

ο Roxane   Kleopatra ∞ Alexander   Thessalonike ∞ Kassander   Europe
　　　　　King of the Molossians　　　　　　　316 - 298

...der IV
308

18. Stemma of the Temenids dynasty.

19. Stater of Archelaos I (413-399 B.C.) with a depiction of a bust of a goat. London, British Museum.

20. Silver tetradrachm of Philip II. The Macedonian king can be recognised in the mounted figure wearing the kausia (Macedonian hat).

mands of the Athenians; despite all this, however, it recovered to some degree with Amyntas III on the throne and, with the accession of Philip II (359 B.C.), succeeded in regaining its self-belief and recovering its former strength. This charismatic ruler, whose strategic genius and diplomatic ability transformed Macedonia from an insignificant and marginal country into the most important power in the Aegean and paved the way for the pan-Hellenic expedition of his son to the Orient, was an expansive leader who had the breadth of vision to usher the ancient world into the epoch of the Hellenism of three continents. During the course of his tempestuous life, he firmly established the power of the central authority in the kingdom, reorganised the army into a flexible and amazingly efficient unit, strengthened the weaker regions of his realm through movements of population, and, abroad, made Macedonia incontestably superior to the institution of the city-state which, at this precise period, was facing decline.

His unexpected death at the hands of an assassin in 336 B.C., in the theatre at Aigai on the very day of the marriage of his daughter Cleopatra to Alexander, the young king of the Molossians, brought to an end a brilliant career, the final aim of which was to unify the Greeks in order

21. Small ivory portrait head of Philip II. Together
with other portrait heads it adorned the wooden
couch in the tomb of Philip II in the Vergina Great
Tumulus. Thessalonike, Archaeological Museum.

22. The Macedonian kingdom and the other Greek
states in 336 B.C., the year in which Philip II died.

Scythians
Istros
Tomis

Getai

Kallatis

Triballians

Odessos

Autariatai

Mesembria
Anchialos
EUXINE
Dardanians
Agrianians
Kabyle
Beroe
Apollonia

Philippopolis

THRACE

Salmydessos

Bylazora
Astibos
Stoboi
Paionia
Idomenai
Sintike
Alkomena
Herakleia
Serrhai
Philippoi
Dikaia
Doriskos
Bisanthe
Selymbria
Byzantium
Kyrrhos
Styberra
Bragylai
Krestonia
Odomantike
Neapolis
Abdera
Stryme
Kypsela
Ornoi
Perinthos
Kalchedon
Lynkos
Tyrissa
Europos
Edonis
Oisyme
Maroneia
Sale
Ganos
Lete
Amphipolis
Apollonia
Ainos
Propontis
Parthinoi
Edessa
Bottia
Bisaltia
Prokonnesos
Apollonia
Dimalle
Pella
Thasos
Kardia
Panion
Priapos
Byllis
Eordaia
Methone
Therme
Mygdonia
Stageira
Thasos
Samothrace
Kallipolis
Parion
Kyzikos
Kios
Beroia
Aineia
Akanthos
Alopekonnesos
Lampsakos
Taulantians
Aigeai
Pydna
Chalkidike
Olophyxos
Sestos
Abydos
Orikos
Argos
Orestis
Aiane
Doliche
Pieria
Dion
Olynthos
Potidaia
Sane
Sermylia
Charadrai
Akrothoon
Imbros
Madytos
Dardanos
Paravaians
Chaonians
Tymphaians
Azoros
Herakleion
Aphytis
Singos
Torone
Eleous
Sigeion
Phoinike
Aignion
Olosson
Homolion
Mende
Skione
Myrinna
Hephaistia
Skepsis
Bouthrotos
Passaron
Dodone
Perrhaibia
Meliboia
Lemnos
Tenedos
Antandros
Korkyra
Orikos
Hestiotis
Larissa
Assos
Adramyttion
Korkyra
MOLOSSIAN
KINGDOM
Trikka
THESSALY
Skotoussa
Pherai
Halonnesos
Antissa
PERSIAN EMPIRE
Ephyra
Pandosia
Pharsalos
Pagasai
Skiathos
Ikkos
Eresos
Mytilene
Atarneus
Kassope
Dolopia
Phthiotis
Oreos
Peparethos
Lesbos
Pitane
Thyrreion
Ambrakia
Ainis
Malis
Nikaia
Euboia
Skyros
Gryneion
Argos
Herakleia
Kyme
Leukas
Stratos
Aitolia
Doris
Chalkis
Phokaia
Magnesia
Oiniadai
Thermos
Amphissa
Elateia
Eretria
Chios
Erythrai
Smyrna
Same
Ithake
Kalydon
Lokris
Delphoi
Boiotia
Klazomenai
Kephallenia
Patras
Naupaktos
Phokis
Thebes
Oropos
Chios
Teos
Kolophon
Dyme
Aigion
Notion
Magnesia
Achaia
Sikyon
Megara
Athens
Karystos
Ephesos
Priene
Elis
Korinthia
Piraeus
Andros
Tenos
Samos
Zakynthos
Elis
Corinth
Attica
Ikaros
Samos
Olympia
Arkadia
Argolis
Epidauros
Keos
Miletos
Tegea
Argos
Troizen
Kythnos
Mykonos
Megalopolis
Thyrea
Hermione
Seriphos
Delos
Patmos
Leros
Halikarnassos
Messene
Messenia
Sparta
Paros
Najos
Kalymnos
Lakonia
Gytheion
Epidauros Limera
Melos
Sikinos
Amorgos
Kos
Knidos
Nisyros
Rhodes
Boiai
Anaphe
Astypalaia
Telos
Ios
Lindos
Kythera
Rhodes
Karpathos

AEGEAN SEA
ADRIATIC SEA
Illyrians
Drilon
Epidamnos
Lychnidos
Apollonia
Athamanes
Penios
Strymon
Nestos
Hebros
Agrianes
Axios
Haliakmon

Istros (Danube)

THE KINGDOM OF THE MACEDONIANS AND THE OTHER GREEK STATES AT THE DEATH OF PHILIP II (336 BC)

kingdom of the Macedonians and dependent territories

Thessaly: bound to the person of Philip

kingdom of the Molossians, allies of Philip

member states of the Hellenic Confederacy

neutral Greek states

Kydonia
Crete
Knossos
Itanos
Gortys

24. *Gold necklace from a female tomb at Sindos. Last quarter of the 6th century B.C. Thessalonike, Archaeological Museum.*

25. *Gold band earrings. Last quarter of the 6th century B.C. Thessalonike, Archaeological Museum.*

23. *Clay Attic two-sided kantharos from the cemetery of Akanthos. 480-470 B.C. Thessalonike, Archaeological Museum.*

26. *Gold earrings from the region of Lete near Thessalonike, ca. 300 B.C. Thessalonike, Archaeological Museum.*

23

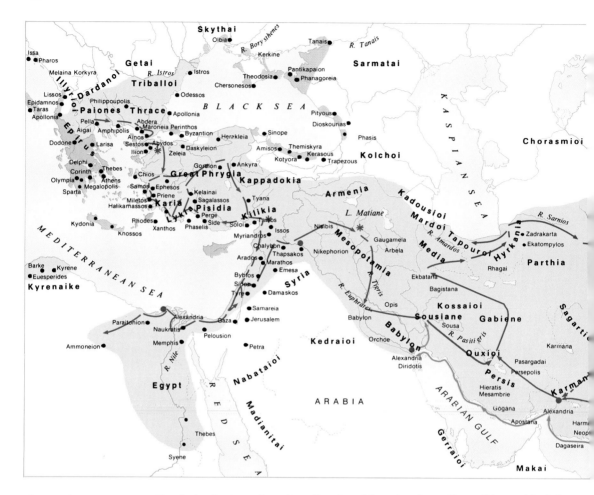

to exact vengeance on Persia for the invasion of 481-480 B.C.; Macedonia, in complete control of affairs in the Balkan peninsula, was ready to assume its new role.

A fascinating sequence of political events with a highly favourable outcome and military victories with world-wide repercussions, the resolution of a number of intractable problems of an inter-state nature, and a series of inspired programmes and visions implemented with great success in a short space of time - these are the component elements in the panorama of the life of the great general and civilizer Alexander III, who was justly called the Great and who has passed into the pantheon of legend. And if his victories at Granikos (334 B.C.), Issos (333 B.C.), Gaugamela (331 B.C.) and Alexandria Nikaia (326 B.C.) may be thought of as sons worthy of their father, bringing about the overthrow of the mighty Persian empire and distant India, the prosperous cities founded in his name as far as the ends of the known world were his daughters - centres of the preservation and dissemination of Greek spirit and culture. From this world of daring and passion, of questing and contradictions, the robust Hellenism of Macedonia carried the art of man to the ends of the inhabited world, bestowing poetry upon the mute and, in the infancy of mankind, instilling philosophical thought. In the libraries that were now founded from the Nile to the Indus, in the theatres that spread their wings under the skies of Baktria and Sogdiana, in the Gymnasia and the Agoras, Homer suckled as yet unborn civilizations, Thucydides taught the rules of the science of history, and the great tragedians and Plato transmitted the principle of restraint and morality to absolutist regimes. Alexander's contribution to the history of the world is without doubt of the greatest importance: his period, severing the "Gordian Knot" with the Greek past, opened new horizons whose example would inspire, throughout the centuries that followed, all those leaders down to Napoleon himself who left their own mark on the course of mankind in both the East and the West.

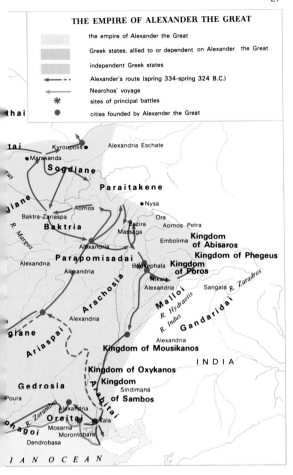

27. The empire of Alexander the Great.

Hellenistic period

In the immense kingdom created by Alexander's III the Great conquests in the East, Macedonia continued to be the cradle of tradition and the motherland, point of departure and return; the object of the innermost desire of the veterans who returned to build, at the time of Philip III and Cassander, the houses lavishly decorated with mosaic floors at Pella, and undoubtedly at other cities in northern Greece, and the imposing funerary monuments at Lefkadia (Mieza). The Hellenistic period, an epoch of doubt and questioning and unalloyed individualism, a restless period in which Greeks and barbarians together stood tall in the face of man's destiny, doomed yet optimistic, was conceived on Alexander's bier at Babylon (323 B.C.) and, like a phoenix born from its ashes, flew towards the future of the world.

From this time to 277 B.C., when Antigonos II Gonatas, the philosopher king, ascended the throne, Macedonia was the field of intense competition for the succession, was ravaged by savage invasions by Gauls, and saw the royal tombs at Aigai dug up, cities abandoned, and celebrated generals fall ingloriously in fratricidal battles. During these fifty years, in which all the cohesion that had been won was lost, Cassander's murder of Alexander IV, son of Alexander the Great and Roxane, in 310 B.C., removed the last representative of the house of the Argead dynasty, Olympias (mother of the conqueror of Asia) and Philip III Arrhidaios having already met with a lamentable death.

Cassander (316-298/97 B.C.), whose cultural achievements included the foundation of Thessalonike and Cassandreia, and after him Demetrios Poliorketes (293 B.C.), Pyrrhos (289/88 B.C.), Lysimachos and Ptolemy Keraunos (281 B.C.) plunged the country into a bloodbath and weakened the kingdom with their clumsy and selfish policies - some of them in the maelstrom of their tempestuous fortune-seeking lives, others in despairing attempts to dominate and acquire influence, setting as their aim the acquisition of the Macedonian crown, a title that undoubtedly conferred enormous prestige upon its bearer.

Despite all this, as is often the case in periods of political instability and demographic contraction, Macedonia, which at the time of Philip II had entertained some of the most famous intellects in Greece (Aristotle, Theophrastus, Speusippos), gave birth to some famous historical figures who -mainly as a result of the stability achieved under the rule of Antigonos - together with others who found protection at the royal court (Onesikritos, Marsyas, Krateros, Hieronymos, Aratos, Persaios), made Pella an important cultural centre in the early and middle Hellenistic period.

The country had to wait for the reign of Philip V, an ambitious Antigonid who ascended to the throne at the age of just 17 years (221 B.C.), to relive times of glory and greatness. Continuously on the alert against the threatening Thracians, Dardanians and Illyrians, the young leader sought to strengthen his kingdom by suitable diplomatic manoeuvres and even terrorism, by employing local leaders to protect the border regions effectively, and by transplanting populations and annexing territory. At the same time he tried, albeit in an opportunistic manner, to assert control over the situation in southern Greece, though here his ambitions foundered on the suspicion and bitter experience that had been accu-

28. Marble head of Alexander the Great by the sculptor Leochares. 4th century B.C. Athens, Acropolis Museum.

29. The famous mosaic from a house at Pompeii, a copy of the famous wall-painting by Philoxenos of Eretria depicting a critical moment during the battle of Issos. Naples, National Museum.

30. Detail from the "Alexander sarcophagus" depicting Alexander on horseback, wearing a lion's head and despatching a Persian infantryman. End of the 4th century B.C. Constantinople, Archaeological Museum.

31

32

mulated there as a result of the policies of previous Macedonian kings, Demetrios II and Antigonos III Doson. The "unionist" policy of Macedonia failed for a variety of reasons - the presence of the Macedonian garrisons in Corinth, Athens, Chalkis and Piraeus, the imposition of despotic regimes, in general, the lack of any convincing rationale for the preservation of the Hellenic League with a Macedonian king at its head - especially since the Persian threat was long since past - and the reconstitution or creation of ethnic federations (Aitolian League, Achaian League); the policy was in any event an anachronism, modelled on earlier, happier times.

Despite the unfavourable outcome of affairs on the external front, however, and despite the restraining intervention of the Romans at the expense of the territorial integrity of the country, which was deprived of its possessions in southern Greece and Asia Minor (197 B.C.), Philip's V

31. Silver tetradrachm of Lysimachos with a horned head of Alexander the Great. Athens, Numismatic Museum.

32. Silver tetradrachm of Demetrios Poliorketes with a portrait head of the ruler. Athens, Numismatic Museum.

33. Silver tetradrachm of Philip V with a portrait head of the great Antigonid king. Athens, Numismatic Museum.

34. Silver tetradrachm of Perseus with the head of the king. Athens, Numismatic Museum.

33

34

prestige and influence was revealed long ago by dedications at the most famous Greek sanctuaries (Delos, Rhodes, Karia). His dynamism with regard to the vision of a great and powerful Macedonia is attested by his internal policy during the final decade of his rule (188-179 B.C.): during these years, the planned exploitation of the mines, the granting to the cities in the kingdom of the right to mint coins, the imposition of harbour dues, the increasing of taxation and the provision of grants to encourage child-bearing, all led not only to recovery but also to the accumulation of wealth.

This prosperity and a sound incomes policy, together with the rise of trade and the liberalisation of local institutions in the major urban centres, filled the royal treasury with liquid funds and the granaries with stores of grain, and armed 18,000 mercenaries under the rule of his successor, Perseus, the last king of Macedonia. The 6,000 talents and the vast quantities of precious vessels that came into the hands of Aemilius Paulus on the morrow of the decisive battle of Pydna (168 B.C.) attest to the economic vigour of the state up to the very eve of its collapse.

Roman period

This, then, was the end of the kingdom beneath Mount Olympos, which had been the common point of reference for all the Hellenistic kingdoms of the East and had supplied succeeding generations with Greek ideals. It was essentially a nation state, in contrast with the "spear-won" kingdoms of the *epigoni* (Successors) in which the Macedonians were always a minority of foreign conquerors, a conservative country, certainly, devoted to its traditional institutions, so different from the immense new empires of the Seleucids and the Ptolemies, with their heterogeneous populations. Far removed from the deification of leaders, from vainglorious titles, from the appellations and dooms of excess, Macedonia

35. Macedonia during the period of Roman rule.

35

36

37

confronted its destiny as once its Stoic king Antigonos II Gonatas had confronted the highest office, which had been bestowed upon him: as glorious slavery!

A menace to the Roman Senate, the land of Alexander was divided into four *merides* (portions), or economic and administrative districts, and the possession or sale of landed property between them was forbidden, as was intermarriage. The Macedonians were described as "free" (in reality, under the tutelage of the Romans), paid a tax and were obliged to maintain an army only large enough to protect their own borders against the barbarian tribes of the north. This regime, however, lasted no more than twenty years: anti-Roman sentiments on the one hand, and social friction between the privileged classes and the masses on the other, and above all the deterioration of the internal situation led to the revolt of Andriskos, an adventurer who claimed to be the son of Perseus. With the crushing of his rebellion by the Roman legions (148 B.C.) Macedonia now belonged to the past, even as a protectorate: the senate decided to turn it into a province *(provincia Macedonia)* - the first Roman province in the East - and incorporate it into the Roman empire, installing a governor with his headquarters at Thessalonike and an army. The period from 148 B.C. to the advent of Augustus (27 B.C.) was undoubtedly one of the most burdensome for the country which, administratively, now stretched from the Ionian sea to the Nestos river, and from mount Olympos to the source of the Axios river: the continuous incursions of barbarian tribes (Skordiskoi, Bessoi, Thracians) throughout the second century B.C., the invasion by the armies of Mithridates VI, supported by the Maidoi, the Dardanians and the Sintoi, at the beginning of the first, and the upheaval, decimation and ravaging inflicted on it during both the first Civil War (Pompey-Caesar, 49-48 B.C.) and the

36. *Milestone from the Via Egnatia, found near the Gallikos river, bearing the name of the proconsul Gnaius Egnatius. 2nd century B.C. Thessalonike, Archaeological Museum.*

37. *Marble stele with a list of ephebes of Beroia. Beroia, Archaeological Museum.*

second (Brutus/Antony-Octavian, 42 B.C.), turned the province into a huge battlefield, with severely adverse consequences for the land and its inhabitants.

The construction of the Via Egnatia from Dyrrachion to Byzantion (in a second stage) as a continuation of the Via Appia on the Italian mainland, and the settling of colonists (Dion, Cassandreia, Pella, Philippoi) and Italian merchants may have transformed the economic and demographic face of the country, but it did not bring about the latinisation of the inhabitants, who retained their Greek personality and speech to the end.

In a pacified empire, living under the protection of the *Pax Romana* in the rearguard of military enterprises, and a senatorial province from 27 B.C. to A.D. 15 and from A.D. 44 onwards, Macedonia moved onto a different plane. In the "free" cities of Thessalonike, Amphipolis and Skotoussa, as in the tribute paying *(tributariae)* cities, the communities in time adjusted to the new state of affairs ordained by Augustus, while preserving their ancient institutions of government (assembly, council and magistrates); new town-plans were laid out, grand building complexes (agoras, temples) now proclaimed the glory of new gods and earthly lords, honorific altars were erected for select members and officials in a display of gratitude, and fine marble funerary buildings were designed to perpetuate the memory of simple mortals and distinguished citizens after their death. And it is the countless inscriptions - often verbose in their attempt to flatter - that preserve names, professions, lists of ephebes, artists' guilds, dedicators, religious associations, immortalizing the passing moment and completing the mosaic of our knowledge of a region of the Roman world that appears to follow the fortune of a disarmed province. It is the inscriptions that inform us about the existence of *koina* - those organisations that stood between the Roman administration and the local authorities; about the holding of games called Pythia, Actia, Alexandreia Olympia; about the occasional transit of emperors and their armies, and the anchoring of fleets. And of course, about the preservation in the memory of the Macedonians of the man who glorified their name to the ends of the inhabited world.

38-39. Gold medallion in the form of a coin (niketerion) from the find at Abukir, with a portrait of Olympias on one side and a mounted Nereid on the other. Struck about the middle of the 3rd century A.D. for the Alexandreia Olympia games held at Beroia, the headquarters of the Macedonian Koinon. Thessalonike, Archaeological Museum.

38-39

40

40. Imago clipeata with a bust of Galerius. Detail from the marble arch of the Octagon in the palace of Galerius. Beginning of the 4th century A.D. Thessalonike, Archaeological Museum.

Forgotten in its wilderness, the province of Macedonia strengthened the fortifications of its cities - often, indeed, demolishing the adjacent buildings - when, in the middle of the 3rd century, the Carpi, the Goths and the Heruls reached the Aegean, laying everything waste.

In the twilight of the Roman gods, and of all the other deities of oriental or Egyptian origins for whom the country had provided fertile ground on which to establish and disseminate themselves, Christianity offered to Thessalonike, Philippoi, and Beroia, resignation, redemption and life beyond death, from as early as 50 A.D., when saint Paul the Apostle of the Nations preached the new religion. It prepared the ground for the resurrection of the dead and also for the regeneration of the empire. An empire tossing and turning amidst the instability of opportunistic government by a host of ambitious contenders for power, an empire in the chaos of economic decline, threatened with the breaching of the integrity of its borders by the repeated incursions of barbarian tribes, and humbled by heavy defeats on the field of battle.

The assumption of power by Diocletian in A.D. 280 - an event that formed a landmark in the history of the Roman empire and laid the foundations for a new era - was of the greatest importance for Macedonia, as for the rest of the empire, leading as it did to a way out of the crisis.

Diocletian's administrative changes returned Macedonia to her natural boundaries. Part of the diocese of the Moesia was assigned to the *praeses* (ruler), who was responsible to the *vicarius* (vicar), the supreme governor. The situation was standardized first as a result of the changes made by Constantine the Great, according to which Macedonia, along with Thessaly, Epirus Vetus and Epirus Nova, Achaia and Crete formed the diocese of Macedonia, and then in the second half of the 4th century A.D. when the diocese of Macedonia, Dacia and Pannonia combined to form the praefecture of Illyricum, with its capital at Thessalonike; there were further changes, however, at the beginning of the 5th century, with Macedonia divided into "Macedonia Prima" and "Macedonia Salutaris".

Byzantine period

Macedonia's strategic importance at the crossroads of the major arterial roads in the Balkan peninsula meant that during the critical period marking the transition from the late Roman to the Byzantine period it was the object of benefactions from the royal house, despite the general upheavals of the times. Manifestations of this interest included the transfer of the capital to Thessalonike by Galerius Maximian, and the erection there of an imposing palace; the construction in the same city of a capacious dockyard by Constantine the Great (A.D. 322/323), and the choice of the capital of Macedonia as the headquarters of Theodosius the Great (A.D. 379/380) for his campaigns against the Visigoths and Ostrogoths. The economic prosperity of Macedonia in the 4th and 5th centuries A.D. is attested by the large numbers of quarries (Thasos, Prilep), furnaces for the smelting of metals, workshops for the construction of weapons and metal objects, pottery workshops and centres producing beads of glass-paste; there is also evidence for the existence of extensive farms, salt-flats, yarn dyers (Stoboi), the organising of trade fairs

("Demetria") and the carrying on of a trade in leather. This prosperity was undoubtedly responsible for the imposing buildings (whether of a religious or secular character) brought to light in many places by the archaeologist's spade: basilicas, villas and fortifications.

It was upon this world, a world deeply influenced by Christianity, a world that slowly and surely cast off its Roman toga to don the Byzantine purple, a world sorely tried by the incursions of the Goths, the Avars, and all the others who had designs on its wealth and power, that faith in mission of the "God of mercy" erected the thousand-year empire of the East, to guide and enlighten the West. It raised the cross of the Resurrection as far afield as the banks of the Danube, in castles, in churches adorned with mosaics, and in bath-houses. Proclaiming the glory of men like Justinian I, the courage of a Heraklios, the majesty of Constantine VII Porphyrogennitus. In the face of the Avars and the Slavs, the Bulgars and the Arabs.

As the countryside was depopulated by the repeated barbarian incursions and the majority of the inhabitants sought refuge and protection in the urban centres, the cities were transformed into centres of intense commercial and cultural activity. Ports like those of Thessalonike and Christoupolis (Kavala), with their granaries and heavy traffic in sea-faring ships, and also prosperous cities in the hinterland, such as Herakleia Lynkestis, Bargala, Serrhai and Philippoi, were adorned with brilliant buildings; their fortifications were strengthened, and their old urban tissue was abandoned as new programmes of urban development were implemented (to which the destructive earthquakes of the 7th century made their contribution).

It was at this period, moreover, that the administrative system of "themes"(districts), already tested in areas of Asia Minor exposed to great danger, was introduced to the European regions of the empire. The characteristic features of this system were the concentrating in one and the same person of military and political au-

42

42. Seventh century mosaic from the church of Saint Demetrios in Thessalonike. Saint Demetrios can be seen at the right with his right arm protectively on the shoulder of a priest who is holding a gospel-book and has his head framed by a battlement.

43. Wall-painting from the church of Saint Demetrios, depicting, according to one view, the entry of Justinian II into Thessalonike after his victory over the Slavs (A.D. 688). The haloed emperor is depicted on horseback.

thority, and a change in the composition of the army. Macedonia was divided between two "themes" - the "theme of Thessalonike" (from the Pindos range to the Strymon river) and the "theme of Strymon" (the modern counties of Serrhai, Xanthe and Rhodope), the latter with its capital at Serrhai.

The integration of the Slavs into Byzantine society (9th century A.D.), the result partly of their conversion to Christianity by Cyril and Methodios and partly of the extension of Byzantine influence to the interior of the Balkans, had direct consequences for Macedonia, whose cities benefited from the peace that now prevailed. Thessalonike evolved into an important cosmopolitan centre to which flowed merchandise from East and West. Churches were erected at Kastoria and Beroia and adorned with wall-paintings in which were crystallized the basic elements of large-scale art after the triumph of Orthodoxy and the triumph of the icons.

Before 1204, the year in which Constantinople was captured by the crusaders of the Fourth Crusade, Macedonia was shaken by the upheavals and the ravaging and taking of prisoners attending successive invasions by the Bulgarians, first under Symeon (A.D. 894-927) and then under Samuel (A.D. 989-1018), and suffered the humiliation of seeing its capital fall into the hands of Arab pirates (A.D. 904); almost three hundred years later, the same city, along with others (Kastoria and Serrhai) was captured after a siege by the Normans of Sicily (A.D. 1185). This is the reason that the 9th and 10th centuries in Macedonia have no great achievements to show in the sphere of cultural activity. A contributing factor in this was, of course, the strict centralization that informed the policy of the Macedonian dynasty. By contrast, the 11th and 12th centuries bestowed upon the north Greek administrative division men of the church and of letters, of the stature of Theophylact Hephaistos (the famous

43

44. The "themes" of the Balkan peninsula in the 10th century A.D.

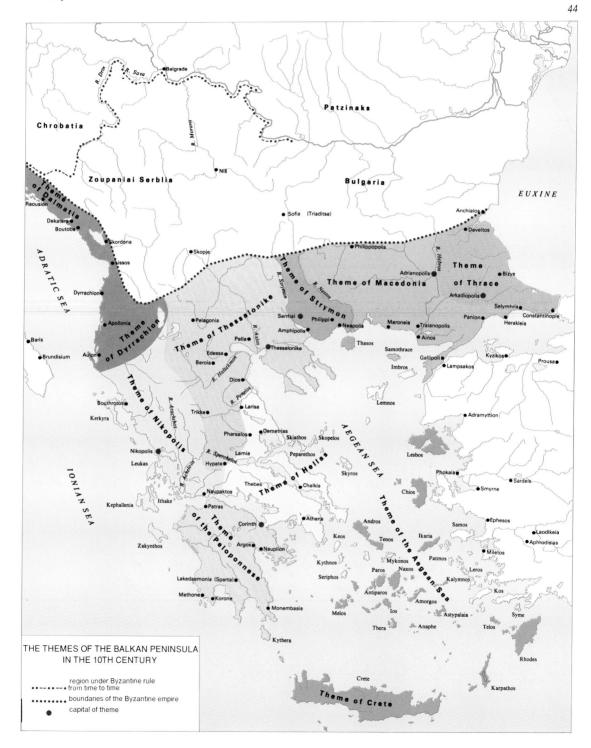

THE THEMES OF THE BALKAN PENINSULA
IN THE 10TH CENTURY

‑‑‑‑‑ region under Byzantine rule from time to time

‑‑‑‑‑ boundaries of the Byzantine empire

● capital of theme

45. Miniature from the Chronicle of Ioannis Skylitzes. The city of Thessalonike is depicted at the left, with the imperial armies in front of it putting the Bulgarian invaders to flight. Madrid, Biblioteca Nacional.

46. Miniature from the Chronicle of Ioannis Skylitzes. At the right is the Arab pirate fleet, with Thessalonike and its last defenders at the left. Madrid, Biblioteca Nacional.

45

46

47

archbishop of Bulgaria, with his see at Ochrid), Michael Choumnos (metropolitan of Thessalonike), and Eustathios Kataphloros (Metropolitan of Thessalonike and a famous scholiast on classical texts). They contributed to a flowering of ecclesiastical architecture and church painting (Beroia, Edessa, Melenikon, Serrhai, Ayios Achillios, Thessalonike, Mount Athos, Nerezi, Kastoria and Ochrid) of such intensity that these churches formed models for creations in other Balkan

47. Twelfth-century wall-painting from the church of the Anargyroi at Kastoria, depicting saints Georgios and Demetrios.

48. The Entombment of Jesus, wall-painting of the second half of the 12th century from the church of Saint Panteleimon at Nerezi.

49. Macedonia and the neighbouring regions after the Fourth Crusade.

50. Coin (billon trachy) of Theodore Komnenos Doukas Angelos, depicting the liberator of Thessalonike being blessed by the hand of God and by saint Demetrios. Athens, Numismatic Museum.

48

49

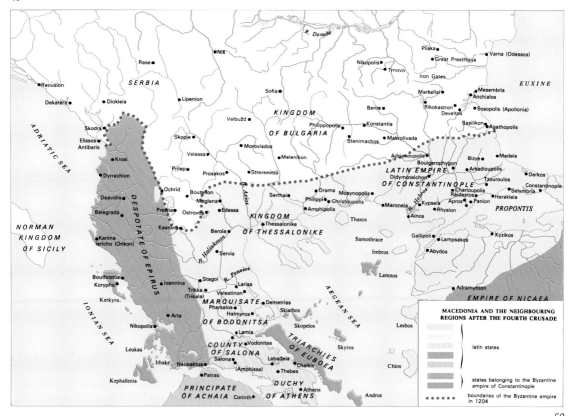

MACEDONIA AND THE NEIGHBOURING
REGIONS AFTER THE FOURTH CRUSADE

latin states

states belonging to the Byzantine
empire of Constantinople

boundaries of the Byzantine empire
in 1204

50

lands and as far afield as Russia and Georgia in the East and Sicily and northern Italy in the West. Wall-paintings of the quality of Saint Panteleimon at Nerezi (1162) - a typical example of Komnenan painting, with its pronounced depiction of passion and its soft lines in the rendering of bodies, tall and elegant in their other-worldly Mannerism - or of the Latomos monastery in Thessalonike (2nd half of the 12th century), and of the Anargyroi at Kastoria and Saint Nikolaos Kasnitzes in the same city (12th century), with their refined academic style; these are all undoubtedly points of reference for the artistic production and achievement of this age, before the empire was dismembered by the Latins and divided into kingdoms, baronies, and counties. And, of course, we should not forget the superb compositions of the portable icons and mural mosaics.

Frankish period

With the collapse of the Byzantine Empire and its dismemberment by the western crusaders *(Partitio Romaniae)*, the whole of Macedonia became subject to the Frankish kingdom of Thessalonike, of which Boniface, marquis of Montferrat was appointed ruler. Despite the fact that

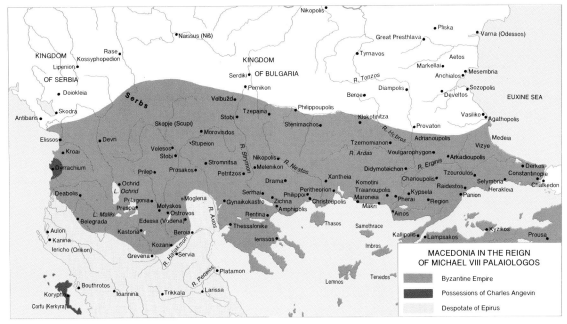

51. Macedonia in the time of Michael VIII Palaiologos.

they had prevailed, however, the new lords had to cope both with rivalries amongst themselves, and with the expansionist visions of Kalojan, the Bulgarian tzar Ioannitzes, who in 1207, the year of his death, arrived with his armies before the walls of Thessalonike, having first captured Serrhai and taken prisoner Baldwin, emperor of Constantinople.

The situation became increasingly confused as time went on: the Bulgarian state was consumed by inter-dynastic quarrels and after the death of Boniface, the Frankish kingdom of Thessalonike fell into the hands of guardians of minors: the new despot of the so-called "Despotate" of Epirus, the ambitious Theodore Komnenos Doukas Angelos (1215-1230), brother of the founder of the state, Michael II Komnenos Doukas Angelos, systematically extended his possessions from Skodra in Illyria to Naupaktos (Lepanto) and, by steadily advancing his armies, succeeded in capturing the bride of the Thermaic gulf and dissolving the second largest Latin bastion in the Balkans (1224). He was defeated, however, by the Bulgarian tzar Ivan Asen II in 1230, at the battle of Klokotnitsa, as a result of which his kingdom contracted to the area around Thessalonike and shortly afterwards became

subject to the rising power of the period, the empire of Nicaea. In December 1246, Ioannis III Vatatzes, after a victorious advance, during which he captured Serrhai, Melenikon, Skopje, Velessa and Prilep, entered the city of saint Demetrios in triumph, and installed as its governor the Great Domestic Andronikos Palaiologos.

Caught at the centre of expansionist designs, struggles for survival and domination and attempts to recover lost prestige, Macedonia repulsed the attacks of the "Despotate" of Epirus, warded off the united armies of king Manfred of Sicily and Villehardouin, ruler of Achaia, and recaptured Kastoria, Edessa, Ochrid, Skopje and Prilep, before eventually being incorporated into the Byzantine Empire, which was reconstituted on the morrow of 1261 with the capture of the Queen of Cities by Michael VIII Palaiologos.

These were ephemeral, "Pyrrhic victories", for the final page of the Byzantine epic augured the demise of a legend that had been kept alive for over a thousand years. The wretched condition of the empire in every sphere enabled the Serbs of Stephen Dušan to make deep advances to the south (1282ff.), and the mercenaries of the Catalan Company to devastate the Chalkidike and Mount Athos (1308ff.), fuelled fratricidal dynastic strife between the Palaiologoi and the Kantakouzenoi, and gave rise to social turbulence such as that provoked by the Zealots in Thessalonike.

And as the fortresses of moral and material resistance, buffeted by the maelstrom of the

52

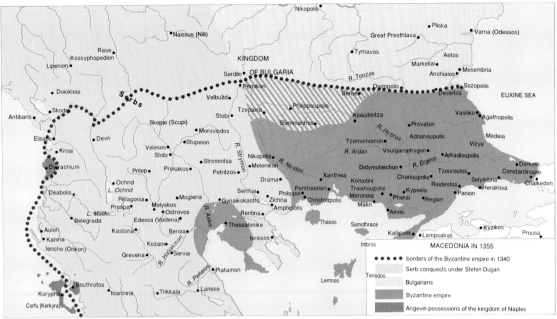

52. Macedonia in 1355.

53. Gregorios Palamas, the great exponent of Hesychasm and metropolitan of Thessalonike, in a 15th century icon. St. Petersburg, Museum of Fine Arts.

times, fell one after the other on the altar of short-term political planning and superstitious delusion, the myopic response to the reality of the situation brought the pagan hordes to European soil and shackled the right hand of Western civilization and Christianity. The last defenders of cities and ideals - an outstanding example of whom was the restless Manuel, governor of Thessalonike from 1369 and subsequently emperor in Constantinople as Manuel II - felt the death rattle of Serrhai (1383) as the 14th century expired, and heard the protracted screams of Drama, Zichna, Beroia, Servia and Thessalonike itself - once in 1395 and once, for the last time, in 1430 - with the crescent moon flying on its battlements.

Amidst the ruins of the nation, the only beacons of endurance for the enslaved population, the only points of reference to the glorious past for those who abandoned the sinking ship in good time, making their way to the West, were the books in which they took refuge in the harsh centuries that followed - the deeply philosophical treatises, the pained verses, the inspired compositions of men like Thomas Magistros, Demetrios

54. Wall-painting from the church of Saint Nikolaos Kyritzes at Kastoria. Detail of the Betrayal.

55-56. Wall-paintings from the small, aisleless church of Saint Nikolaos Orphanos in Thessalonike. The paintings date from the second or third decade of the 14th century. Top: the Marriage in Cana, bottom: scenes from the miracles of saint Nikolaos.

Triklinios, Theodore Kabasilas, Gregorios Palamas, Demetrios Kydones, and the wise jurist Constantine Armenopoulos. The strikingly warm monuments of the Christian faith, created by named and anonymous mosaicists, painters of cosmic universe, architects of the undomed divine: in the Peribleptos at Ochrid (1295), in Saint Nikolaos Orphanos, in the Holy Apostles (1312-1315), in Saint Elias (at Thessalonike), in Saint Nikolaos Kyritzes (at Kastoria), in the Church of Christ at Beroia (1315), in the Basilica of the Protaton at Karyes on Mount Athos (end of the 13th century). In the field of myth, masters of the palette such as the painter Manuel Panselinos and his fellow artists Eutychios and Michael Astrapas and Georgios Kalliergis.

And it was precisely at this period, when the rumoured impending judgement of the souls in heaven was menacing terrified mortals on earth with its sword, that there occurred a change in the consciousness of the Byzantine world which led oppressed Hellenism to an unprecedented self-awareness, taking it back to the roots of its origins.

Faced with Ottoman predomination, the imposition of the Muslim religion by forced conversions to Islam where necessary, the arrival in Macedonia a few years after the fall of Constantinople of thousands of Jewish refugees from Spain, and the migrations of Vlach- and Slav-speaking groups, the Greek element in the Empire - the "Romaioi"(Romans) as they were called by the Turks - acquired an inner strength and rallied round the Great Idea of casting off the foreign yoke and its alien language and religion. Through the encouragement of the crusading Orthodox Church, the preservation of Greek-speaking schools, and revolutionary remittances from the Greeks of the diaspora, especially those in Italy, it kept alive its knowledge, its language and its dreams. And as time went on and the deep wounds of the first decades of slavery were forgotten, it achieved great things in commerce and trade, on the diplomatic front, in administration, and in public relations.

57. *Fourteenth century wall-painting from the church of Saint Nikolaos Orphanos in Thessalonike. Detail from the Mocking of Christ.*

58. *Wall-painting of saint Merkourios from the basilica of the Protaton at Karyes. Thought to be the work of a painter of the end of the 13th and*

beginning of the 14th centuries A.D., who is known by the name Manuel Panselinos.

59-60. *Georgios Kalliergis, "the finest painter in the whole of Thessaly (=Macedonia)", painted the superb wall-paintings in the church of Christ in Beroia in 1315. Top right: the prophet Malacchi, bottom: the Dormition of the Virgin.*

57

58

59

60

Macedonia under Turkish Rule (the Tourkokratia)

61. Macedonia and the expansion of the Ottoman Turks (1402).

62. View of Yanitsa (Yenice = New City) from a 19th century engraving.

63. Macedonian woman. 18th century coloured woodcut.

64. Archon (noble) of Thessalonike. Engraving of the end of the 18th-beginning of the 19th centuries.

While ruined cities like Thessalonike, victims of the conquest, were repopulated with peoples from every region of the Ottoman Empire, others, such as Yanitsa (Yenice), were new creations with a purely Turkish population. About the middle of the 15th century, Monastir had 185 Christian families, Velessa 222 and Kastoria 938. Thessalonike, a century later, counted 1087 families and Serrhai 357. In Drama, Naousa and Kavala, the main language spoken was Greek. The same was true of Servia, Kastoria, Naousa and Galatista. Stromnitsa, like Yanitsa, was a Turkish city. Jewish communities of some importance were to be found in Beroia, where there were equal numbers of Moslems and Christians, and in Serrhai, Monastir, Kavala and Drama. Few Slav-speakers remained in the countryside of Eastern Macedonia - the remnants of Stephen Dušan's empire - though there were more in Western and the north of Central Macedonia.

The inhabitants, new and old, lived in separate communities, and were jointly responsible for the implementation of orders from the central authority, for the preservation of order and, most importantly of all, for the payment of taxes. The administration of the community was in the hands of the local aristocracy, which was permitted certain initiatives of a philanthropic or cultural nature. This local autonomy in matters of adminis-

tration also extended to the hearing by archbishops of cases involving family and inheritance law, in accordance with Byzantine custom-law.

The administrative system of the Ottoman Empire was based on its military organisation and, at the beginning of the period, the European conquests formed a single military and political district (the Eyalet of Roumelia), governed by the beyrlebey, a high-ranking official. In time, this broad unit was divided and Macedonia was broken up into smaller sections, of which Western Macedonia was assigned initially to the sanjak of Skopje and later to those of Ochrid and Monastir. By contrast, both Central and Eastern Macedonia formed separate sanjaks, with their capitals at Thessalonike and Kavala respectively. The northern areas were assigned to the sanjak of Kyustendil.

62

63

64

65

65. Ioannis Kottounios, the scholar from Beroia. From his first book published in 1628.

As during the Byzantine period, cereals, apples, olives, flax and vegetables were cultivated on the fertile plains of Macedonia. As the centuries passed, tobacco, cotton and rice were added to them. The creation of settlements in the mountainous areas and the intensification of stock-raising led to a reduction in the forested area. Trout from the rivers and lakes supplied the markets of Constantinople. From the numerous metal, silk and textile workshops - which owed much to the skills of the Jewish element - the empire ordered objects for daily use and also luxury goods. Goldsmiths, builders, chandlers, furriers, armourers, dyers of thread and cloth-makers in a few years turned the villages and towns in which they settled into bustling production and distribution centres. They were a source of prosperity, economic strength, building activity, and

intense competition. The caravans that transported the labour and skills of these craftsmen to Vienna, Sofia and Constantinople competed with the boats from the ports of Thessalonike and Kavala, which discharged their cargoes at both ends of the Mediterranean. And since Hermes Kerdoos (the god of commerce) invariably walked hand in hand in Greece with Hermes Logios (the god of letters), as soon as the tempest of the conquest had subsided and the Greeks had gained control of trade and production, the Greek expatriates achieved great things in the free lands of Austro-Hungary, Germany, France and Italy (both before and after the fall of Constantinople); the church assumed a leading role, supplanting the imperial authority; thirst for knowledge and the imparting of knowledge led initially to the foundation of church schools and then to the building of community educational institutions, to which flocked not only the Greeks but also the Greek-speakers of the Balkans.

Through benefactions from wealthy Macedonians such as Manolakis (1682) and Demetrios Kyritzis (1697) from Kastoria, young men were educated in Beroia, Serrhai, Naousa, Ochrid, Kleisoura and Kozani. Thanks to the inspired teaching of men like Georgios Kontaris, scholarch (head of school) at Kozani (1668-1673), Georgios Parakeimenos, headmaster in the same city (1694-1707), Kallinikos Varkosis, scholarch at Siatista (until 1768), and Kallinikos Manios in Beroia (about 1650), the Macedonians were able to partake of ancient and ecclesiastical literature and were initiated into the new achievements of science, which the intellectual pioneers of the Greek spirit were transporting from the educated West. There were many too, however, who, either as refugees to the West or as willing emigrants, transmitted their own precious lights to the regenerated world of Europe: men like Ioannis Kottounios (1572-1657), lecturer in the Universities of Padua, Bologna and Pisa, Demetrios, the Patriarch's envoy to Würtemberg (1559), and Metrophanis Kritopoulos, teacher of Greek in Venice (1627-1630).

Up until the beginning of the 19th century, though with a substantial break during the period of the Russian-Turkish confrontations (1736-38 and 1768-77), the Macedonian countryside prospered greatly and was at the same time the scene of unprecedented building activity. New villages were constructed and existing townships extended and beautified; amidst a climate of prosperity and expanding trade, two-storey *archontika* (mansions) were erected at Siatista,

Kozani, Kastoria, Beroia and Florina; their tiled roofs, carved wooden ceilings, and elegant built-in wooden cupboards, their reception rooms lavishly painted with floral, narrative and other motifs, and their spacious cellars and shady courtyards, all reflected the wealth of their owners and the achievements of a popular art that skilfully combined the lessons of tradition with a wide variety of borrowings from East and West.

For some time after the collapse of the Byzantine Empire, the subject Christians of Macedonia were content to fulfil their Christian duties by using the churches that had escaped pillaging by the conquerors. As the flock steadily increased, however, and the old buildings began to feel the adverse effects of time, while the inhabitants grew more prosperous, the need to repair and beautify the houses of God under the jurisdiction of the Greek communities and also to erect new ones became inescapable. Painters from Kastoria, and then from Crete, Epirus, and Thebes, in guilds or individually, criss-crossed Macedonia from as early as the 15th century, and hymned the glories of the Orthodox faith with their palettes, some in a primitive style, others with a more academic, refined intent. Yet others from Hlonades, Samarina, and Selitsa near Eratyra immortalised human vanity in secular buildings and, in the encyclopedic spirit of the age, portrayed philosophers, fantastic landscapes, the dream of the soul - Constantinople - and the vision of progress - cities of Western Europe.

66. The wedding dress worn at Roumlouki, villages near Gidas. Athens, Benaki Museum.

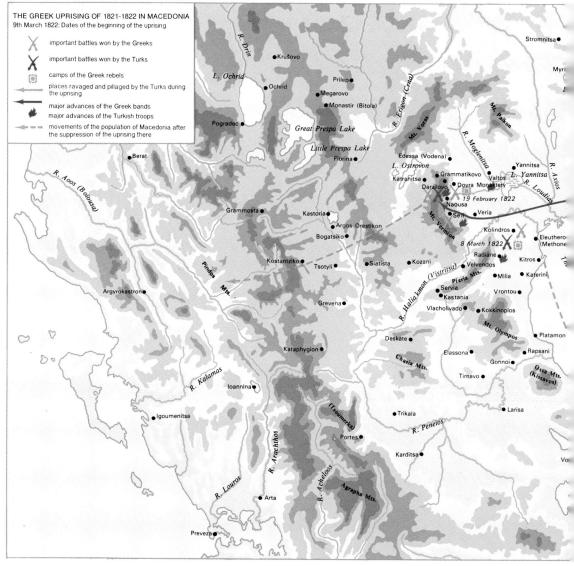

THE GREEK UPRISING OF 1821-1822 IN MACEDONIA
9th March 1822: Dates of the beginning of the uprising

✕ important battles won by the Greeks

✗ important battles won by the Turks

⬚ camps of the Greek rebels

← places ravaged and pillaged by the Turks during the uprising

◀ major advances of the Greek bands

🔥 major advances of the Turkish troops

◀- - - movements of the population of Macedonia after the suppression of the uprising there

Modern times

And as the wheel of destiny, after many centuries, furrowed the roads of the final decision, and an unquenchable desire for freedom consumed petty interests and levelled out vainglorious vacillation, the national desire to cast of the unbearable yoke began to awaken. The year 1821 of the Uprising in the Peloponnese lit up the peaks of mount Olympos and mount Athos. Although the repressive measures taken by the Turkish army and the seizure of hostages in Thessalonike did not dishearten the rebels of Emmanuel Pappas and the archimandrite Kallinikos Stamatiadis on Mount Athos and Thasos, who were thirsting for action, the insurrectionaries'

ignorance of military affairs and their lack of supplies, together with the ease with which the Turks were able to mobilise large armies, strangled the movement at its birth. The uprisings on Olympos and Bermion met with a similar fate, ending in the tragedy of the holocaust of Naousa.

After the liberation of southern Greece and the foundation of the free Greek state - the furthering of the Great Idea -spirits were restored and, with the invisible support of the Greek consulate in Thessalonike, incursions began into Turkish-held Macedonian areas, to stir up arm bands. Tsamis Karatasos roused Chalkidike. So, too, did Captain Georgakis. The unfavourable turn taken by the Cretan Struggle, however, and the inability of Greeks and Serbs to make common cause once again prevented a general up-

67

68

69

67. *The Greek Uprising of 1821-1822 in Macedonia.*

68. *Emmanuel Pappas from Serrhai, member of the Philike Hetairia (from a drawing by the sculptor K. Palaiologos). Athens, National Historical Museum.*

69. *Tsamis Karatasos, a major in the Greek army and later aide-de-camp to King Otto, played a leading role in every attempted uprising in Macedonia in the first decades of the 19th century. Athens, National Historical Museum.*

70. *The National Liberation Struggle at the lake of Yanitsa.* →

71. *Captain Agras (Tellos Agapinos) and his comrades on the lake of Yanitsa. Athens, J. Mazarakis Collection.*

72. *Pavlos Melas, the national hero, wearing the uniform of a Macedonian fighter, from a painting by G. Iakovidis. Athens, National Historical Museum.*

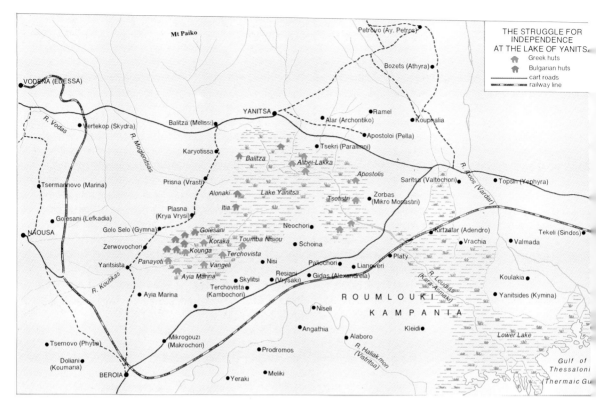

THE STRUGGLE FOR
INDEPENDENCE
AT THE LAKE OF YANITS.

🏠 Greek huts
🏠 Bulgarian huts
— cart roads
railway line

Mt Paiko

Petrovo (Ay. Petros)

Bozets (Athyra)

VODENA (EDESSA)

R. Vodas

Vertekop (Skydra)

R. Moglenitsas

YANITSA

Ramel

Balitza (Melissi)

Alar (Archontiko)

Kouphalia

Apostoloi (Pella)

Karyotissa

Tsekri (Paralimni)

Balitza

Alibei-Lakka

Tsermarinovo (Marina)

Prisna (Vrasti)

Apostolis

Saritsa (Valtochori)

Topsin (Yephyra)

R. Axios (Vardar)

Alonaki

Lake Yanitsa

Tsotistri

Zorbas
(Mikro Monastiri)

Plasna
(Krya Vrysi)

Itia

Golesani (Lefkadia)

Golo Selo (Gymna)

Golesani

Neochori

Kirtzalar (Adendro)

Vrachia

Valmada

Tekeli (Sindos)

NAOUSA

Koraka

Toumba Nisiou

Schoina

Zerwovochori

Kounga

Terchovista

Platy

R. Loudias
(Kara Asmaki)

Koulakia

Yantsista

Panayoti

Vangeli

Nisi

Paliochori

Lianoveri

Ayia Marina

Skylitsi

Resiani
(Vrysaki)

Gidas (Alexandrela)

Yanitsides (Kymina)

Terchovista
(Kambochori)

R O U M L O U K I

Ayia Marina

Niseli

K A M P A N I A

Kleidi

Lower Lake

Tsernovo (Phytia)

Mikrogouzi
(Makrochori)

Angathia

Alaboro

R. Koutikas

Doliani
(Koumaria)

Prodromos

R. Haliakmon
(Vistritsa)

Gulf of
Thessaloni

BEROIA

Yeraki

Meliki

(Thermaic Gu

Χατί

73. The triumphal entry of king Georgios I and his successor prince Constantine into the liberated city of Thessalonike. Athens, Gennadeios Library.

rising of the Macedonians.

In the second half of the 19th century, the international conjunctures tended to favour the other peoples of the Balkan peninsula and international diplomacy adopted a hostile stance towards Greek affairs. With the nationalist movements of Bulgaria rivalling the Turkish rulers in their anti-Greek attitudes, Macedonia, the apple of strife of the south Balkans, strove to preserve its Greek integrity by building schools and founding educational societies; it countered Slav expansionism with the historical reality and the Orthodoxy of the Ecumenical Patriarchate, and mobilised yet again its armed hopes and the youth of Free Greece. The Macedonian Struggle was in preparation. From the ill-fated year of 1875, from the inauspicious 1897, despite the genocide and the hecatombs of victims, the marshes of Yanitsa, the mountain peaks of Grevena, the forested ravines of Florina were transformed into pages on which, at the turn of the 20th century, men like Pavlos Melas, Constantine Mazarakis-Ainian, Spyromilios, Tellos Agapinos (Agras) and so many others, known and anonymous, wrote the name of Macedonian regeneration in their blood. In an empire on its way to collapse, despite the Young Turks' movement for renewal, and in opposition to a heavily armed, irrevocably hostile Bulgaria, with Serbia as an unreliable ally, Hellenism countered with the rights of the nation and, on 26th of October 1912, raised the flag of the cross in the capital of Macedonia, Thessalonike. Behind it, 500 years of slavery that had not succeeded in creating slaves. Half a millennium of torture, persecution, murder, plotting, disappointment and falsification of history donned once more the blue and white and, with the sword of justice, opened the road to the modern age. The age of the Balkan epic and progress.

CENTRAL (LOWER) MACEDONIA

According to Thucydides (II, 99), Lower Macedonia *(Kato Makedonia),* included Bottiaia, Pieria, Eordaia, part of ancient Paionia, Almopia, Mygdonia, Crestonia and Bisaltia. It extended, that is to say, over the modern counties of Pieria, Emathia, Thessalonike, Pella and Kilkis. Of these regions, Pieria, and above all Bottiaia, formed the kernel of the Macedonian kingdom prior to the extension of its geographical borders to west and east under Archelaos and especially under Philip II. The fertile plains of this region were watered by broad rivers - the Axios, Haliakmon and Loudias - and enjoyed a mild climate, and it is not difficult to account for the evolution and flowering here in historical times of the earliest cities of the Makedones (Aigai, Beroia, Pella, Mieza, Dion, and later Thessalonike), and also, much earlier, of powerful settlements on sites that at the time were on the shores of lakes or the banks of rivers: in the Neolithic period (Nea Nikomedeia, Yanitsa and Mandalo in the county of Pella), in the Bronze Age (Spathes on Olympos and Assiros) and in the Iron Age (Pydna, Palaio Gynaikokastro in Kilkis, Toumba in Thessalonike and Vergina). Nor is it surprising that the enchanting shores of the Thermaic Gulf, with their sheltered bays, saw the development of harbours like those of Herakleion (Platamon), Pydna and Methone, and the flourishing of centres such as Chalastra (possibly modern Sindos), Therme and Aineia (Mikhaniona), from the Archaic to the late Classical periods. The ruins of these settlements and the artistic treasures that have come to light and now adorn the Museums of Thessalonike and Dion are of exceptional importance; the richness, sensitivity and perfection of technique constitute a major contribution to our knowledge of ancient Greek civilization.

Discoveries such as the *kouros* from Europos in Kilkis, superb jewellery, weapons, black- and red-figure vases from the cemeteries of Sindos and Ayia Paraskeve, wonderful examples of toreutic art in bronze and silver from Sevasti in Pieria, from Pydna and Makrygialos, from Vergina (Aigai) and the city of Thessalonike (Oreokastro, Stavroupolis), marvellous ivory compositions from Lefkadia, Vergina and Dion are all indicative of the high cultural level of the region from Archaic times until the period after Alexander the

Great, from which date brilliant achievements in the sphere of town-planning (Pella) and funerary architecture (Vergina, Lefkadia). Examples of the vast wealth that flowed into the country after the campaign in the East. Forebear of the Hellenistic kingdoms of the *epigoni* (Successors), Lower Macedonia embraced the two capitals of the Macedonian kingdom - Aigai and Pella - and the great sanctuary at Dion (the Delphi of the north); after the dissolution of the kingdom (168 B.C.), it formed the second and third of the four *merides* into which the Roman Senate divided the country before it was incorporated into the *Provincia Macedonia* (148 B.C.). A theatre of military operations in the last centuries before Christ, first between the Roman legions on the one hand and the menacing barbarians of the north (Sintoi, Dardanians, Maidoi and Skordiskoi) and the armies of Mithridates VI of Pontus on the other, then between Julius Caesar and Pompey, and finally between Brutus and the duumvirate of Octavian and Mark Antony, the area yearned for peace, which was secured to it after many decades of upheaval, by the rule of Augustus (27 B.C. onwards).

Coloniae - Dion, Pella - free cities - Thessalonike - and tribute-paying cities - Beroia, Edessa and others - were in time transformed into pulsating centres of Greco-Roman civilization, with *fora, caesarea, curiae,* theatres, gymnasia, libraries, temples of the imperial cult, and wide streets paved with stone. They evolved into staging posts in the carrying trade, through which passed merchants from the West, in which were the headquarters of professionals and guildsmen from the East, at which were stationed squadrons of the Roman army and to which came caravans from Illyria and Thrace, following the Via Egnatia. They became storehouses of the glorious past of the land and erected monuments to the legendary conqueror, Alexander, organising games in his name (Alexandreia Olympia) and issuing coins (issues of the *Koinon ton Makedonon).* Greek cities, their old local institutions preserved in the assembly of the people, the council and the magistrates. Cities which, down to the middle of the 3rd century A.D., rejoiced in the mosaic floors of the wealthy houses, took pride in their agoras and sanctuaries, and mourned their dead with carved sarcophagi. Arks of Hellenism, until they were threatened by the Heruls and the Goths, that refused to forget their history and that cultivated philosophy, literature and poetry, and the theatre, and also the body. At the great turning point, with the divine message now firmly rooted in the Christian population - initially of Thessalonike and Beroia, and then of many of the Macedonian cities (Stoboi, Edessa, Pella) - and with the old administrative divisions subjected to repeated modifications, according to the needs of the times (reforms of Diocletian and Constantine the Great), the Roman personality of the land gradually donned the Byzantine purple. Early Christian basilicas and baptistries replaced triumphal arches, and hippodromes and bloody spectacles gave way to processions of the devout. In Thessalonike the ancestral god Kabeiros was displaced by the martyr Demetrios. The emperors, who were called upon to defend the northern and eastern borders of the empire, now leaders "by the mercy of God" of an Orthodoxy which rolled back the clouds of paganism and the barbarian hordes with equal zeal, increasingly spent their winters in this blessed land that offered rest and resignation: Constantine the Great in A.D. 322, Theodosios I in A.D. 379/80, and in A.D. 387-88, Valentinian II, regrouped their armies in the Macedonian capital to meet either rival claimants to power or the invading Goths. The region did not escape plundering, however, and cities like Pella, Stoboi and Edessa experienced the ferocity of the barbarians (A.D. 473-483), while Thessalonike only just escaped capture by the Huns (A.D. 540) and the Avars (A.D. 597). Despite all the turbulence and ravaging of the land, however, stock-breeding and farming prospered in the fertile plains of Central Macedonia, marble was exported from its harbours, and its urban centres were home to workshops of purple dyers and bronze-smiths, while leather was worked by specialist craftsmen. Salt-flats produced the salt for the curing of meat. The inhabitants around lakes Koroneia (Ay. Vasileios) and Bolbe harvested copious catches of fish with which they supplied the surrounding area (10th century A.D.). From this period of early Christianity date splendid monuments to the Christian faith, attesting to the prosperity of the region - monuments like the church of Saint Demetrios and the Acheiropoietos in Thessalonike, the episcopal basilica at Stoboi, and others at Edessa and Dion, strong fortification walls and brilliant houses (Thessalonike, Vargala and Stoboi). The achievements of sculpture competed with the conquests of metal-working, and mural mosaics rivalled the wall-paintings of tombs and religious buildings.

In the centuries that followed, Central Macedonia was once again tested by the perfidious foes of her integrity and prosperity: the Avars penetrated in waves, their plundering frenzy reaching the heart of the Byzantine Empire (A.D. 586-618, sieges of Thessalonike), Arab pirates marauded the Thermaic Gulf (A.D. 904), the Bulgarians took advantage of the weakness of the state to capture Beroia (A.D. 989), Kolindros, Servia and Edessa, and the Normans (A.D. 1185) sowed death and destruction amongst men and monuments. Usurpers, who coveted the economic prosperity, the flourishing culture and the intellectual prestige of the urban centres, which at this period could boast of brilliant, lavishly painted cathedrals and smaller churches (Beroia, Edessa - 11th century A.D.) and outstanding intellects. And while the dangers from the north abated as time passed, either because of internal weaknesses in the new states created in the Balkans (Serbia, Bulgaria), or as a result of the flexible policy pursued by Byzantine diplomacy (conversion of the Serbs by Cyril and Methodios of Thessalonike in the 9th century, followed by their assimilation to Byzantine civilization), the structure of the Byzantine Empire was shaken to its foundations by the Fourth Crusade of the "faithful" Christians of the West (A.D. 1204). The Crusade that dissolved institutions and authorities and looted the treasures of generations had by 1224 made this part of Byzantine Empire subject to the Franks of Boniface of Montferrat, under the name of the "Kingdom of Thessalonike". A Latin bishop was installed in Beroia, and the churches of Saint Demetrios and the Saint Sophia (Wisdom of God) in Thessalonike were given over to the western creed. The fortress at Platamon became a prominent fortification. At Pydna, a ruined church was converted into an army barracks.

Back in the bosom of the Byzantine Empire of Michael VIII Palaiologos, having for a short period formed part of the so-called Despotate of Epirus (A.D. 1224-1246), Central Macedonia was threatened by the Catalan Company, was thrown into turmoil by the conflicts between Andronikos II and Andronikos III Palaiologoi (A.D. 1328), was occupied by the armies of the Serb kral Stephen Dušan (A.D. 1334) and, finally, was bathed in blood by the confrontation between Ioannis Kantakouzenos and Ioannis V Palaiologos, before it eventually capitulated to the Ottoman Turks (1430, Capture of Thessalonike). More than two hundred years of disorder provoked by the Latin conquest, years of destruction, but also years of great achievement in the spheres of the art of fortification (Gynaikokastro on the Axios, Chrysi in Almopia), of architecture, mosaic, painting (Thessalonike), literature and philosophy, with prestige and influence on a world-wide scale.

The coming of the Turks, the planting of the countryside with Ottoman intruders (the *toparch* Ahmet Evrenos already owned the entire plain of Thessalonike in A.D. 1426), the settling of Jews from Spain in the urban centres (Thessalonike, Beroia), the creation of new cities (Yanitsa), and the depopulation of the plains as a result of the terrorism of taxation and the *paidomazoma* (child-levy) - all these factors led to a gradual change in the aspect of the region, and to the creation of new conditions, with Hellenism rallying before its destiny, seeking in visions and ideals the outlet of which it was deprived by its slavery. In Naousa, founded at this period, in Beroia (Karaferia under the Ottoman occupation), Vodena (Edessa) and Thessalonike (Selanik), commerce flourished, churches were erected in the neighbourhoods, *archontika* (mansions) concealed wealth and advancement, cottage industries supplied free Europe and Constantinople itself, ships carried merchandise and knowledge, foreigners and fellow-countrymen, secretly at first, though later openly, too, and schools preserved the memory of the past and laid the foundations for the future. At the same time, the news at various times of the defeat of the conqueror in international conflicts (1571, crushing of the Turkish fleet at Lepanto, 1645-69 Venetian-Turkish war, Austrian-Turkish embroilment 1716-18, Russian-Turkish confrontation 1768-1774) heartened the subject Greeks who, despite the harsh domestic policy of the *Sublime Porte* and the horrors perpetrated by irregular bands of armed bandits, did not hesitate to show their rejoicing, and engaged in practical movements of rebellion. *Armatoles* on Bermion, in Pieria and at Naousa, and *klephts* in Edessa added strength to courage and lent boldness to endurance to cast off faint-heartedness, and, in the midst of untold adversities, imitated Thermopylai. The army that marched under the leadership of the successor to the throne Constantine into the maelstrom of the Balkan Wars of 1912-13, drew many inspiring examples, and had much to learn from the unsuccessful uprisings of Olympos and the holocaust of Naousa (1822), from the victims of Turkish bestiality in the capital of Macedonia on the morrow of the revolt in Chalkidike, from the named and unnamed warriors of the pen, from the charismatic diplomats of the Greek consulate in Thessalonike, from the clergymen bathed in blood, and from the insurgents of the marshes of Yanitsa and Pieria. Despite Bulgarian interventions and machinations to the contrary, the blue and white flag finally fluttered in the breeze on the White Tower, gazing steadfastly at History.

60

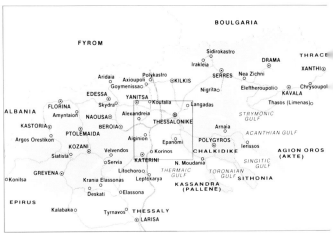

THESSALONIKE
and its region

74

HISTORICAL REVIEW

Ancient times

The *toumbes* and *trapezes* (artificial tumuli) in the immediate environs of Hellenistic Thessalonike have yielded rich evidence of continuous habitation, testifying to a concentrated, continuous and organised human presence from the Neolithic period onwards. The tumuli, formed from the ruins and foundations of successive layers of settlement, are distributed around the edge of the Thermaic Gulf (which was wider in antiquity and penetrated further inland) and attest to vigorous commercial communications with southern Greece and Ionia.

Archaeologists are not agreed as to the location of the site of Therme, the precursor of Hellenistic Thessalonike. According to one view, it is to be identified with the ancient settlement now being excavated in the neighbourhood called Toumba in Thessalonike, and according to another, with the ancient settlement at Mikro Embolo (Karambournaki), while a third, finally, holds that Therme should be sought in the centre of modern Thessalonike. When, in 315 B.C., Cassander, king of Macedonia, decided to found a new city in the heart of the Thermaic Gulf, by bringing together the inhabitants of twenty-six townships in Krousis, Anthemous and Mygdonia,

74. The old Waterfront (Paralia) of Thessalonike with the White Tower.

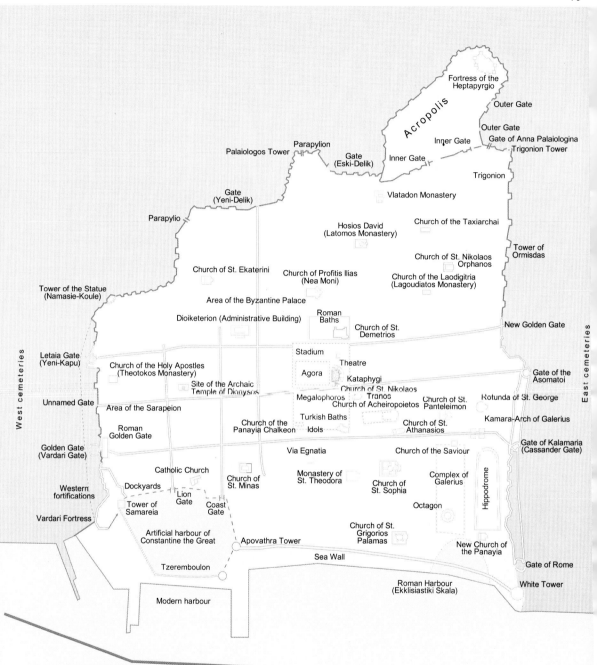

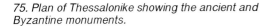

75. Plan of Thessalonike showing the ancient and Byzantine monuments.

76. Relief head from the sculptured frieze of the temple at Therme. End of the 6th century B.C. Thessalonike, Archaeological Museum.

77. Marble sima with a water-spout in the shape of a lion's head, from the ionic temple at Therme. End of the 6th century B.C. Thessalonike, Archaeological Museum.

78. Column capital from the ionic temple at Therme. End of the 6th century B.C. Thessalonike, Archaeological Museum.

76

77

78

79. Grave stone.
440 B.C.
Thessalonike,
Archaeological
Museum.

80. Head of
Serapis from the
area of the
Serapeion, a
Roman copy of an
original by the
sculptor Bryaxis.
Thessalonike,
Archaeological
Museum.

81. Bronze situla
from a tomb at
Kalamaria. 430-420
B.C. Thessalonike,
Archaeological
Museum.

Therme probably formed the kernel of the new unit, which was named after the wife of the Macedonian ruler (Thessalonike), and quickly became the "metropolis" of Macedonia.

Although for the first centuries of the city's existence (3rd-1st centuries B.C.) only scanty remains are preserved, confined mainly to discoveries yielded by excavation of cemeteries and/or isolated "Macedonian" tombs, recent studies of the street-plan of the modern city dating from before the fire of 1917 have revealed that in the centre of the city at least, the urban tissue of ancient Thessalonike was preserved: broad streets oriented north-south and east-west and intersecting at right angles enclosed large building blocks, rectangular in plan, in accordance with the principles of the so-called Hippodameian system. This system of urban lay-out, which was designed to secure the optimum location of the various functional areas within the urban grid - special areas for sanctuaries, agoras, residences, and so on - and was already known at an earlier date, was diffused on a spectacular scale in the 5th and 4th centuries B.C., and especially through the successors to the empire of Alexander the Great, when it became identified with the dynastic ambitions of the Hellenistic princes.

The fortifications of the new city, which were contemporary with its foundation, do not appear to have differed, at least in the line that they followed, from those of later periods, with the single exception of the eastern section, which must have been demolished when the area was levelled in order to incorporate the complex of Galerius into the plan at the end of the 3rd and the beginning of the 4th centuries A.D.

No traces have survived either of the Hellenistic port or of the palace of this period, which is mentioned in the sources at the time of Perseus (before the middle of the 2nd century A.D.). By contrast, the Forum (Agora) of the city, attested by inscriptions of the 1st century B.C., should be sought in the centre of the modern city, in precisely the place where the Roman agora has been excavated - that is, in the centre of the inhabited area. The commercial agora may possibly be located in the modern Plateia Emboriou, and the Gymnasium is perhaps to be placed in the area around and to the west of the church of Saint Demetrios.

The area devoted to public sanctuaries is located by discoveries made during excavations in the area between the agora and the west fortification wall; here was the temenos of Dionysos, and the Serapeion, in which other Egyptian gods,

80

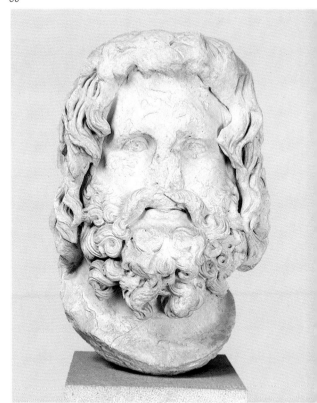

81

82. Alexandrian faience kalathos from the cist-grave at Neapolis, near Thessalonike. Beginning of the 2nd century B.C. Thessalonike, Archaeological Museum.

83. Clay "West Slope" vases from the "Macedonian" tomb in Syntrivaniou Square. First half of the 3rd century B.C. Thessalonike, Archaeological Museum.

84. Gold bracelets from a cist-grave at Neapolis, near Thessalonike. Beginning of the 2nd century B.C. Thessalonike, Archaeological Museum.

85. Clay figurine of Aphrodite from the tomb at Neapolis, near Thessalonike. Beginning of the 2nd century B.C. Thessalonike, Archaeological Museum.

84

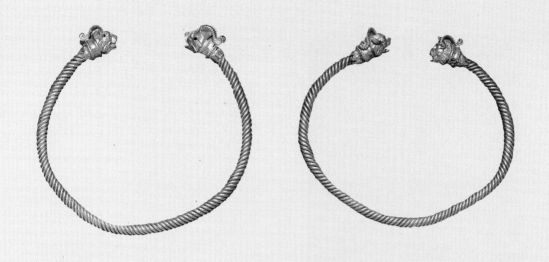

85

86

Isis, Osiris and Harpokrates were worshipped alongside Serapis. The latter building was particularly prestigious, as can be deduced from a letter of Philip V relating to it and from the revealing discoveries that have come to light during its excavation; later, at the time of Mark Antony and under the influence of Cleopatra, it was extended and acquired great fame.

In accordance with the ancient custom, the classical cemeteries of the city lay outside the fortified enceinte, and usually along major roads. However, in addition to these organised cemeteries, with groups of cist graves - some of which had rich grave offerings - there were also a number of isolated monuments in the wider region of Thessalonike (Stavroupolis, Neapolis, Mikhaniona), sometimes on private estates and sometimes on the edges of ancient townships.

From the 3rd century B.C. onwards date the monumental funerary structures known as "Macedonian" tombs, which have been found some

86. The "Rescript" of Philip V, dated to 187 B.C., in which the king took measures to protect the Serapeion of Thessalonike. Thessalonike, Archaeological Museum.

87. Silver tetradrachm of the "second meris" of Macedonia. 168-148 B.C. Athens, Numismatic Museum.

88. Altar with an inscription referring to the Asklepias tribe of Thessalonike. 2nd century A.D. Thessalonike, Archaeological Museum.

87

of the Antigonid dynasty, and entered into relations with famous - mainly religious - centres of Hellenism. Antigonos II Gonatas took refuge here after his defeat by Pyrrhos in 274 B.C. and it was here that Philip V withdrew after the battle at Kynoskephalai (197 B.C.) in order to turn his attention to the Romans. It was to Thessalonike that the Roman embassy came in 185 B.C. to settle the problem of the Thracian cities, and it was in its docks that Perseus burned the ships of the Macedonian military fleet to prevent them from falling into the hands of the enemy.

An autonomous city with institutions, organisation and magistracies modelled on the Greek cities of the south, Thessalonike was made dependent on the central authority, represented by the royal officer *(epistates),* flanked by five judges *(dikastai).* The citizens were divided into tribes - those known are Antigonis, Dionysias and Asklepias - and belonged to demes - Bukephaleia and Kekropis, for example. The main political organs were the council *(boule)* and the assembly of the people *(ekklesia).* The executive organs were the treasurers *(tamiai)* and the *agoranomoi.* The city also had its own eponymous magistrate, the priest of a deity whose name is not mentioned in the sources.

In 187 B.C., in the context of the reorganisation of the state after the treaty of Apameia (188 B.C.), Thessalonike was the first of the Macedonian cities, acting with the consent of Philip V, to issue its own coins - exclusively bronze. During this first phase of its operation the mint functioned for twenty years -that is, until 168 B.C., the year in which the Macedonian kingdom was dissolved.

The city did not lose its importance in the region in the years that followed, however. Capital of the second *meris* - the second of the four administrative districts into which the Romans divided Macedonia in 168 B.C. - and an extremely important strategic centre throughout the entire 2nd and 1st centuries, it attracted the interests of the Roman administration in its attempts to repel both the incursions of the Thracian tribes and the invading armies of Mithridates VI, king of Pontus.

quite close to and others far from the limits of the Hellenistic city. The majority, though they had frequently been robbed in antiquity, reveal through their structure, their painted decoration in its preserved form and the grave gifts that they contained (those that have survived) the wealth of their owners, most often members of great families. The monuments in question are the "Macedonian" tomb in Syntrivaniou Square, the one at the Maieuterion, the tomb of Charilaou, that of Phoenix, one in Monastiriou street and one in Neapolis, the first four in the east, and the other two in the west of the city.

Thessalonike, perhaps the most important military base in the kingdom and the largest commercial port in northern Greece, a city of international renown and prestige, played host to large numbers of foreigners during the troubled years

Roman period

Well defended in the heart of the Thermaic Gulf, in the foothills of mount Kissos, and in a favourable position for East-West and North-South trade, with four rivers in its immediate environs, possessed of a safe harbour, and standing on one of the most sensitive road networks, the Via

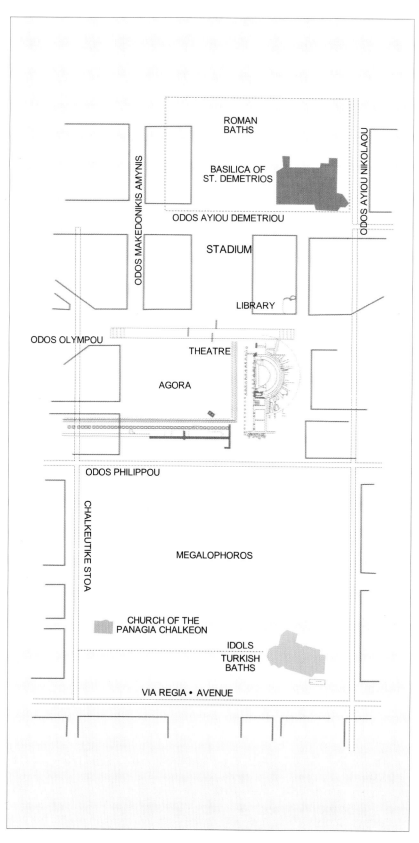

ROMAN
BATHS

BASILICA OF
ST. DEMETRIOS

ODOS MAKEDONIKIS AMYNIS

ODOS AYIOU NIKOLAOU

ODOS AYIOU DEMETRIOU

STADIUM

LIBRARY

ODOS OLYMPOU

THEATRE

AGORA

ODOS PHILIPPOU

CHALKEUTIKE STOA

MEGALOPHOROS

CHURCH OF THE
PANAGIA CHALKEON

IDOLS
TURKISH
BATHS

VIA REGIA • AVENUE

89. Plan of the Agora
(Forum) of
Thessalonike (Ch.
Bakirtzis).

90. Bronze coin of
Thessalonike with the
figure of Kabeiros, the
patron god of the city.
2nd century B.C.
Athens, Credit Bank
Numismatic Collection.

91. Pedestal for a
statue of queen
Thessalonike from the
Library in the area of
the Roman Forum. End
of the 2nd century A.D.
Thessalonike,
Archaeological
Museum.

Egnatia (laid in the second half of the 2nd century B.C.) the most glorious of the foundations of Cassander remained throughout the Roman Empire the administrative and economic centre that it had been in the period of the Hellenism of three continents and during the Roman Republic.

Under the new order imposed by the rule of Augustus (27 B.C.-A.D. 14), the city of Thessalonike was now in the rearguard of military enterprises and was already recognised in the middle of the 2nd century A.D. as the most populous city of the province of Macedonia. Two centuries earlier - about the middle of the 1st century B.C. - it was the place of exile of the Roman orator Cicero and, shortly afterwards, in 48 B.C., it served as the headquarters of Pompey before the battle of Pharsalos. Given the status of a free city *(civitas libera)* immediately after the victory of the Triumvirate of Octavian, Mark Antony and Lepidus at Philippoi (42 B.C.), it escaped plundering at the hands of the soldiers of Brutus, and in time became the birthplace of brilliant men of letters, and a centre to which flocked a host of scholars, merchants and craftsmen, both Greek and Roman. The importance of the city under the emperor Hadrian is indicated by the fact that it was one of the founding members of the *Panhellenion* - the pan-Hellenic amphictyony founded by the philhellene emperor in A.D. 131/132, with its headquarters at Athens. The cosmopolitan character of Thessalonike and the Roman presence there did not lead to any substantial changes in

the composition of its population and, most importantly, did not lead to the Latinisation of the inhabitants: this much is clear from the vast number of Greek inscriptions. On the other hand, not a few Thessalonikans, each for their own reasons, left their native city, either permanently or temporarily, and are attested in regions of the vast Roman empire as far afield as the west of north Africa, parts of former West Germany, Serbia and Rome, and as close to home - as is to be expected - as Philippoupolis (Plovdiv), Stoboi, Thasos, Philippoi and Athens.

The almost square town plan probably remained unchanged after the Roman conquest: the centre of the city continued to be occupied by the market-place (Agora), with its various building complexes. And while the wealth of the city is revealed by its public buildings, the economic prosperity of the inhabitants is attested by the uncovering of the brilliant mosaic floors that adorned private residences, the considerable number of representational busts of high quality, and other works of large-scale sculpture. And also by the great number of carved marble sarcophagi and the graves with their rich offerings.

With regard to the religious life of the city, the inscriptions refer to the cults of a variety of deities: Dionysos, Apollo, Aphrodite Omonoia, Zeus Hypsistos, the Nymphs, the Dioskouroi, and Nemesis. Although there is no direct evidence, the sites can be determined fairly accurately of the temple of the god Fulvus - the son of Marcus

90

91

Aurelius, who was deified after his premature death in A.D. 165 (the area to the west of Saint Demetrios) - that of the patron god of the city, Kabeiros (on the site of the later church of Saint Demetrios), the temple of the deified Julius Caesar, that of Zeus Eleutherios and Roma, and perhaps that of Augustus (in the area of Strategou Doumbioti street). The city had not forgotten the ancient glory of the time of the Macedonian kingdom, however: statues of Alexander the Great, his son Alexander IV and his sister Thessalonike were erected in a prominent position in the Library. And it did not remain unmoved by the messages of Christianity brought to it by saint Paul, the Apostle of the Nations, in A.D. 49/50: the Christian community of Thessalonike was one of the firsts to be founded on the European soil, and quickly became one of the most active.

Despite all the reverses that the 3rd century A.D. held in store for the surrounding region and for the city in particular, Thessalonike, at this period of inner retraction and questing for ethical support in the past, successfully exploited the honours showered upon her by the philhellene emperor Gordian III, who in A.D. 241 bestowed upon her the right to hold the ecumenical Pythian games every five years and to maintain a temple dedicated to the cult of the emperor. She also achieved the granting of the honorary titles of "Metropolis" and "Colonia" by Trajan Decius (A.D. 249-251). Danger was before the gates, however: Goths, Carpi, and Heruls flooded the Balkan peninsula, laid waste the cities and the countryside and, in the spring of A.D. 254, laid siege to Thessalonike, which escaped capture thanks to the bravery of its inhabitants and its recently repaired fortification walls, and also, according to tradition, thanks to the decisive presence on her battlements of the patron god of the city, Kabeiros. The same "deus ex machina" again saved his beloved city from the rapacious designs of the barbarian hordes in A.D. 268.

92. Detail of a mosaic floor with a depiction of a mature male figure, the personification of a sea demon. 3rd century A.D. Thessalonike, Archaeological Museum.

93. Detail of a mosaic floor: a female figure and a dolphin symbolise the sea. 3rd century A.D. Thessalonike, Archaeological Museum.

The situation became bleak, however, and the frequent rebellions of ambitious contenders to the Roman throne, combined with the increasing raids of the German tribes from the north and the Sassanids from the east, brought the empire to the brink of dissolution and economic collapse.

The rise to power of the emperor Diocletian (A.D. 284) and the creation of the so-called first Tetrarchy, prevented its total decomposition, restored the unity of the state and preserved the "Roman ideal". As capital of that part of the Roman Empire that included the Balkan peninsula, and seat of one of four *tetrarchs,* Galerius (C. Galerius Valerius Maximinianus), Thessalonike flourished once more and acquired great prestige through its building activity, which was now designed mainly as an expression and assertion of dynastic policy: the brilliant complex of buildings, of grandiose architectural design (the official residence of the ruler, the hippodrome, the triumphal arch, popularly known as Kamara, and further north the Rotunda -Galerius' mausoleum) is irrefutable evidence for the nature of the enterprise, and for a shift in the centre of gravity from the political centre of the city - the agora - to the administrative centre - the palace. It was at this period that the history of Thessalonike was marked by the martyrdom of saint Demetrios, later the patron god of the city; after the Edict of Milan (A.D. 313), the wise adminstration of Constantine the Great, thanks to whose interest the city acquired an artificial harbour (A.D. 322), and the establishment of Christianity as the official religion, Thessalonike gradually assumed its medieval character and broke with its pagan past.

Byzantine period

Although the end of the 4th century A.D. was marked by the hideous slaughter of 7,000 Thessalonikans in the city's hippodrome, on the orders of Theodosios I the Great, and barbarian raids were a daily danger to its inhabitants, Thessalonike pursued the destiny marked out for it by its position as the second largest city in the eastern half of the empire. Solid fortification walls were erected together with an outwork, guaranteeing safer defence. The Rotunda was converted into a church and decorated with superb mosaics. In A.D. 412/13, the provincial governor Leontios erected a brilliant church dedicated to saint Demetrios, and in the middle of this same century (5th century A.D.) was built the large church of the Virgin, known as the Acheiropoietos. By the end of the century the transformation of the city

94

95

into a centre of Christianity of wide prestige and influence was complete, and to the two churches mentioned above were added the huge basilica that has been identified beneath and around the modern church of Saint Sophia, the church of Saint Minas (original phase), and the enormous octagonal church near the modern "Phoenix" Turkish baths in the west part of the city. Dark centuries, however, and testing times were waiting at the end of each creative interval. Thessalonike was besieged by the Ostrogoths of Theoderic the younger (A.D. 479), threatened by tribes of Huns (A.D. 540), and cut off by hordes of Slavs (6th-7th centuries A.D.). In 610 and 630 earthquakes destroyed large areas of the city and the ensuing fire consumed the church of Saint Demetrios (A.D. 629-634). Avars and Bulgars, and vast numbers of Sklavenoi from the depths of the Balkans, attempted to capture the "bride of the Thermaic Gulf" by land and by sea.

From the middle of the 7th century to the beginning of the 9th, the central authority was concerned to strengthen the Greek element in Macedonia, decimated and wearied by the repeated raids of the Avar and the Slav tribes. Unhappily, the progress of Thessalonike was interrupted in the first days of August A.D. 904, when the city was captured by Arabs pirates: the cost of the sack was high, with as many as 22,000 prisoners thrust onto the slave markets of Crete and other parts of the East, and countless numbers falling victim to the slaughter. After the death of Ioannis Tzimiskes (A.D. 976), Thessalonike experienced from afar of the expansionist enterprises of the Bulgars who, under tzar Samuel, captured Beroia and Larisa, and reached Central Greece. They were driven back and annihilated by the emperor Basil II Bulgaroktonos ("Slayer of the Bulgars"), and Bulgaria was turned into a province of the Byzantine Empire (1018). The strengthening of the fortification walls and the defence of the Macedonian capital at this period, though it discouraged the attacks of the Bulgars (1040)

94-95. Saints; detail from the third zone of the mosaic decoration of the dome of the Rotunda. End of the 4th century A.D. Thessalonike.

96. Part of the defence walls of Thessalonike. 4th century A.D.

97. Coin (billon trachy) of Manuel Komnenos Angelos Doukas, emperor of Thessalonike (A.D. 1230-1237). Washington, Dumbarton Oaks Collection.

and the Cumans was still not enough to withstand the danger from the West, particularly in view of the advanced state of dissolution of the empire: in 1185 the Normans of Sicily laid siege to Thessalonike by land and sea, made themselves masters of it and held it for a year. Their acts of barbarity went as far as the destruction of the silver Chalice inside the basilica of Saint Demetrios. And Thessalonike was rich in these years of the dynasty of the Komnenoi. Birthplace of Cyril and Methodios, the apostles of the Slavs, city of saint Demetrios, to whose great festival flocked hosts of visitors every year on the 26th October and for several days afterwards, spiritual centre that produced prelates, theologians and literary scholars of the stature of Michael Choumnos and Eustathios, bustling commercial port, the second city of the empire, with countless churches adorned with wall-paintings and mosaics, capital of the "theme of Thessalonike", and later the ad-

ministrative unit of "Thessalonike-Strymon-Voleron", Thessalonike had a theatre and a library, was governed by a local aristocracy the *dynatoi* (powerful) or *aristoi* (best) of the sources owning mansions and large estates, had a vast number of workshops, and counted a population approaching 100,000. In its mint were struck gold, silver and bronze coins. In its churches, the art of the palette and the mosaic immortalized the cultural achievements of a robust and creative society.

The dismemberment of the Byzantine state by the crusaders of the Fourth Crusade in 1204 assigned Thessalonike - along with the rest of Macedonia - to Boniface, marquis of Montferrat, the first king of the Frankish kingdom of Thessalonike. From the moment of his installation, however, the conqueror had to deal with both the reaction of the Greek element and the raids of the Bulgarians who, already in A.D. 1205 and 1207, were laying siege to the capital of the kingdom, albeit without success.

The powers of the Greek states created in Epirus and Nicaea on the morrow of the fall of Constantinople to the Franks were biding their time, however. Thessalonike was to be freed by the despot of Epirus, Theodore Komnenos Doukas Angelos, in 1224, and was later annexed to the empire of Nicaea in 1246 by Ioannis III Vatatzes. The recovery of the "queen of cities" by Michael VIII Palaiologos in 1261 restored the city of saint Demetrios to the bosom of the Byzantine Empire. In the period that followed, which is characterised by the dynastic strife between the Palaiologoi and the Kantakouzenoi, the endeavours of the Serb kral Stephen **Dušan** to extend his state, the plundering raids of the Catalans, and the movement of the Zealots and Hesychasts created great upheaval and tumult within the Empire and in Thessalonike in particular, and prepared the ground for the inevitable weakening of the state in the face of the threat that lurked in the East. In 1354, the Turks crossed to Europe and with them began the twilight of a thousand years of history, the history of Eastern Roman Civilization.

99. Glass plate with an incised depiction of a bird. 13th century A.D. Thessalonike, Archaeological Museum.

With Manuel II, son of Ioannis V Palaiologos, playing a leading role, Thessalonike was transformed in the period 1382-1387 into a vigorous centre of resistance to Turkish expansionism. No other ruler of the time worked as hard as Manuel to revive the ancient spirit and awaken the historical and national consciousness of the Greeks. The period was doomed, however, and time overtook events. Victim of the defeatism of certain circles, the city was to surrender to Murad I, becoming a tax-paying subject until 1391, when it was annexed to the Turkish state by Bayezid I.

Scions of distinguished families, artists and intellectuals, faced with slavery and the danger of forced conversion to Islam, abandoned their ancestral homes and either sought refuge in inaccessible areas or fled to regions that had not been vanquished, taking their knowledge and their art with them. An art that had shone in the Macedonian capital in the century prior to its subjugation, illuminating the artistic firmament of the Balkan peninsula. An art that endowed the gallery of known artists with names such as Georgios Kalliergis, the Astrapas brothers, Manuel Panselinos. The city of saint Demetrios, a

98. Mosaic depiction of an angel, from the 9th century A.D. Detail from the scene of the Ascension on the large dome of the church of Saint Sophia, Thessalonike.

78

brilliant centre of Greek culture and education, was to nurture within its bosom jurists and philosophers, philologists and theologians, whose writings for a long time formed the points of reference for later research.

The defeat of Bayezid I by the Mogol Tamerlane outside Ankara in A.D. 1402 led to the liberation of Thessalonike, which tried to exploit the respite secured to her by the blows suffered by the Ottoman state. The tranquillity was transient however. Despair at the turn taken by affairs gripped the hearts of the "free besieged". The city gradually emptied and its buildings were abandoned and fell into ruin. Those that remained on the battlements of patriotism went hungry.

In the end, after being ceded for a short period to the Venetians (1423-1430), the fortress could not hold out and surrendered to Murad II. In the space of the three days that the looting, sacking of monuments, slaughter and taking of prisoners lasted, the city was razed to the ground. A prelude to the Fall of Constantinople, the capture of Thessalonike symbolized the beginning of the end. Symbolized the Dark Ages of Turkish occupation.

The Tourkokratia and Modern times

Despite the settlement in Thessalonike of Moslems and the influx of thousands of Jewish refugees from Western Europe, the city continued under the new order to be the bastion of Hellenism, the second city after Constantinople, preserving its traditional local institutions and internal autonomy. Its connections - mainly economic - with wider geopolitical areas (the Balkans, south-east and central Europe, and the eastern Mediterranean) brought the city wealth, transformed it into a cosmopolitan centre and healed the wounds of the past. The 7,000 inhabitants of 1430 increased by 1478 to 11,000. By 1519 the population of the city had reached 29,000 inhabitants. To serve the needs of the Moslems, Christian churches were converted into mosques (the Acheiropoietos, 1430), Turkish baths were built (Bey Hamam, 1444, Pasha Hamam, 1520-30), markets were erected (Bedesten, 15th century) and inns were founded. And of course, during the implementation of the new building programmes, the name of Allah was worshipped in new, splendid houses (Hamza Bey mosque, 1467/68, Alaça Imaret mosque, 1484).

In time the face of the city was transformed. The basic kernel of the urban network was now formed by the Turkish neighbourhoods (mahal-

lades) with a different ethnic composition and different methods of organisation. In 1478, ten Greek districts are reported (6,094 inhabitants) and ten Turkish (4,320 inhabitants). In contrast with the comfortable, spacious houses of the conqueror, those of the Greeks and Jews were cramped, built closely together, and had tiny courtyards, frequently causing problems of cleanliness and health. Gardens of Turks and Greeks (bahçedes and perivolia) filled the uninhabited areas on the slopes of the fortified region of the city.

Anyone who attempted in 1621 to travel to Thessalonike from the coasts of Epirus would have crossed a region full of brigands. This period saw an increasingly menacing paralysis of the state machine, leading even to the adulteration of precious metals. A period during which there were embroilments in the Macedonian capital between the Greek and Jewish elements on the one hand, and the Turks on the other, arising out of the lack of justice and the venality and greed of the state organs who illegally exacted inflated taxes. Clashes with the Venetians in Crete, too, led to unusual to-ing and fro-ing in Macedonia in the middle of the century: detachments of local inhabitants of Thessalonike, a kind of citizens' militia, patrolled the coasts day and night, in fear of Venetian descents. The majority of the inhabitants, however, faced with insecurity and outbursts of brigandage, emigrated, leaving behind them their few compatriots who rallied defensively in the bosom of the communities and the Church. And it was here, precisely, that the education of the nation scraped by, with ecclesiastical writings as its only textbooks. Here, where the ancient glories were preserved beneath birth certificates/christening clothes on which survived names of the great Byzantine families. The institution of the church-school now became reduced in stature. At the same time, the copying of manuscripts continued.

Seat of a sanjakbey, with a molla (supreme interpreter of the law and judge) with a genitsar aga (commander of the Janissaries), and a base of a strong military power, Thessalonike, the Selanik of the Turks, was a commercial centre which, on account of the transit trade, played an important role in this sensitive part of the Ottoman empire as the largest harbour in the region. This role was not diminished even when the English and the Dutch, exploiting the sea routes opened up by the western European explorers, transported the exotic products of the Indies direct to London or to Amsterdam. Trade now

100

100. The Bezesten, the indoor market of Thessalonike. 15th century A.D.

passed into the hands of the Greeks, while the Jews succeeded Venice, now in decline, as the sole carriers of trade in the Mediterranean.

The houses of Thessalonike, facing east and south, are high, tiled, stone-built, many-storeyed buildings with two or three courtyards. They have balconies *(sahnisia),* sheds *(çardak),* and kiosks *(kioskia).* There were 30 churches in the city at this period, with 48 mosques and 36 synagogues. *Mendresedes* (theological schools), *tekkedes* (Dervish monasteries), *hamams* (baths) and *hans* (inns). Evliya Çelebi, the famous 17th century Turkish traveller, admired the bezesten - the closed market of Thessalonike. According to this writer, there were in the city 4,400 establishments of craftsmen, cottage-industries and merchants. The blue silk *pestemalia* (bath-towels), and the keçe (felt) carpets were renowned throughout the empire.

A stout wall along the shore protected Thessalonike from attack from the sea, and huge towers with canon, guaranteed the security of the port, one at the east and one at the west end. The east tower, the famous White Tower [about

the middle of the 15th century with repairs and additions by Süleyman I the Magnificent (1520-1566)], was also used as a gaol.

From the hundreds of boats, filled with a variety of merchandise, that put in at the city poured a colourful crowd of merchants and sailors from every part of the world.

The importance of Thessalonike, especially in the years following the Austrian-Turkish war and the treaty of Passarowitz, can be seen from the eagerness of the major economic powers of Europe to establish consulates there. The French were followed by the English, the Dutch and the Venetians. Coffee, sugar, tin, cinnamon and pepper were succeeded by silks, glassware, paper, nutmeg and ivory. Luxury goods were unloaded from Constantinople, and cargoes of oil, citrus fruit and sponges arrived from the Aegean islands. Timber was despatched to Crete. Cereals, tobacco and unworked silk were conveyed to the East. Every week, caravans of 120 animals set off for Sofia, Skopje and Vienna.

About 1733 the city was still confined within its fortification walls. There do not appear to have been any villas or suburbs outside these. The garrison consisted of 700-800 Janissaries. The inhabitants numbered about 40,000: 10,000 were Turks, 8,000-9,000 Greeks, with a few Bulgarians, and 18,000-20,000 Jews. As in the Byzantine period, 1/3 of the city was occupied by gardens and *alanes* (open spaces - the area outside the old hippodrome was a similarly unbuilt area). In the cathedral, a three-aisled timber-roofed basilica honouring the name of Gregorios Palamas, the relic of this wise saint was preserved, while the church of Saint Demetrios, which had been converted into a mosque, had a spacious crypt.

The head of the Greek community was the archbishop. The local rulers - the *demogerontes* - managed local finances and, along with their fellow citizens, were responsible amongst other things for the expense of running the schools, in which were taught ancient Greek, Latin, philosophy and theology. The Jews also had small schools. The Greeks of Thessalonike maintained links, mainly of an economic nature, with their fellow countrymen in Venice, entered into partnership with French and German capital, and looked after Austrian interests in the Aegean.

As early as the end of the 18th century, trade guilds *(roufetia)* with a wide variety of names are mentioned in the city - the result of an undoubtedly growing economy. Life does not seem always to have been pleasant, however, for any internal disturbance in the Ottoman empire or turbulence resulting from international embroilments had direct repercussions on the subject population. Turks and "Franks", each for their own reasons, endeavoured in a variety of different ways to obliterate the ethnic identity of the inhabitants. Enforced conversions to Islam, seductive proselytising on behalf of Catholicism and the destruction and looting of the remains of historical memory in the name of a dubious cult of the ancient world, alternated with convictions and hangings for participation in revolutionary movements, confiscations, and enslavement. Despite the adversity and stagnation stemming from subjugation to the Turks, the wind of the Enlightenment was not slow to freshen the waters of the Thermaic Gulf. Schools were built (the "Greek School" was now founded), wealthy individuals expended large sums on the painted decoration of churches, and affluent Greeks resident abroad funded

the erection of charitable foundations (Papaphis). The messages of the French Revolution and the Serbian Uprising touched the urban class that was now in the process of formation and, when the new century dawned, the representatives of the commercial and intellectual world were becoming increasingly conscious of their obligations in response to the inspired summons of Righas Pheraios.

Those who had emigrated returned to their birthplaces, where they erected brilliant town houses. Unlike the Jews who, as children of the diaspora, felt less closely bound with the land, the Greeks looked on Greece as a legacy from their forefathers and the Turks as merely passing lords. News of the revolt in Moldavia and Wallachia, and later the uprising in the Peloponnese and Central Greece, and even rumours of an impending invasion by Russian armies of liberation aroused men's spirits, called to mind ancient glories, and set hands to weapons. Chalkidike and Mount Athos, with the aid of an expeditionary force of Psarianoi and under the leadership of Emmanuel Pappas from Serrhai, were transformed into explosive centres of resistance and revolt against the Turkish yoke. In 1821, however, Macedonia was drowned in blood. Monks were abused, villagers murdered, holy water fouled, settlements given up to the frenzy of fire. Caravans of slaves made their way to Thessalonike to be sold on the slave-markets there, hostages were executed, and the city reeked with the stench of the unburied bodies of the hanged. Harshness and fear ruled where once prosperity had blossomed. The Macedonian capital, which now numbered about 60,000 inhabitants, of whom 30,000 were Turks, 16,000 Greeks and 12,000 Jews (the remainder were mainly foreigners, with a few gypsies and negroes), became the scene of indescribable suffering. The decimation of the Greeks contrived by the Turkish authorities in the city was intensified by the wave of those fleeing to various parts of southern Greece (in 1825, the population of Thessalonike had shrunk by about 4,000 Greeks).

In the end, however, the genius of the nation

101. The White Tower, a building dating from the middle of the 15th century, in its present form.

104

102-103. Gold waistcoat embroidered from Kastoria, and smoked silver buckle from Naousa. End of the 19th century. Thessalonike, Folklore Museum.

104. The Mordoch villa, by the architect X. Paionidis. Built in 1905, it is a good example of the eclectic architecture characteristic of the "towers" on Vas. Olgas Avenue in Thessalonike.

arrested the decline and the situation soon changed, mainly in the economic sphere. After the plague of 1838, which laid waste half the Jewish population and accelerated the end of the carpet and textile industries - the former already moribund as a result of the steadily increasing imports of English cashmeres - the Greek element became the main promoter of trade. Meanwhile, the face of the city was also transformed. New neoclassical buildings were erected alongside the old houses, large sections of the fortification walls were demolished (in the east and along the coast), avenues were laid out and army barracks constructed. On February 2nd 1835, the *Sublime Porte* announced the appointment by the Greek Kingdom of the first Greek consul in Thessalonike. The history of the city had entered upon a new phase.

The introduction of steam-propelled boats in the middle of the 19th century led to the revival of commercial links between Thessalonike and the ports of the western Mediterranean. At the same time, rail links were established between the city and Skopje (1871), which opened up the road to Central Europe, and also with Dedeagac (Alexandroupolis) (1896), which allowed direct communications with Constantinople. The penetration of Macedonia by capitalism, with the foundation of industrial units, endowed it with a gas factory and a horse-drawn tramway. However, caught between East and West, the inhabitants of Thessalonike faced the 20th century with mixed feelings, in a climate of unease at the state of international affairs and at events within a dying empire. Thessalonike faced the future while bound to the past. Faced the 26th October 1912, which was to return it to the bosom of the Greek state after almost half a millennium of slavery.

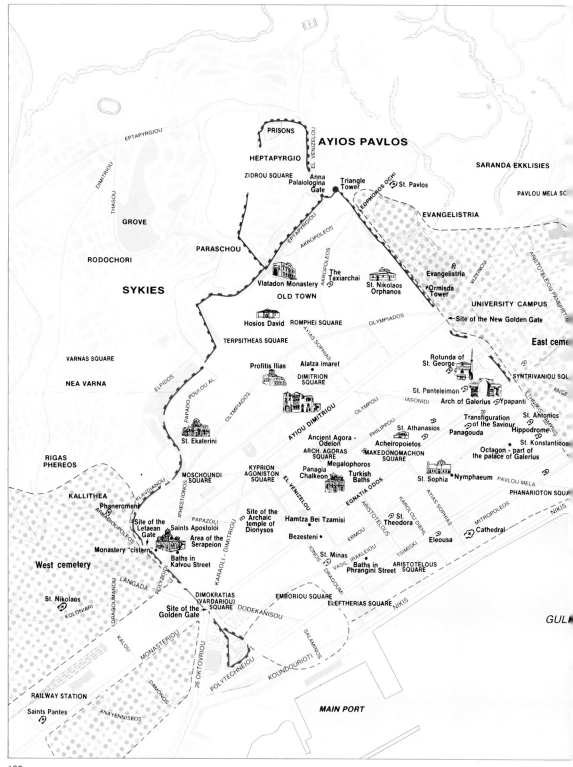

PRISONS

AYIOS PAVLOS

HEPTAPYRGIO

SARANDA EKKLISIES

ZIDROU SQUARE

Anna
Palaiologina
Gate

Triangle
Tower

St. Pavlos

PAVLOU MELA SC

EVANGELISTRIA

GROVE

PARASCHOU

Evangelistria

RODOCHORI

The
Taxiarchai

Ormisda
Tower

SYKIES

Vlatadon Monastery

St. Nikolaos
Orphanos

UNIVERSITY CAMPUS

OLD TOWN

Hosios David

ROMPHEI SQUARE

OLYMPIADOS

Site of the New Golden Gate

TERPSITHEAS SQUARE

East ceme

VARNAS SQUARE

Rotunda of
St. George

SYNTRIVANIOU SQ

NEA VARNA

Profitis Ilias

Alatza imaret

DIMITRION
SQUARE

St. Panteleimon

Arch of Galerius

Ypapanti

ANGE

St. Antonios

IASONIDI

Transfiguration
of the Saviour

Hippodrome

St. Konstantinos

AYIOU DIMITRIOU

Ancient Agora -
Odeion

St. Athanasios

Panagouda

ARCH. AGORAS
SQUARE

Acheiropoietos

MAKEDONOMACHON
SQUARE

Octagon - part of
the palace of Galerius

RIGAS
PHEREOS

MOSCHOUNDI
SQUARE

KYPRION
AGONISTON
SQUARE

Megalophoros

Panagia
Chalkeon

Turkish
Baths

St. Sophia

Nymphaeum

PAVLOU MELA

KALLITHEA

EL. VENIZELOU

EGNATIA ODOS

PHANARIOTON SQUA

Phaneromeni

Site of the
Archaic
temple of
Dionysos

Hamtza Bei Tzamisi

St.
Theodora

NIKIS

Site of the
Letaean
Gate

Saints Apostoloi

PAPAZOLI

Eleousa

Cathedral

Bezesteni

Monastery "cistern"

Area of the
Serapeion

Baths in
Kalvou Street

St. Minas

Baths in
Phrangini Street

ARISTOTELOUS
SQUARE

West cemetery

St. Nikolaos

KOLONIARI

DIMOKRATIAS
(VARDARIOU)
SQUARE

EMBORIOU SQUARE

ELEFTHERIAS SQUARE

NIKIS

GUL

Site of the
Golden Gate

DODEKANISOU

RAILWAY STATION

Saints Pantes

ANAYENNISEOS

POLYTECHNEIOU

KOUNDOURIOTI

MAIN PORT

105. Thessalonike: plan of the modern city and its monuments.

THE MONUMENTS

In the space of a few decades from the year of its foundation (316/5 B.C.), Cassander's Thessalonike progressed in leaps and bounds, ascended the surrounding hills, and evolved into one of the most important centres in northern Greece. From this time onwards, and for the rest of its life, the city was renowned for its cultural prestige and influence (which reached first the Hellenistic Aegean and then the Christian Balkans) for its political importance in the Roman East and in Byzantine Orthodoxy, and for its commercial activities along the Via Egnatia and the river Axios.

The archaeological remains from the early period of the city's life are scanty: continuous habitation, earthquakes, pillaging and fires, along with the ambitious building plans of the Augustan period and the Tetrarchy of Galerius have not only effaced most of the Hellenistic buildings, but were also the cause of the razing of entire neighbourhoods.

The scattered - mainly portable - finds are supplemented by the ruins of the sanctuary of Serapis in the basement of an apartment building near Antigonidon Square in the west of the city (model in Thessalonike Museum), the remains of houses in Kassandrou, Gr. Palama, Mitropoliti Genadiou and other streets, small sections of the original defensive wall incorporated into the later Byzantine fortifications in the north wall of the city and, finally, a number of "Macedonian" tombs.

During the Roman Empire and the Byzantine period, from which the majority of the surviving monuments date, Thessalonike was adorned with a large number of splendid buildings. Churches and exedres were erected, luxury houses with elegant decoration were built, statues of gods and rulers were raised, and triumphal arches constructed. Large areas were converted into majestic building complexes for public use (Agora/forum, stadium, etc.), or to provide for the central authority its earthly residences and its resting places after death (Palace of Galerius, Rotunda, etc.)

The heart of the city, which withstood the blows of the centuries, which beat faster when Hellenism prospered and mourned at other, more inauspicious moments for the nation, is today as robust as ever behind the eye of time, and beats through the monuments of the past, an indefatigable interpreter welcoming its guests.

THE CITY WALLS

When he founded Thessalonike, Cassander also provided for the defences of the city - a city that the archaeological finds tend to place in the area to the north of Olympou street. Sections of the Hellenistic phase (masonry courses) have been observed in the north-west part of the walls, incorporated as foundations into a super-structure of later date. Despite the fact that this enceinte received some attention in later decades, the fortification was neglected in the 1st century B.C., as attested by Cicero. The city's defence is believed to have been rein-forced under the Late Republic, however: to this period dates the construction of the Golden Gate, which formerly stood on the site of the present Vardari Square- probably a triumphal arch for the victors of Philippoi (42 B.C.), Octa-vian and Mark Antony. Parts of the fortifications again needed repairing in the middle of the 3rd century A.D., when hordes of Heruls and Goths threatened the Macedonian capital with suffocat-ing sieges; the city by now covered a greater ar-ea, mainly towards the south, and the sea wall ran parallel with and to the south of Ermou street. A coin of Thessalonike dating from the time of Gallienus (A.D. 253-268) bears a scene of Kabei-ros on the walls of the city, indicating that this demon-god, the protector of the city, just like saint Demetrios many years later, appeared, or was believed to have appeared as a vision in the front line, to defend his beloved city and wreak vengeance on her enemies. Galerius' initiative at the beginning of the 4th century, with the creation of an extensive palace complex in the east sec-tor of the city, undoubtedly involved a major modification of the fortification walls of Thessalo-nike: the line followed by the wall was shifted to-wards the plain in order to enclose the royal resi-dence, the hippodrome, the triumphal arch (Ka-mara) and the Pantheon (Rotunda).

In the following centuries, the walls continued to embrace the city of Cassander in two parallel, ascending arms, to east and west, which ended at the triangle of the acropolis in the north. Rein-forced by towers, posterns, gates and a bastion bestowed by the later Roman and Early Byzan-tine/Byzantine periods (4th-10th centuries A.D.), the walls resisted the plundering raids of the Bul-gars and Avars, though they capitulated to the siege of the Arabs were then left for a time to their fate, and later failed to withstand the Nor-mans of Sicily (A.D. 1185). Repairs are attested at the time of Basil II the Bulgar Slayer and during

the Palaiologan period (Gate of Anna Palaiologi-na on the Acropolis), and particularly under the Ottoman occupation when, in view of the new conditions prevailing in siege and military tech-niques, there was significant remodelling and ad-ditions (White Tower, Heptapyrgio, Top-Hane, Triangle Tower).

In recent years the Archaeological Service has expended much effort and money to embel-lish and restore the city walls, which today are preserved to a length of about four kilometres (the original length is reckoned to have been twice this). The sea-wall and a section of the south-east and south-west wall no longer exist: they were demolished on the altar of modern civ-ilization at the end of the 19th-beginning of the 20th centuries A.D.

The defensive enceinte of Thessalonike - the height of whose walls ranged from 10 to 12 me-tres - was the shape of a trapezium, with the acropolis at the top. On the east and west side, there was a double wall in the flat areas to the south. According to the literary sources, the inner wall was called *teichos* (the wall) or *endoteron* (the inner), and the outer wall, 10 m. away from

106. Part of the east section of the Byzantine defence walls of Thessalonike.

the main wall, was known as the *exo teichos* (outer wall) or *proteichisma* (outwork) Only a few parts of this outwork are still preserved, near Syntrivaniou Square. The masonry of the walls consists of wide zones of bricks alternating with narrower zones of stones, or, more rarely, brickwork relieved at intervals by brick arches.

Of the towers set at intervals about fifty still guard the city today. All of them are square in plan, with the exception of the White Tower at the south-east corner of the enceinte and the Triangle Tower or Tower of the Chain at the northeast corner, both of which are circular. The Tower of the Vardaris fort is octagonal. The Heptapyrgio, a complex of seven towers, as its name suggests, inside the Acropolis near the north wall, was converted into a gaol in the last years of Turkish occupation: Yedi Koule was until recently a byword for the fate of prisoners serving long sentences.

The White Tower, the emblem of Thessalonike, constructed in the middle of the 15th century A.D. probably by Venetian craftsmen, was erected next to the old Byzantine tower, already destroyed, that had defined the southern end of the

east wall towards the sea, and it, too, served as a prison for people under sentence of death. (An exposition of christian antiquities is housed here).

Other indispensable features of the wall, in addition to the towers, were the gates. Of those known in the east wall, we may note: 1) the Gate of Rome, near the sea and not far from the tower at the south-east corner that was replaced by the White Tower; 2) the Cassandreia Gate or Gate of Kalamaria, at which ended the main avenue in the city, the modern Egnatia Street; 3) the Gate of the Asomatoi, just to the north of the Rotunda; and 4) the Gate of Anna Palaiologina in the wall connecting the Triangle Tower or Tower of the Chain (*Alyseos*) with the enceinte of the acropolis. The following gates were known in the west wall: 1) the Golden Gate, at which the main avenue ended in the west; and 2) the Letaia or Litaia Gate, at the west end of modern Ayiou Demetriou street. On the side towards the sea, near the inner harbour in the south-west, was the Gate of Leon.

THE AGORA/FORUM

Excavation work carried out in the 1960s for the construction of the Thessalonike Lawcourts led to the undertaking of archaeological excavations that brought to light the Ancient Agora and its out-buildings, to the south of the church of Saint Demetrios in the middle of the ancient city.

Despite the fact that this same area must also have been the site of the Hellenistic Agora - black-glaze sherds and a larger-than-life size poros Atlas clearly belong to this building phase - the extensive structural remains covering the area between Olympou, Philippou, Agnostou Stratioti and Makedonikis Amynas streets belong to the period of the Antonines and Severi (2nd-3rd centuries A.D.). At this time, in what appears to have been an ambitious plan, the entire area up to Egnatia street (the Via Regia of the Romans) was modelled into two contiguous, stepped terraces (of which the one to the south -known in the Byzantine period by the name Megalophoros- is still unexcavated) and covered with greenery and rows of trees. Between the two terraces ran a paved way oriented west-east.

On the northern terrace, a large uncovered courtyard, square in plan and paved with marble (original dimensions 145 m. x 90 m.) is surrounded on all four sides by stoas which formerly had colonnades in two orders and decorated floors (at present only the east and south side have been uncovered). Appended to the rear of the east stoa, on the ruins of an earlier building, the city Odeion - the theatre that was also called the "Stadion" -had a paved marble orchestra with a chord of 16.30 m, a *cavea* supported on vaulted porticoes and a stage with a proscenium, on which, in antiquity, stood statues of the Muses (some of these are preserved in the Museum); in late Antiquity, the building was modified in keeping with the manners and beliefs of the day and converted into an arena for gladiatorial combats.

The descent from the Upper to the Lower Plateia (the Megalophoros) was by way of a stone staircase at the south-east edge of the northern terrace. The difference in height due to the slope led to the ingenious creation below the south stoa of a *cryptoporticus,* a portico with two aisles standing at both basement and ground-level and facing the Lower Agora, which was used as a place of refuge in times of bad weather and also as a retaining wall for the terrace of the Upper Agora.

107-110. In the 18th and 19th centuries, the stoa of the Incantadas, known by the Greeks as "Idols", was in the courtyard of a Jewish house in Thessalonike that probably stood on a side street on the north side of Egnatia street. Illustrated are, at the top: relief figures of Ganymede, a Maenad and Dionysos. Paris, Musée du Louvre, below: 19th century engraving of the stoa of the Incantadas.

The facade of the entire complex facing the Via Egnatia was of monumental appearance; the stoa with two orders bordering the south side of the Lower Plateia, which was known to the Spanish Jews of Thessalonike as Las Incantadas (the "Idols" of the Christians) had pillars on the upper storey carved with relief figures of a Maenad, Dionysos, Ariadne, Ganymede, Leda, Nike, Aura and one of the Dioskouroi (now in the Louvre). The monumental arrangement was completed by an elegant exedra to the south-east of the Megalophoros, on the Via Regia (in front of the Paradeisos Baths) - and possibly by another one like it at the south-west corner, near the church of the Panagia Chalkeon.

109

110

111

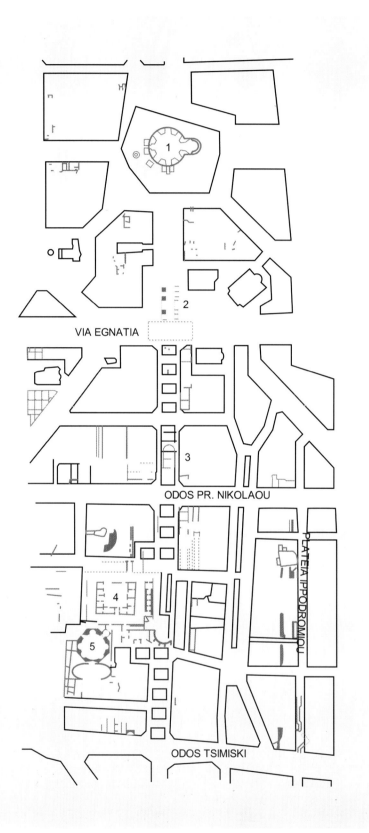

VIA EGNATIA

ODOS PR. NIKOLAOU

PLATEIA IPPODROMIOU

ODOS TSIMISKI

111. Plan of the Galerian complex.

112. The Rotunda of saint Georgios, one of the buildings in the Galerian complex. Beginning of the 4th century.

THE COMPLEX OF GALERIUS

At the beginning of the 4th century A.D. the tetrarch Galerius transferred the capital of his province from Sirmium in Pannonia to Thessalonike and proceeded to erect a series of new buildings, mainly for his personal use, as part of a broad programme of urban renewal on the eastern limits of the city, where it was specially extended for the purpose.

Organised in a straight line with a north-south axis, the complex included the Rotunda (the Pantheon or Temple of Zeus), the triumphal arch (known popularly as Kamara), the Palace complex, with the Octagon attached to it, and the Hippodrome.

1. The Rotunda.

Generally considered to be a Pantheon or Temple of Zeus, though it has also been thought to be the Mausoleum of Galerius, the Rotunda is an imposing brick-built building, circular in plan, standing at the junction of Apostolou Pavlou street and Philippou street. With a diameter of 24.15 m., it is covered by a huge hemispherical dome, at the crest of which an *opaion* (opening) allowed daylight to bathe the interior in mystery; the structure, with its plain exterior, was converted into a Christian church in the reign of Theodosios the Great, after a number of modifications had been made to meet the needs of the new religion. The house of God was dedicated to His only begotten Son, under the name Dynamis or, according to others, was consecrated to the memory of the Asomati (the Archangels), and in the early Byzantine period it was embellished with superb mosaics with full-length depictions of the saints of the first eastern church, portrayed frontally before a composite architectural backcloth.

A Cathedral from the 10th to the 12th centuries A.D., the Rotunda was converted into a mosque in 1591, with the name Hortac Efendi Camisi. The building owes its name of Saint Georgios to the small church next to it. It is now used for exhibitions and cultural events.

112

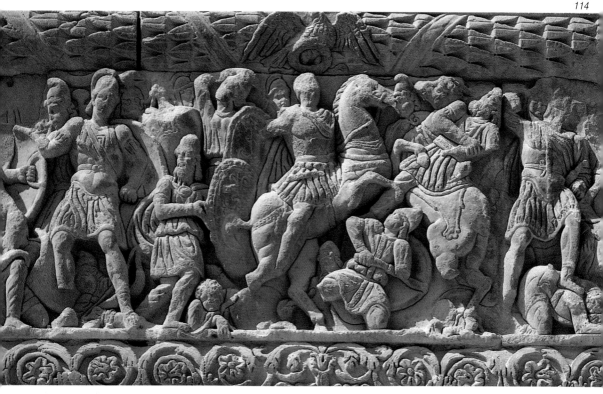

115

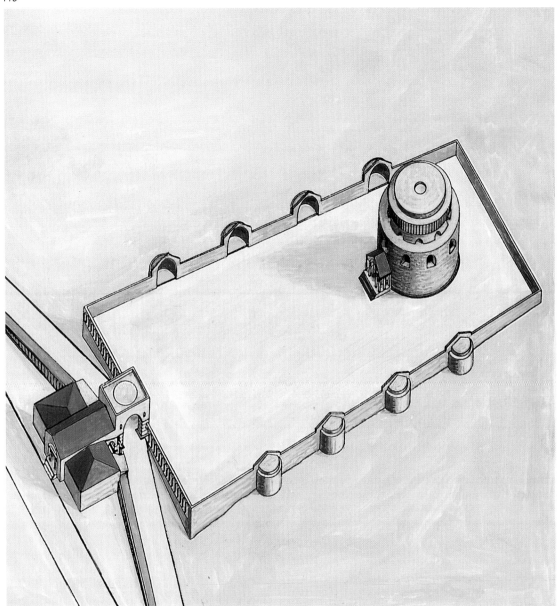

113. The "Kamara", the triumphal Arch of Galerius. Beginning of the 4th century A.D.

114. Detail of the sculptural decoration of the "Kamara", which comprised narrative episodes from Galerius' confrontation with the Persians in A.D. 296-297. Thessalonike.

115. Hypothetical reconstruction of the Rotunda and the triumphal Arch of Galerius. Beginning of the 4th century A.D. (G. Velenis).

2. The Triumphal Arch (Kamara).

The majestic arch was erected on the original line of the Via Egnatia (the Leophoros of the Byzantines) shortly before A.D. 305, to extol the victories of Galerius against the Persians (A.D. 297) in four superposed zones of relief scenes; today only two of the four original pillars of which the monument was composed (the two to the west) are preserved.

Contiguous with the south side of the arch was a large roofed hall with a mosaic floor, which formed the monumental entrance to the proces-

sional way leading from the Kamara to the Rotunda.

3. The finds in D. Gounari street

Closely connected with the palace complex in Navarinou Square, the finds yielded by excavations in Gounari street, on the axis leading from the Rotunda to the sea, have yet to be explained: a large hall, rectangular in plan with wall-paintings and a mosaic floor, and a second room, contiguous with it, paved with marble and equipped with a semi-circular apse at the north, external buttresses and two niches at the south, do not of themselves alone supply the connecting link in the general arrangement.

4. The Palace

A four-sided, two-storey building complex in the modern Navarinou Square, with rooms and open areas decorated with marble and wall-paintings set around a central open peristyle courtyard, is now an imposing ruin, with an ar-

rangement similar to that of a Roman barracks; it is usually identified with the palace of Galerius (the *basileia* of the sources) - the counterpart of the palatial residence of Diocletian at Spalato (Split) in Dalmatia.

Its main entrance was on the south, towards the sea and the pre-Constantinian harbour of the city, known as the Ekklisiastiki Skala, and it had stately rooms with probably twice the area of the four-sided complex that has survived. The scattered remains on building plots around Navarinou Square are certainly evidence for a structure of majestic size and impressive decoration (mosaics, marble revetment, wall-paintings), worthy of the office of its occupant.

5. The Octagon

Appended to the south-west side of the Palace, the Octagon had a spacious, elliptical anteroom added to the south, at the ends of which spiral staircases led to a second storey, and is thought by some to have been the throne room.

116. Part of the Palace Complex of Galerius in Navarinou Square. Thessalonike.

117. The Octagon is part of the Palace of Galerius; according to one theory, it was the throne-room of the Palace.

The seven niches, one in each side of the Octagon - the eighth side was occupied by the entrance - and the main area were paved with diamond-shaped and square slabs of marble. The walls, too, were decorated with marble revetment. The portable finds from the excavation of this unusual building and the immediately surrounding area - now in the local Archaeological Museum - include four marble pilaster capitals with scenes of Zeus, one of the Dioskouroi, Hygeia and Kabeiros, and a marble decorative arch with a bust of Galerius and the Fortune of Thessalonike in two round medallions, each supported by the god Attis.

THE HIPPODROME

Closely connected with the Palace and its ancillary buildings, the Hippodrome of the city lies beneath the modern square bearing its name; it has been identified by sporadic finds in the basements of apartment buildings (barrel-vaulted brick-built corridors, substructure of the seats on the long sides, and of the *cavea)* and covered an area of 30,000 sq. m. In contact with the east wall, it was the counterpart of the Palace complex proper, and at the same time an integral part of it, for according to the Roman beliefs of the time, the centre of secular authority had to be close to and communicate with the centre of popular authority and the place in which the popular will was expressed. The Hippodrome ceased to function after the bloody events of A.D. 390, when the emperor Theodosios the Great, in response to an uprising of the citizens against the garrison of Goths and their leader Butherichus who was killed in the fracas, gave the order for all the spectators gathered in the Hippodrome to be killed. The area was abandoned, the building was used as a quarry for stone, and the horror was covered by the earth piled up on it by time. The Ottoman occupation and the modern period planted houses and plane trees on the abomination. Until the archaeologist's spade and rebuilding came, the one to awaken what the other is concerned to preserve in oblivion.

THE CHURCHES

Saint Demetrios

In the middle of the 5th century, the prefect of Illyricum, one Leontios, built a magnificent basilica in the name of Demetrios, the great martyr of the Christian faith, in the north-west of the Roman Forum, on the site of an earlier bath and in the neighbourhood of the Gymnasium - possibly on the ruins of the temple of Kabeiros; this building burned down during the great earthquake that occurred some time between A.D. 629 and A.D. 634, to be replaced a short time later by another equally majestic structure. The church of the patron saint of Thessalonike, with dimensions of 43.58 m. x 33 m., was restored and renovated after the fire of 1917; it retains the form of the basilicas of the 5th and 7th centuries A.D., and belongs to the type of the five-aisled basilica with a transverse aisle projecting from the body of the church. The central aisle, 12 m. wide, is separated from the side aisles by two rows of columns, in two orders, interspersed with pillars, and is roofed with a saddle-vault; the side aisles have pitched roofs.

Time, the great destroyer, has deprived the eyes of the pious and of art-lovers of a great number of works from the rich painted and marble decoration - revetments, mosaics, wall-paintings. Those that remain, however, attest to the size of the wealth that has been lost.

Of the marble decoration, the capitals are distinguished by their variety of types and decoration. The mosaics and wall-paintings do not form part of a specific iconographic programme, but are dedications by the devout, created at various periods from the 5th to the 15th centuries. The earliest mosaics, which escaped the fire that broke out between A.D. 629 and A.D. 634, are on the west side, and belong to the 5th century. One of them depicts saint Demetrios in military dress, with angels, and the other has a scene with two children being dedicated to the saint. The other surviving mosaics date from after the 7th century fire, and adorn the two pillars to

118

right and left of the sanctuary (the Virgin and saint Theodore, saint Demetrios and the founders of the church).

The chapel of Saint Euthymios, appended to the south-east corner of the original building is an interesting example of Palaeologan architecture, in which some important wall-paintings are preserved from the beginning of the 14th century. Beneath the sanctuary is a labyrinthine area that is now a basement (the Crypt) - part of the Roman baths that stood here before the church, in which, according to tradition, saint Demetrios was imprisoned and met a martyr's death; here is the holy of holies of the building: a semi-circular cistern, in the form of a ciborium, received the holy myrrh/oil that flowed from the walls at the back, an elixir of atonement and purification for the faithful worshipper.

Grafted onto the north-west corner of the middle aisle, the funerary monument of Lucas Spandounis is an exceptionally fine example of Florentine art, dating from 1481, according to the inscription on it.

118. The exterior of the church of Saint Demetrios in Thessalonike, from the south-west.

119. Ninth century mosaic from the north-west pillar of the bema in the church of Saint Demetrios in Thessalonike. It depicts the Virgin and saint Theodore in an attitude of Deesis.

119

120

120. Seventh century mosaic from the church of Saint Demetrios in Thessalonike, showing the dedication of children to the patron saint of the city.

121. Seventh century mosaic from the church of Saint Demetrios in Thessalonike. Saint Demetrios is depicted between the bishop and the eparch, who rebuilt the church. The city walls can be seen in the background.

Saint Sophia

The famous church of the Wisdom of God, surrounded by a large number of out-buildings, was erected in the middle of the 7th century on a site occupied in the early Byzantine period (5th century A.D.) by a large five-aisled basilica dedicated to the memory of saint Mark (dimensions 163 m. x 50 m.). Saint Sophia is square in plan, with the tripartite sanctuary *(bema, prothesis, diakonikon)* projecting to the east; the articulation of the space is equally simple, though impressive in its implementation: the interior of the church was divided into three aisles by alternating pillars and columns carrying barrel-vaults which, with the aid of pendentives, support the hemispherical dome. The side aisles are open at the west end and connect with the narthex, thus forming a Π-shaped peristyle embracing the central core of the church. The repetition of the ground floor plan at the level of the upper storey, through the creation of wood-roofed, tiled galleries that encircle three sides of the building, lends the cruciform shape of the main space a transcendental dimension, and places the pious worshipper directly at the heart of the Christian symbol of redemption - at the centre of an enormous cross.

The mosaic decoration gives the building an air of brilliance: the barrel vault over the sanctuary has founders' inscriptions and stylized floral ornamentation, the narrow front of the arch between the vault and the apse, and the semi-dome of the apse itself (period of the "battle of the icons" onwards) has an imposing cross at the beginning (the ends of the arms can be made out), followed by a scene of the enthroned Virgin Brephokratousa, and most imposing of all, the dome has magnificent composition (perhaps about A.D. 885), in which the scene of the Ascension takes on a particular dogmatic and metaphysical dimension, set within an impressive expressionistic landscape.

The great lesson is completed by the wall-paintings on the large exonarthex dating from the beginning of the 11th century, which has figures of local saints.

122. Exterior view of the church of Saint Sophia in Thessalonike.

123. Mosaic scene of the Ascension, from the large dome of the chutch of Saint Sophia in Thessalonike, 9th century.

122

123

The church of the Acheiropoietos

The large basilica of the Virgin, known also from as early as the 14th century A.D. as the Acheiropoietos - clearly from the cult icon of the Virgin housed in it - is a building to the east of the ancient Agora generally dated to the middle of the A.D. 5th century; it was the first house of prayer to be converted by sultan Murad into a Moslim place of worship (Eski Cuma Cami), immediately after the capture of the city in 1430.

Built on the ruins of a complex of bath houses dating from Roman times, which was adorned with mosaic floors and hypocausts, the three-aisled wood-roofed basilica near the Via Egnatia (the "Leophoros" (Avenue) of the Byzantines), with which it communicated through a monumental propylon, has a strikingly simple design and austere proportions; its sturdy row of fluted columns on the ground floor, made of Peloponnesian and Thessalian marble, set off the acanthus leaves blowing in the wind on the capitals, and the scintillating mosaics on the intrados of the arcades.

Despite later interventions on the building, the reconstruction work, the blocking up and tearing down, mainly of sources of light for the interior of the building, the wonder felt by the learned Constantine Armenopoulos (14th century A.D.) for the building, who said that the church seemed to be carried only on columns, suspended in the air, and not on walls, still conveys, beyond the rhetorical flourish, the immediacy of the devout pilgrim's spontaneous reaction.

A structure with a single room attached to the south-east side of the church was formerly considered to be a baptistery. Modern thinking identifies it with the original diakonikon of the church.

The question of whether the Acheiropoietos also had an atrium will be answered by future excavations in Makedonomachon Square.

Latomos Monastery (Hosios David)

The small church of Hosios David, climbing the steep narrow streets of the upper city, at the end of Ayias Sophias street and to the south-west of the Vlatadon Monastery, was once the katholikon of the Monastery of Christ the Saviour of Latomos, or Latomoi, erected in the 5th century A.D., according to the "Narrative" of Ignatios. Its name probably derived from the quarries (latomeia) that were once worked in the neighbourhood.

A forerunner of the domed cross-in-square type of church, with original dimensions of 12.10 m. x 12.30 m., the church was erected on the ruins of a Roman bath; today only two thirds of the early Christian building survive.

The interior decoration consists of wall mosaics and paintings dating from the end of the 5th century A.D. (mosaic representation of the Epiphany on the semi-dome of the apse) to the third quarter of the 12th century A.D. (wall-paintings on the south vault), and from the period at the end of the 13th -beginning of the 14th centuries ad (wall-paintings on the east wall of the north arm of the cross).

Panagia Chalkeon

Built to the north of the Via Egnatia, the church of the Virgin, known popularly as the "Red Church" after its brick construction, is a cross-in-square church with four columns, an architectural type that first made its appearance at the time of the Macedonian Dynasty. According to an inscription carved on the lintel over the main entrance, the erection of the church is dated to ad 1028. Its modern name "Panagia ton Chalkeon" is a translation of the name Kazançilar Cami by which it was known in the Ottoman occupation, on account of the copper utensils made and sold in the area.

Of the decoration that once covered the entire monument, the wall-paintings still survive in fragmentary condition (the majority of the scenes date from the 2nd quarter of the 11th century, with remains of others on the west wall of the nave dating from the 14th century A.D.).

Saint Panteleimon

The church of Saint Panteleimon is the name given, probably in A.D. 1568-1571, to the elegant church of Saint Isaac, named after its founder Isaac - whose secular name was Jacob, Metropolitan of Thessalonike (A.D. 1295-1314). The katholikon of a monastery, it is a cross-in-square church with four columns, in this case encircled by a portico (demolished at the beginning of the 20th century A.D.). The few wall-paintings date from the transition from the 13th to the 14th centuries, or were perhaps created during the Ottoman occupation.

Holy Apostles

One of the finest monuments in Thessalonike, the church of the Holy Apostles, in the west section of the city a short distance away from the fortifications, was the katholikon of a monastery dedicated to the Virgin and built by the Patriarch Nephon I between A.D. 1310 and 1314. Although the interior decoration was never completed, owing to Nephon's removal from the throne, the brilliance of the wall mosaics and the splendour of the wall-paintings reflect the high artistic climate and the spiritual flowering of the "second-in-rank" city of the empire in the 14th century A.D.

The church was the composite cross-in-square type with four columns, and had a narthex and portico and five domes; with its refined, tiled decoration, and skilfully articulated volumes, it is a characteristic example of the ecclesiastical architecture of the Palaiologan Period.

Saint Nikolaos Orphanos

Originally a three-aisled basilica with a narthex at the west, the elegant church of Saint Nikolaos Orphanos, standing in the tranquillity of the tall, shady cypress trees on the slopes of Apostolou Pavlou street, was founded in the years A.D. 1310-1320, during the period when Thessalonike was at its zenith.

With its marble decoration preserved intact, and retaining all the freshness of the rich colours of the wall-paintings, the church is a splendid monument for the study of Byzantine ecclesiastical painting at the time of the Palaiologan dynasty.

Saint Katherine

A composite cross-in-square church with four columns, the church of Saint Katherine, close to the north-west fortifications of the city - Yakoub Pasha Cami of the Ottoman occupation - was founded in A.D. 1320-1330 and is thus another monument from the brilliant Palaiologan Period in Thessalonike. The wall-paintings, now preserved in fragmentary condition, mainly cover themes from the life of Christ.

Church of the Saviour

South-west of the Arch of Galerius (Kamara) and close to modern Egnatia street, the Church of the Saviour, dedicated to the Transfiguration, was once a funerary chapel dedicated to the Virgin, and was built in the years after A.D. 1340. With a square plan and a relatively high dome, the church also retains parts of its wall-paintings which, with their conservatism, are stylistically removed from the rest of the roughly contemporary creations by other craftsmen in the city of saint Demetrios. The narthex is a modern fabrication.

Vlatadon Monastery

Close to the gate leading to the Acropolis, the patriarchal monastery of Vlatadon, also known as Tsaous Monastery, occupied a privileged position, since it once controlled the water that came from Chortiates to slake the city's thirst. It was founded by Dorotheos Vlatis in the period A.D. 1351-1371, when he was Metropolitan of Thessalonike, though only the sanctuary, the south chapel, the nave and the bigger part of the south portico belong to the original phase; the other buildings and a number of modifications date either from the period of the Ottoman occupation or later.

The wall-paintings decorating the church, which have suffered particularly badly at the hands of unbelievers, date from the period A.D. 1360-1380, and are one of the last examples of the local artistic school, a few years before the final capture of the city by the Turks (A.D. 1430).

Saint Elias

The church conventionally known as "Profitis Elias" occupied an eminent position to the north of the church of Saint Demetrios, from which it once overlooked the lower city; the katholikon of a monastery, probably dedicated to Jesus Christ, it is one of the most complex structures created by Byzantine architecture in the years following the middle of the 14th century A.D. With a spacious triconch plan, surrounded at the four corners by centralized domed buildings, and with a square narthex, the church combines features of the monastic architecture of Mount Athos with others from the local ecclesiastical architecture of Thessalonike. The badly damaged wall-paintings date from the second half of the 14th and the beginning of the 15th centuries A.D.

124. Mosaic decoration on the intrados of an arcade in the church of the Acheiropoeitos in Thessalonike.

125. Mosaic depiction of the Epiphany from the chapel of Hosios David in the Latomos Monastery, Thessalonike.

126. Mosaic depiction of the Transfiguration of Christ from the church of the Holy Apostles in Thessalonike.

THE ARCHAEOLOGICAL MUSEUM

The Archaeological Museum of Thessalonike - a 1962 building with a wing added in 1980 - houses mainly antiquities brought to light from time to time by the archaeologist's trowel, from building plots within the city, from sites in the surrounding area, and generally speaking, from locations that fall under the jurisdiction of the XVI Ephorate of Antiquities (Counties of Thessalonike, Kilkis, Pieria, and Chalkidike). It also houses finds from other parts of northern Greece (Vergina) however, and a few objects from regions outside Greece (Redestos).

A. Thessalonike and its region

Rooms 1, 2, 3, 4, 5, 6, 7 and 8 (ground floor)

A special room (6) is devoted to the "state and society" of the ancient city, in which are exhibited finds from the excavations at two settlements that are possible candidates for identification with ancient Therme, the predecessor of Thessalonike - Toumba and Karambournakl (pottery from the Mycenaean to the Classical periods), along with grave offerings from the Hellenistic period (vases, jewellery), statues and votive reliefs from the sanctuary of Serapis and the Egyptian gods, mosaic floors (Ariadne on Naxos and a depiction of a chariot) from wealthy residences and a complex of baths (thermae) dating from the 3rd century A.D., and funerary altars. A special section relates to the city as capital of Galerius (Galerian complex - 3rd century A.D.); the display case containing coins issued by Thessalonike (2nd century B.C. - 3rd century A.D.) is of some interest.

The picture of the artistic production of the city is completed by items exhibited in the relevant rooms(3, 4, 5, 7, 8): architectural remains from a large temple (of Dionysos?), that presumably adorned ancient Therme, Roman copies of sculptures of the Classical period (parts of an acrolithic statue of Athena in the type of Pheidias, Aphrodite in the Fréjus type etc.), a statue of Augustus in the Primaporta type, dating from the reign of Tiberius, and portraits of emperors and private citizens dating from the early centuries of the Christian era. The wealth of the Hellenistic cemeteries is revealed by the valuable discoveries from the cemeteries at Sedes and Stavroupolis (room 9, Vergina room).

The townships (cemeteries and cult areas) near Thessalonike [Derveni (ancient Lete, room 9), Sindos (possibly ancient Chalastra, room 1), Ayia Paraskeve and Potidaia (room 2), Epanomi, Mikhaniona (ancient Aineia, room 9) and Nea Kallikrateia] have furnished the Museum with a rich collection of imported vases from Attica, Corinth and Ionia, a cylindrical papyrus containing a philosophical text in a poem dealing with the origins of the gods, attributed to the mythical poet Orpheus, a gilded bronze krater with relief decoration, a wonderful marble funerary stele with a figure of a kore, carved in a Parian workshop, a marble funerary double door with bronze decoration and two marble funerary couches with superb painted decoration, local gold jewellery, elegant vessels of precious metal, children's toys, gold mouthpieces, gold funerary masks, offering tables, delicately worked wreaths, very fine necklaces and a host of other objects illuminating the high cultural level of the Macedonian kingdom from the 6th to the 4th century B.C., and the earliest of them linking it with the Mycenaean tradition.

B. Vergina

Room 9 (ground floor)

A special room houses the unique finds from the unplundered royal tombs of ancient Aigai (Vergina), the first capital of Macedonia and burial place of its rulers, together with models of the tombs in the Great Tumulus in which they were contained and a photographic record of the excavations (silver table vessels, jewellery, weapons and equipment, gold funerary boxes, lampstands, silver hydrias, ivory decorative plaques from furniture, etc.).

It is the intention in the near future to transfer the finds from the royal tombs at Aigai to Vergina, where they will be exhibited in the covered area of the tombs, which is to be converted into a Museum.

C. Coast of Pieria - Chalkidike

Room 11, (lower floor)

The coast of Pieria and Chalkidike was settled by colonists from Eretria, Chalkis, Andros and

Corinth as early as the 8th century B.C., who founded colonies that flourished and prospered, extending knowledge and trade to the east and the west; the area is represented in a special room by brilliant finds from Mende, Polychrono, Pyrgadikia, Akanthos (modern Ierissos), Nikiti, Torone, Pydna, and Olynthos. The series of artistic creations is completed by exceptionally fine examples of sculpture from Nea Kallikrateia (440 B.C.), Potidaia (380-370 B.C., stele of a lyre player), Olynthos (head of a youth - end of the 5th century B.C.), and Kassandra (420 B.C. - stele of a hunter or athlete), and supplemented with items from the brilliant decoration of the "Macedonian" tomb at Potidaia (marble door with two leaves, marble couches); together with the finds from Hellenistic Pydna, these attest to the vigour of the Macedonian kingdom at the time of Alexander III and the first of his successors.

D. The prehistoric past of Macedonia

Room 10 (lower floor)

The prehistoric past of Macedonia (vases, figurines, bronze objects and sherds from settlements) is displayed, accompanied by explanatory charts and samples of sherds in chronological order, in a room that illustrates the role played by the region in the formation and evolution of culture in this critical part of the Balkan peninsula from the Neolithic Period (7,000-2,000 B.C.) to the Early Iron Age (1,100-700 B.C.). Examples of pottery are exhibited from Servia near Kozani, settlement III at Vasilika, Olynthos, Mesimeri, Armenochori near Florina, Axiokhori in Kilkis, Ayios Mamas, Petralona, Assiros, Kastanas, Ayios Panteleimon and Vergina.

127. Diagram of the galleries in the Archaeological Museum of Thessalonike.

127

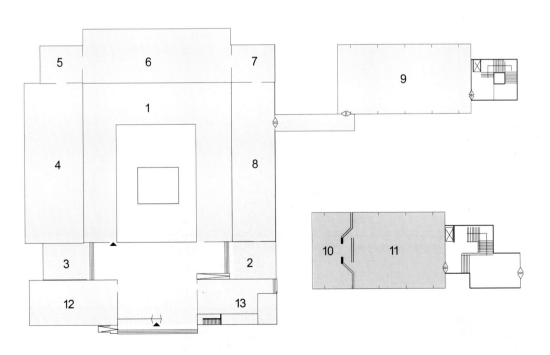

128

129

130

128. Late Bronze Age jug from the tumulus at Sedes. Thessalonike, Archaeological Museum.

129. Clay Mycenaean skyphos from the prehistoric settlement at Kastanas (local workshop). Thessalonike, Archaeological Museum.

130. Plemochoe from Sindos (Chalastra). 520 B.C. Thessalonike, Archaeological Museum.

131. *Gold necklace from a female burial at Sindos, ca. 510 B.C. Thessalonike, Archaeological Museum.*

131

132

132. *Superb marble grave stele of a girl from N. Kallikrateia (from a Parian workshop), ca. 440 B.C. Thessalonike, Archaeological Museum.*

133. *Clay female protome from a female burial at Sindos. 480-460 B.C. Thessalonike, Archaeological Museum.*

134. *Red-figure pelike from a grave tumulus at Aineia. Second half of the 4th century B.C. Thessalonike, Archaeological Museum.*

135. *Bronze hydria/cinerary urn from a grave tumulus at Aineia. 430 B.C. Thessalonike, Archaeological Museum.*

133

134

135

137-139. Three gold necklaces. The two above have been found in a tomb at Derveni of the last quarter of the 4th century B.C. and the one below, from Sedes, dates back to the end of the 4th century B.C. Thessalonike, Archaeological Museum.

136. Gold myrtle wreath from a tomb at Derveni (Lete). Last quarter of the 4th century B.C. Thessalonike, Archaeological Museum.

136

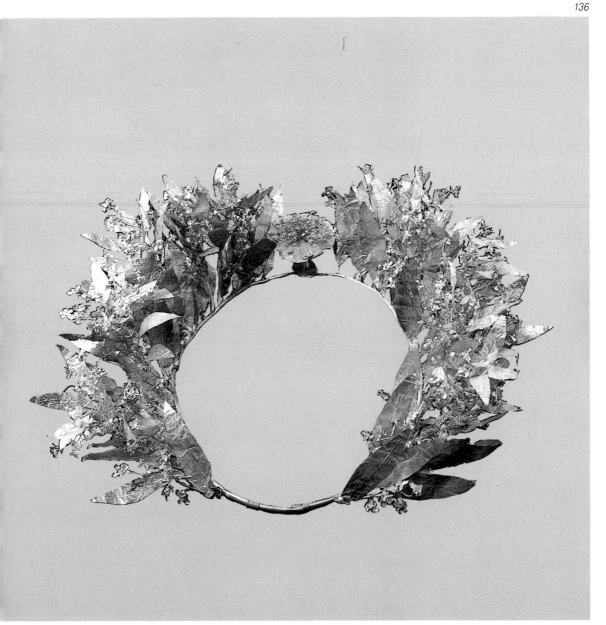

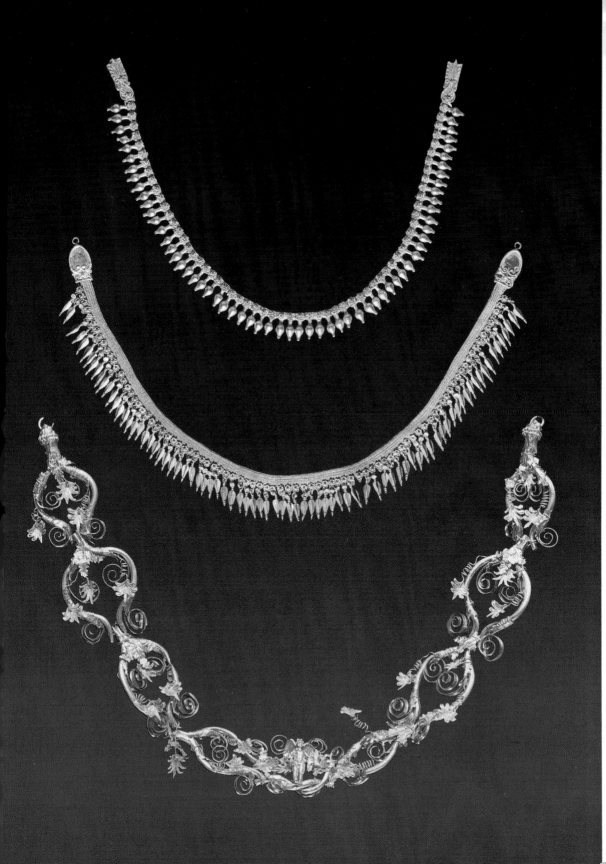

140

141

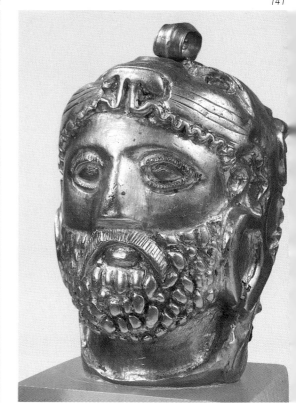

142

140. Small decorative piece of gold sheet in the form of a Macedonian shield, from the "Macedonian" tomb at Katerini. Second half of the 4th century B.C. Thessalonike, Archaeological Museum.

141. Jewellery attachment in the form of a head of Herakles, from a tomb at Derveni. Last quarter of the 4th century B.C. Thessalonike, Archaeological Museum.

142. Leather pectoral covered with bronze scales, from a tomb at Derveni. Last quarter of the 4th century B.C. Thessalonike, Archaeological Museum.

143. Gold earrings from Derveni. Last quarter of the 4th century B.C. Thessalonike, Archaeological Museum.

144. The magic "Knot" of Herakles; detail of a gold thigh ornament from Sedes. Last quarter of the 4th century B.C. Thessalonike, Archaeological Museum.

144

145. Gold diadem from a tomb at Derveni. Last quarter of the 4th century B.C. Thessalonike, Archaeological Museum.

146. Gilded-silver royal diadem from the tomb of Philip II at Vergina. Second half of the 4th century B.C. Thessalonike, Archaeological Museum.

147. The superb bronze krater from tomb b at Derveni, 320-300 B.C. Thessalonike, Archaeological Museum.

145

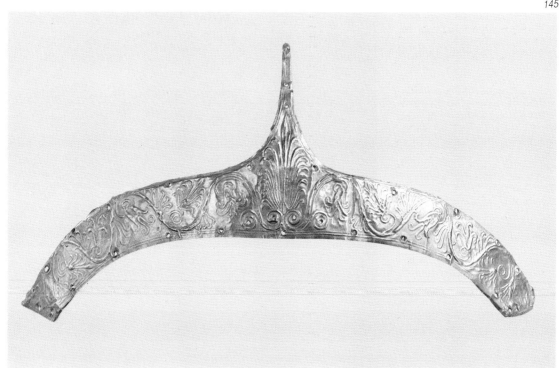

146

148. Gold oak wreath, found in the chest in the tomb
of Philip II at Vergina, on the bones of the dead king.
Second half of the 4th century B.C. Thessalonike,
Archaeological Museum.
←

149

149. Gold sheet with repoussé decoration which adorned the gorytos (combined bow and arrow case) in the tomb of Philip II at Vergina. Thessalonike, Archaeological Museum.

150. Iron helmet from the tomb of Philip II at Vergina. Thessalonike, Archaeological Museum.

151. Gilded greaves from the tomb of Philip II at Vergina. There is an interesting difference in height and shape between the right and the left legs. Thessalonike, Archaeological Museum.

150

151

153

154

152. Copper lantern
from the tomb of Philip
II at Vergina.
Thessalonike,
Archaeological
Museum.

153-154. Clay vases
from the tomb of Philip
II at Vergina: black-
glaze oinochoe and
red-figure askos (from
an Attic workshop).
Both were unused
when they were placed
in the tomb.
Thessalonike,
Archaeological
Museum.

157

155. Glass birds from
Roman tombs at
Thessalonike.
Thessalonike,
Archaeological
Museum.

156. Glass vases from
Roman tombs at
Thessalonike.
Thessalonike,
Archaeological
Museum.

157. Bronze portrait
head of Alexander
Severus (A.D. 222-235),
from Ryaki, in Pieria.
Thessalonike,
Archaeological
Museum.

158

158. Marble statue of Aphrodite in the Fréjus type, Roman copy of a 5th century B.C. original. Thessalonike, Archaeological Museum.

159. Female portrait head. 2nd century A.D. Thessalonike, Archaeological Museum.

160. Statue of Augustus (27 B.C.-A.D. 14) from the area of the imperial Sanctuaries in Thessalonike (to the west of the Town Hall). Thessalonike, Archaeological Museum.

161. Statue of Harpokrates from the Serapeion of Thessalonike. End of the 2nd century B.C. Thessalonike, Archaeological Museum.

159

160

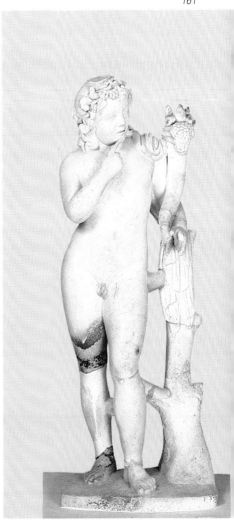

161

128

163. Detail of a mosaic floor from a 2nd century A.D. house, found in Sokratous street. Thessalonike, Archaeological Museum.

162. Part of a 3rd century A.D. mosaic with a scene of a four-horse racing chariot (found at the junction of Egnatia street and Antigonidon street). Thessalonike, Archaeological Museum.

162

163

THE EXHIBITION OF CHRISTIAN ANTIQUITIES IN THE WHITE TOWER

The exhibition of Christian antiquities in the Tower that is the emblem of the city of saint Demetrios was organised on the occasion of the 2,300th anniversary of the foundation of Thessalonike; it includes objects dating from A.D. 300 to A.D. 1430, mainly from Thessalonike itself.

On the ground floor are displayed coins, funerary inscriptions, lamps, vases, and mosaic floors of the Early Christian period, accompanied by photographs and explanatory texts, maps and drawings.

The first floor houses architectural members, fragments of wall mosaics, vases, slabs of marble wall-revetment, a silver *enkainion*, statues, "hoards" of coins, silver reliquaries etc. accompanied by explanatory wall-charts.

The second floor is devoted to life after death and includes funerary stelai, grave offerings (jewellery, pieces of cloth, clay and glass vases) and wall-paintings detached from the walls of the tombs.

With the third floor, the exhibition completes its philosophical cycle: parapet slabs, both carved on each side and plain, relief marble icons, funerary slabs, funerary glazed vases, gold jewellery, pieces of cloth, icons and fragments of wall-paintings, ecclesiastical liturgical vessels, coins and lead seals offer a picture of Thessalonike and its region in the middle Byzantine period, until the coming of the Ottomans.

On the fourth floor, an attempt is made to sketch the history of Byzantine monumental painting, through the display of characteristic examples of the achievements of the palette up to A.D. 1387.

164. Silver reliquary dating from the 4th century A.D., from Nea Herakleia in Chalkidike. Thessalonike, Exhibition of Christian Antiquities in the White Tower.

165. Wall-painting from a vaulted tomb in the East Cemetery of Thessalonike. It depicts the story of Sosanna and its allegorical interpretation. Second half of the 4th century A.D. Thessalonike, Exhibition of Christian Antiquities in the White Tower.

164

THE MUSEUM OF BYZANTINE CIVILIZATION

In September 1994, the new Museum of Byzantine Civilization was inaugurated with a temporary exhibition presenting some of the Byzantine antiquities of Thessalonike that had been taken to Athens in 1916 and housed since that date in the Byzantine Museum of Athens. These exhibits, along with others that have returned to Thessalonike but which, for a variety of reasons, are not included in the present exhibition, will be included in the permanent exhibition, which will be organised in groups dealing with distinct themes and will come into full operation over the next few years.

The temporary exhibition, which serves the dual purpose of celebrating the completion of the Museum building and the return of the antiquities, comprises portable icons, ecclesiastical embroideries, sculptures and inscriptions.

Outstanding amongst the portable icons are one depicting Christ Pantokrator as the "Wisdom of God", dating from the beginning of the 14th century; an icon of the Virgin and Child from about 1300; a large icon whose main subject is the Ayioi Pantes, from a local workshop, probably located in Thessalonike, of the early 18th century; an icon of Ayios Minas, a notable work of the 18th century that was probably part of the artistic production of a Thessalonike workshop; and an icon of superb artistic quality with six saints in two rows, which is dated to the Late Byzantine period (14th-15th centuries) and is a representative work of the Constantinopolitan School.

The exhibition is completed by the display of two ecclesiastical embroideries (a *sakkos* worn by a prelate and the famous gold-embroidered "Thessalonike Epitaphios"), and a number of representative sculptures and inscriptions.

In addition to the Archaeological Museum, the Exhibition of Christian Antiquities in the White Tower, and the Museum of Byzantine Civilization, the visitor to Thessalonike may also wish to see the Folk Museum and the Museum of the Macedonian Struggle.

166. Gold-thread "Aer" from Thessalonike. Outstanding work of art of the early 14th century. This liturgical piece of cloth was destined to cover the chalice with the bread and wine; consequently, the representations of the Holy Community and Christ-Amnos (The Lamb) refer to the mystery of the Eucharist. Later, this kind of cloth, with the same central representation, served as an "epitaphios" during Holy Week. The embroidery has been executed so skillfully that the subjects are rendered in the manner of a painting, while fully exploiting the possibilities of expression provided by the special technique, with its use of costly materials, gold and silver wire, silks and a variety of stitches with different reflections which create an effect of delicate constantly changing tones. Thessalonike, Museum of Byzantine Civilization.

166

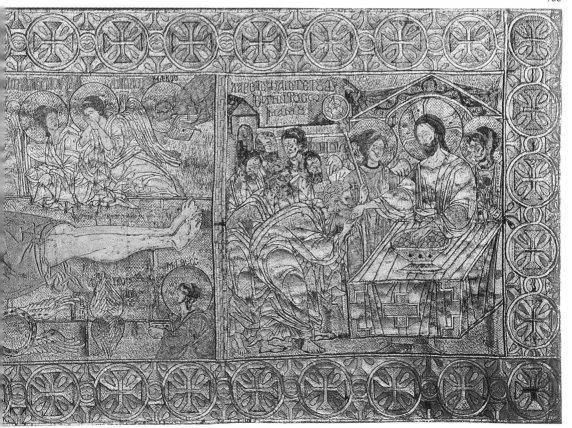

134

167. *The icon of the Virgin and Child. The rendering of the personal features of the figures points to Palaeologan painting, about 1300. Thessalonike, Museum of Byzantine Civilization.*

168. *The large icon of Christ Pantokrator as the "Wisdom of God", an outstanding work of the Palaeologan period (beginning of the 14th century). Thessalonike, Museum of Byzantine Civilization.*

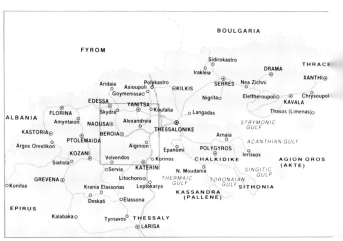

PELLA
and its region

169

HISTORICAL REVIEW

At the centre of a series of satellite settlements, with a "territory" that extended as far as the quarries of Kyrrhos, the former lake Loudias, Platanopotamos and the gulley of Yanitsa, Pella was fortified from the time of Philip II, the ruler who transformed it into a city of international (for the period) influence, and was the most important city in south-eastern Bottiaia, a region enclosed by the Axios and the Haliakmon and bounded by the mountain ranges of Bermion and Paikon.

The surrounding area was inhabited from as early as the Neolithic Period (about 16 settlements have been located) and had a large number of sites in the Bronze Age. The local inhabitants - colonists from Crete, according to tradition - were displaced by the Makedones when the latter crossed from Pieria to the vast pasturages in the modern counties of Emathia and Pella.

Pella was already known to Hekataios, Herodotus and Thucydides (5th century B.C.); at

169. View of a house at Pella. The main courtyard can be seen, and the superb mosaic of white and blue-grey diamonds that adorned the antechamber. End of the 4th century B.C.

138

Leptokarya

Platanorema

Dytiko

ATALANTE (?)

Agrosykia

Platanopotamos

REGION OF THE ATALANTAIANS

Pentaplatanos

Rachona

Γ. Αxιός

Damiano

TYRISSA (?)

Archontiko

"REGION OF THE TYRISSAIANS"

PELLA

Ichnai

"REGION OF THE ICHNAIANS"

PHAKOS

N

LAKE LOUDIA

170. The area of Pella
in the Hellenistic period.

171. Plan of Pella,
capital of the ancient
Macedonians.

the beginning of the fourth century, having become the capital of the Macedonian kingdom at
the wish of Archelaos I, it was known as "the
greatest of the cities in Macedonia". Figures like
Euripides and Agathon were invited here. Here,
too, men like Timotheos and Choirilos were entertained in the royal residence, and Zeuxis, one of
the greatest painters of antiquity, worked here.
The birthplace of Philip II, it increased in size
under his reign and was adorned with a large palace. Attracted by the new regime, artists, poets
and philosophers found at the royal court a warm
supporter of the arts and a generous Maecenas.
At the time of Cassander, the city was extended
according to the "Hippodameian" system and acquired splendid public buildings and spacious private houses with mosaic floors and fine wall-
paintings. It now occupied an area of about
2,500,000 sq.m. and was defended by a fortification wall, with a circuit of around 8,000 m. Initially
a coastal site, it was already by the Classical period at the innermost recess of a lake formed by
the alluvial deposits carried by the river Loudias,
though it continued to be an important harbour,
since the latter waterway was navigable. A small
island in the swamp, called Phakos, communicated with the city by a wooden bridge, and was

used at one and the same time as a gaol and the
treasury of the Macedonian state (gaza).

Having experienced its last decades of glory
with Philip V and Perseus, Pella surrendered to
the Roman general Aemilius Paulus, who en-
camped beneath its walls - its stout fortification
walls - after his triumph at Pydna in 168 B.C.
Headquarters of the third of the four merides (administrative districts) into which Macedonia was
divided between 167 and 147 B.C., it continued,
thanks to the Via Egnatia, to be, like Beroia, one
of the "most illustrious" cities of Macedonia even
after the dissolution of the Macedonian kingdom.
It quickly lost its position to Thessalonike, however, which was chosen as the capital of the Roman province in the East. Earthquakes, the occupation of the city by the armies of Mithridates
VI, the major economic crisis of this period, and
above all the foundation (probably in 150 B.C.) of
the Colonia Pellensis - that is, the Roman colony
of Pella -to the west, on the site of the modern
community of Nea Pella, all brought an end to the
city that had seen the armies of Alexander the
Great pass before it on their way to the conquest
of Asia: Dio Chrysostom was to write, indicative-
ly, at the turn of the 1st to the 2nd century A.D.
that in his time all that remained of (Hellenistic)

171

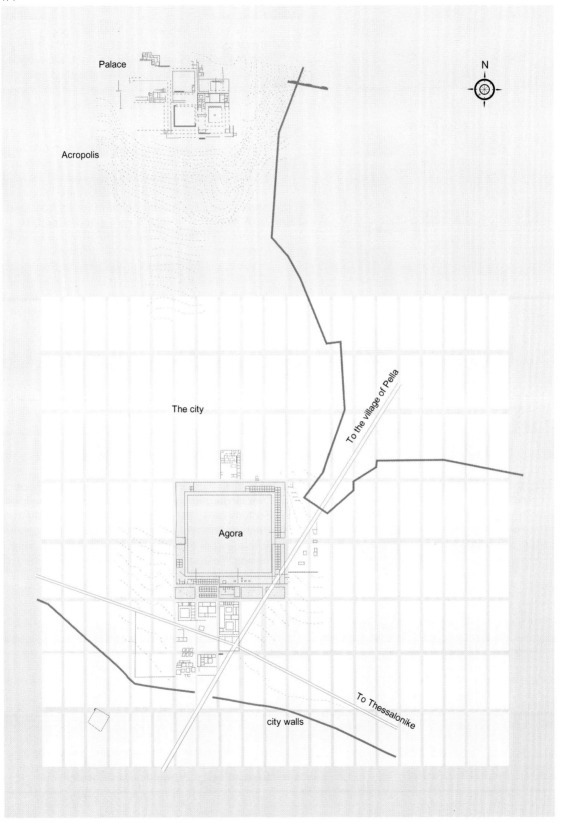

Palace

Acropolis

The city

To the village of Pella

Agora

To Thessalonike

city walls

N

172

Pella was a great quantity of broken roof tiles scattered over the site. Under Diocletian, the colony was probably named Diocletianopolis, though the old name Pella soon came back into vogue. In A.D. 473, Theoderic the Goth settled with his armies in the fertile area to the west of the Axios, and the Drougoubitai, a Slav tribe, dwelt for a time in the area around Pella (7th century). A settlement seems to have survived until the end of the Byzantine period. In the Ottoman occupation, the ruins of the Hellenistic city and the Roman colony formed an ideal source of building material for the holy city of the conquerors, Yanitsa; clearly the East taking revenge for its conquest by Alexander. Though it may also be the fate of all ancient cities as they are transformed by time into the past.

The first excavation of the site, by Professor G. Oikonomou in the summer of 1914, directly after the liberation of Macedonia from the Turks, was followed four decades later by the systematic investigation of it by the Archaeological Service, which still continues to uncover the rich secrets of the city that once controlled the fortunes of the then known world. At the edge of the former lake of Yanitsa, the poor settlement of Ayioi Apostoloi will acquire a new name, and the place will rediscover its former glory.

THE CITY

Little is known of the pre-Cassandreian city. The larger part of the inhabited area, as well as the cemetery dating from the first half of the 4th century B.C., appear to have been razed during the laying-out of Cassander's ambitious urban design. To the time of Philip II, however, belong a number of cist graves to the east, and possibly also the main part of the palace on the so-called

172. *Funerary stele of a Macedonian warrior, by a local workshop. End of the 5th century B.C. Constantinople, Archaeological Museum.*

173. *Aerial photograph of a house at Pella. End of the 4th century B.C.*

acropolis. The grid used in post-Alexandrian Pella consists of two sets of straight, parallel streets, intersecting at right angles to form rectangular blocks of buildings. In this system, known as the "Hippodameian" plan, the short side of the rectangle is invariably 47 m. The long side (north-south), in contrast, varies in a set pattern (125, 111, 125, 150, 125 m. etc.). The width of the streets running through the city from east to west is about 9 m., that of those oriented north-south about 6 m.

The Agora

This area, of great importance in every ancient city, is integrated harmoniously into the urban tissue, covering five building blocks in an east-west direction. It is narrower on the south, to allow the creation of five small blocks of buildings that were given over to commercial establishments and workshops. With dimensions of roughly 200 m. x 182 m., the main area of the Agora, together with the stoas encircling it, and the shops on the sides, formed a building complex of imposing scale. A broad avenue, 15 m. wide, started in the centre of it and ran to east and west through the entire width of the city, connecting it with Edessa in one direction and Thessalonike in the other. The construction of the Agora in the form known today is probably not much earlier than the last quarter of the 3rd century B.C., and may well date from the early years of the reign of Philip V. The complex was destroyed, either by an earthquake or by the raids of barbarian Thracian tribes, probably in the first twenty years of the 1st century B.C.

The houses

Following the articulation typical of the ancient Greek house, the private residence at Pella in the late Classical period has a distinctly introverted character. The plain, undecorated exterior stands in contrast to the interior of the rooms, arranged around a square courtyard, with their richly decorated walls and multi-coloured mosaic floors. Two types of house have been identified in the Macedonian capital: one with an interior peristyle, and one with a *pastas* (a kind of portico). The rooms in daily use, and the rooms for the reception of guests were on the northern side, which was usually two-storeyed, while the storerooms and the ancillary areas in general were grouped on the south side.

One of the wealthier houses with a peristyle,

the House of Dionysos, with its brilliant mosaic floors depicting Dionysos riding on a panther, and a Lion Hunt, has two internal peristyle courtyards. An equally spacious house is that with mosaic floors depicting a Deer Hunt, the Abduction of Helen by Theseus, and the fragmentary scene of an Amazonomachy. Breaking new ground in their conception, the mosaics of Pella, with their subtle use of foreshortening and chiaroscuro, successfully convey a feeling of three-dimensional space. Their technique is more advanced than that of the mosaic floors of Olynthos, and their main features are the use of alternating colours, and of fine strips of clay or lead to pick out detail; the representational scenes, whether used as the main motifs - as "paintings" adorning the *androns* (banquet rooms) - or as decoration for the thresholds of the anterooms, are brilliant examples of painting from antiquity.

The residences of post-Alexandrian Pella were costly structures, reflecting the wealth that flowed into Macedonia on the morrow of the campaign in Asia, and form points of reference for urban architecture in later centuries.

175

174

174. Reconstruction of the painted decoration of a room in the "House of the Plaster" at Pella. (Reproduction of a drawing by N. Sfikas and K. Palian).

175. Mosaic floor from the "House of Dionysos" at Pella, with a scene of a lion hunt. Last quarter of the 4th century B.C. Pella, Archaeological Museum.

ΚΥΝΗΓΙΟΝ ΛΕΟΝΤΟΣ

176. Mosaic floor from the "House of Dionysos" at Pella. Last quarter of the 4th century B.C. Dionysos is depicted holding the thyrsos with one hand and with the other round the neck of the panther on which he is riding. Pella, Archaeological Museum.

176

177. Mosaic floor from the "House of the Abduction of Helen" with a scene of a deer-hunt. Last quarter of the 4th century B.C. Pella.

177

178

178. Mosaic floor from the "House of the Abduction of Helen" with the scene of the abduction. Last quarter of the 4th century B.C. Pella.

179

180

179. Part of the palace at Pella, on the acropolis.

180. The upper part of an ionic column from the palace at Pella. Pella, Archaeological Museum.

THE PALACE

Occupying the entire extent of the hill dominating ancient Pella on the north side of the city, the palace complex of the Macedonian kingdom has an area of 60,0000 sq. m. Articulated into three independent though interconnected units set side by side, the overall complex of buildings is integrated harmoniously into an urban grid that consists of vertical and horizontal zones. Each one of these building units is articulated around a central courtyard, around which are set roofed residential areas. The central unit is an exception, since it includes two open peristyle areas. Along the entire south side, the complex takes the form of a veranda (belvedere) of impressive size, from which the residents on high gazed upon the boundless plain and even the Thermaic Gulf, with the city spreading immediately in front of them. Fragments of doric and ionic columns of various diameters suggest that there was an upper storey on some of the wings of the building complex, which also had a swimming pool.

The successive building phases detected during the excavation of the area undoubtedly make it difficult to define precisely the chronological sequence of the structures. However, on the basis of certain data, it seems fairly sure that the central part of the complex belonged to the end of the first half of the 4th century B.C. Modifications, additions and repairs were carried out mainly during the second half of this same century and throughout the 3rd.

THE CEMETERIES

The earliest tombs in the area that is now the site of the ancient Agora were individual graves cut into the soft limestone of the region, dating from the last quarter of the 5th to the third quarter of the 4th centuries. They gave way to built cist graves in an area to the east of Pella (middle to end of the 4th century B.C.) and to family vaulted rock-cut chamber tombs that survived the Roman conquest. The rich grave offerings - vases, jewellery, decorative attachments for wooden funerary furniture, metal objects, etc. - adorn the display cases of the local Museum and attest both to the piety of the inhabitants of the Macedonian kingdom towards their dead, and to the prosperity of the city.

181. Bronze statuette of Poseidon. Late Hellenistic period, a copy of the statue by Lysippos. Pella, Archaeological Museum.

CULTS

To the gods, heroes and daemons known from the literary and epigraphic traditions (Great Gods, Herakles Phylakos and Asklepios), excavation has added the sanctuaries of Demeter (Thesmophorion), Cybele, Aphrodite and Darron, and has indicated the existence of cults of Poseidon, Dionysos, Athena, with the epithet Alkidemos, and Pan.

THE ARCHAEOLOGICAL MUSEUM

Pending the construction of a spacious Museum in keeping with the importance of the site, a small, though charming, kiosk in the area of the excavation trenches houses a selection of the most important antiquities brought to light by the investigation of the ancient city and the surrounding region: architectural members, metallic objects, vases, jewellery, mosaic floors, reliefs and sculptures carved in the round. The following is a selection of the most important exhibits: An exceptionally fine dog (middle of the 4th century B.C.), and a headless rider contemporary with it, with the volumes of man and animal well balanced, are two of the masterpieces of the Classical period. A marble head of Alexander with wavy hair is a late Hellenistic work which has personal facial features along with certain heroized elements. The bronze statuette of the god of the sea, Poseidon, from this same period translates the lustre of a lost larger-than-life size model, the work of the famous statue-maker Lysippos. There is an impressive restoration of part of the painted decoration of the walls of an interior room of the so-called "House of the Plaster" to the south-west of the present Museum (end of the 4th century B.C.).

182

184

182. Marble equestrian statuette. Middle of the 4th century B.C. Pella, Archaeological Museum.

183. Funerary stele of a dog. Second half of the 4th century B.C. Pella, Archaeological Museum.

184. Marble funerary stele from the cemetery in the area of the Agora at Pella, with a relief figure of Xanthos, according to the inscription at the bottom of the stele:
Ξάνθος/Δημητρίο-/υ καί Ἀμα-/δίκας υἱός
"Xanthos, son of Demetrios and Amadika"
End of the 5th century B.C. Pella, Archaeological Museum.

183

186

185. Red-figure hydria with a scene of the contest between Athena and Poseidon for the name of Athens. End of the 5th-beginning of the 4th centuries B.C. Pella, Archaeological Museum.

186. Stone alabastron. Middle of the 4th century B.C. Pella, Archaeological Museum.

187. Glass alabastron. Middle of the 4th century B.C. Pella, Archaeological Museum.

188. Clay black-glaze pelike. Third quarter of the 4th century B.C. Pella, Archaeological Museum.

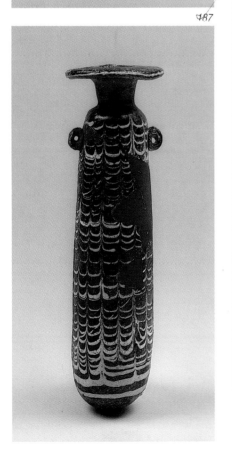

187

188

189

189-191. Heads of clay female figurines. Hellenistic period. Pella, Archaeological Museum.

192. Clay female figurine (Aphrodite). 2nd century B.C. Pella, Archaeological Museum.

193. Clay figurine of Eros. 2nd century B.C. Pella, Archaeological Museum.

190

191

192

193

194. Head of Alexander the Great. Chance find from Yanitsa, near Pella. End of the 4th century B.C. Pella, Archaeological Museum.

195. Marble statuette of Alexander-Pan. Hellenistic period. Pella, Archaeological Museum.

196

197

198

199

200

196. Clay lid for a black-glaze lekanis. Third quarter of the 3rd century B.C. Pella, Archaeological Museum.

197. Clay mould for making relief "Megarian" bowls, with a scene of the Destruction of Troy. Beginning of the 1st century B.C. From a local workshop at Pella. Pella, Archaeological Museum.

198. Deep conical clay vase with appliqué figures. Second half of the 2nd century B.C. Pella, Archaeological Museum.

199. Clay female bust. Beginning of the 1st century B.C. Pella, Archaeological Museum.

200. Clay figurine of Athena "Alkidemos". Late Hellenistic period. Pella, Archaeological Museum.

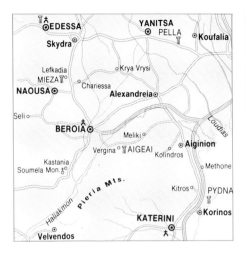

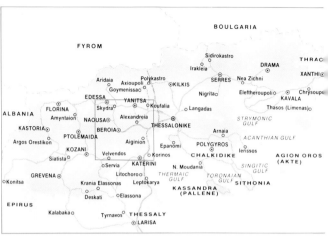

BEROIA
and its region

201

HISTORICAL REVIEW

Standing on the (ancient) road from Thessalonike to Thessaly and "Upper Macedonia", in the eastern foothills of mount Bermion, and on a protected, strategic site, Beroia was the second most important city after Thessalonike, the foundation of Cassander, and always played an important role both in its immediate vital area and in the rest of northern Greece.

The region around the plateau on which the modern city still stands - a region that extends to the north-east as far as the village of Nea Nikomedeia, Stavros and Alexandria, south-east as far as the river Haliakmon and to the south-west and west as far as the village of Asomatoi and to the foothills of Bermion in general, and to the north as far as the village of Patrida - has yielded a vast quantity of archaeological and historical evidence from which to sketch the face of the land from as early as the Neolithic period.

Outside Nea Nikomedeia, for example, at the edge of the lake that formerly covered the entire area as far as Yanitsa and Pella, the earliest settlement in Europe of "settled farmers" has been excavated (7th millennium B.C.). Prehistoric settlements - of later periods - have been identified at Yanitsa, Angelochori and Polyplatano. Re-

201.The city and plain of Beroia.

mains of the Hellenistic and Roman periods have been located as follows: buildings at Alexandria (Hellenistic), villa at Nisi (Roman), "Macedonian" tomb at the Haliakmon Dam (Hellenistic), etc.

Two versions of the etymology of the name of the city have been handed down from antiquity. Both were cited by the historian Theagenes in his now lost *Makedonika,* and were stored by the lexicographer Stephanus of Byzantium (6th century A.D.) in his *Ethnika.* According to the first version, Beroia owed its name to the "founder" of the city, Pheron > Beron, while according to he second it was named after Beroia, the daughter of the Macedonian Beres.

202. Clay red-figure bell-krater, Kerch ware, with a scene related to the cycle of Dionysos and Aphrodite. It was used as a cinerary urn and was discovered in a tomb at Beroia, indicating commercial connections with Attica. Just after the middle of the 4th century B.C. Beroia, Archaeological Museum.

202

Ancient times

A cist grave on a building plot immediately to the north of the Museum building, the finds from which date from the early Iron Age (10th-8th century B.C.) may not actually be representative of this period, for grave offerings like those contained in it have also been found in funerary monuments of later periods. There is, moreover, no certain evidence that the plateau occupied (and still occupied today) by the city was inhabited not only in this, but also in the following - Archaic and Geometric -periods. The first certain reference to Beroia is still the passage 61.4 of the first book of Thucydides' Histories, recording the unsuccessful attempt of the Athenians to take the city by siege (432 B.C.) during their campaign to the Chalkidike in the course of the Peloponnesian War.

This date and the period immediately following it are connected with finds from the Classical cemetery of the end of the 5th and the first half of the 4th centuries B.C., which lies along and beneath the road from the railway station to the northern entrance to the city. However, no architectural monument or building remains located by excavations inside the city can be dated to these years of the reigns of Archelaos I and his successors Perdikkas, Amyntas II, Philip II, and Alexander the Great.

Life in Beroia did not come to an end, of course, and the Athenian orator Kallimedon, a friend of Philip and Alexander the Great, visited the city in 338 B.C. and was married there. The gold that flowed into Macedonia in such great quantities after the conquests in the East will certainly have been used in Beroia, as has been shown to have been the case at Pella, to erect costly buildings, mainly in the reign of Cassander. And it is to precisely these and the following years that should be ascribed the application of the principles of the "Hippodameian" town planning system, which one suspects governed the architectural remains found in the building plots in the centre of the modern city. Mylleas Zoilou, trierach in the camp of Alexander the Great, was from Beroia, as were Koiranos, later a tax-collector in Phoiniki, and probably also Harpalos, who robbed the royal treasury after the death of Alexander the Great.

The 4th century cemetery consists mainly of pit graves, and some of the tombs have the same technology as those belonging to the 3rd century B.C.

Within the city, whose history was marked at

203. Bronze statuette of
a young woman
bathing, said to have
been found at Beroia.
One of the finest
examples of miniature
sculpture, probably
from the period after
Lysippos. Munich,
Staatliche
Antikensammlungen
und Glyptothek.

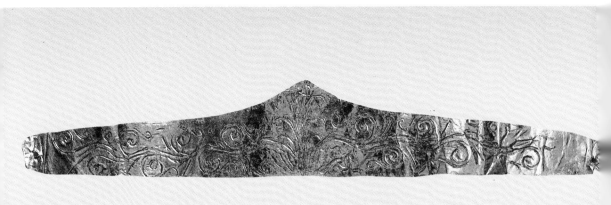

205

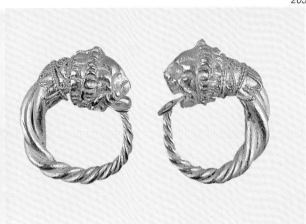

204. Gold diadem with floral decoration and holes by which it was attached to the head of the dead woman. From a female burial at Beroia. End of the 4th century B.C. Beroia, Archaeological Museum.

205. Pair of gold earrings with lion's heads, from a female burial at Beroia. End of the 4th century B.C.. Beroia, Archaeological Museum.

206. Pair of gold earrings, a gold finger ring and a gold necklacc (with rings of gold and cornelian), from a female burial at Beroia. Middle of the 2nd century B.C. Beroia, Archaeological Museum.

this period by the reign of Demetrios Poliorketes, followed by those of Antigonos II Gonatas and Philip V, there are few ancient structures, or rather building remains. However, it is highly unlikely that Beroia did not flourish and prosper in the 4th century B.C. Particularly as the new royal house of the Antigonids (294-168 B.C.) was descended from the city. Men from Beroia are attested as *proxenoi, thearodokoi* and *hieromnemones* at the pan-Hellenic sanctuaries and in cities in Greece. Royal envoys at the court of the king of Illyria and at the Roman Senate pressed the interests of the state.

The large numbers of middle and late Hellenistic funerary stelai, moreover, and especially the many chamber tombs cut into the soft, yellowish rock of the region on the fringes of the city, attest, with their rich grave offerings, to the economic prosperity of the inhabitants. The general aspect of the city's environs, especially the part extending to the east of the plateau, can be in-

ferred from Plutarch's account of the siege of Beroia by Demetrios Poliorketes in 288 B.C., when the city was occupied by Pyrrhos. The entire hillside now occupied by worker's houses appears to have been covered with oak-trees. His description of the siege also leads to the conclusion that the city already had strong fortification walls at the beginning of the 3rd century B.C., parts of which, complete with later additions, are still preserved in places. It was clearly these walls that saved Beroia some time later - in 280/79 B.C. - from the attacks of the Gauls; a few years afterwards (274 B.C.), these same Gauls robbed and plundered the royal tombs at Aigai (Vergina) in their mania for destruction.

Beroia, like the other Macedonian cities, was governed by a group of prominent citizens, the *politarchs,* while at an earlier date royal authority had been represented by an epistates. The inhabitants were organised in "tribes", the known names of these being Peukastike, Berike, Paion-

206

is, and one that may perhaps have been called Antigonis. In the city there were sanctuaries of Herakles Kynagidas, Asklepios, Aphrodite, Artemis, Apollo and Dionysos.

According to one view, the Macedonian *Koinon,* an assembly of a religious character con-sisting of representatives of the Macedonian cities, which is known mainly from inscriptions of the Roman imperial period, had its roots in this late period of the Macedonian kingdom. In which case it is almost certain that Beroia was its head-quarters at this period, as it was at a later date.

207

208

209

207. Red-figure askos, from the Classical cemetery of Beroia. Second half of the 4th century B.C. Beroia, Archaeological Museum.

208. Clay bust of a female deity from a tomb at Beroia. End of the 4th century B.C. Beroia, Archaeological Museum.

209. Clay pyxis with a lid, from a female burial at Beroia. It has "West Slope" floral decoration and a relief bust of Artemis on the raised part of the lid. First half of the 2nd century B.C. Beroia, Archaeological Museum.

210. Clay figurine of Aphrodite and a small Eros, from a female burial at Beroia, product of a local workshop. Beginning of the 2nd century B.C. Beroia, Archaeological Museum.

211. Larger than life-size head of Medusa. 2nd century A.D. It was built into the north gate in the city walls, to ward off enemies. Beroia, Archaeological Museum.

Roman Period

On 22nd June 168 B.C., Perseus, the last king of Macedonia, was defeated by the Roman consul Aemilius Paulus in the battle of Pydna, and Macedonia was converted into a Roman protectorate, and then (148 B.C.) incorporated into the Roman empire as the first province in the East *(Provincia Macedonia).* Hippias of Beroia, leader of the Macedonian phalanx, and his fellow Beroians Medon and Pantauchos, surrendered the city to the Romans the day after the battle and inaugurated a new epoch for Beroia and for Macedonia in general.

In the first century B.C. and at the beginning of the 1st century A.D. the city was to experience at first hand the dramatic events first of the latter years of the Roman Republic and then of the early Roman Empire. It was threatened by the barbarian hordes, formed the training ground for the armies of Pompey shortly before the battle of Pharsalos (48 B.C.), and eagerly embraced Christian teaching when it was visited in A.D. 50 by saint Paul the apostle, who preached in the Jewish synagogue there. Under Roman suzerainty, and enjoying the benefits of the *Pax Romana,* situated behind the front line, with a fertile plain and prosperous trade, Beroia quickly evolved "into a large and populous city of Macedonia", as it is called by Lucian of Samosata.

Headquarters of the *Koinon ton Makedonon,* it organised events in honour of the emperors, involving both athletic and artistic and literary competitions. Spectators and competitors came from all parts of the world, giving the city great prestige every five years, when these meetings were held. It acquired further prestige as the meeting place of the representatives of the Macedonian cities - *the synedroi* - who gathered to conduct the prescribed formalities of the cult of the emperor, in whose name special temples had been erected. Powerful and mighty, Beroia successfully requested from the emperor Nerva, just before A.D. 56, the granting - to it alone of all the cities of Macedonia - of the honorary title of metropolis. Furthermore, it succeeded in eliciting the

212

direct interest of Trajan (A.D. 98-117) and the emperors Marcus Aurelius and Lucius Verus (A.D. 161-169) in various of its internal problems and issues; it gratefully erected statues to Claudius and Septimius Severus and through inscriptions immortalised the names of all its chosen sons who had striven to embellish the city, to succour the citizens in times of grain shortage, to alleviate the burden of the provincial tax, and finally to construct works for the public welfare.

A Greek city, with a Council *(boule)* and an Assembly of the People *(ekklesia),* local magistrates - such as the *politarchs* - and officials - like the *eirenarchs,* the *sitones,* the *tamiai* and the *oikonomoi* - with doctors, architects and a strong priesthood, Beroia was a primarily Greek-speaking city with a special interest in its youth. Great importance attaches to the surviving lists of the ephebes of the city gymnasia, and also to the famous "gymnasiarchal law" - a regulatory document carved on a fine white stele, now in the local Museum - which laid down rules for their organisation.

A city of international repute, it gathered within its fortification walls a large number of foreigners from all over the world. Greeks, Asians and Romans. Some of them permanently resident, and others merely staying for a short time. Merchants, craftsmen, artists, athletes, gladiators. And it was the foreigners who brought with them the cults of Isis, Harpokrates, the Syrian goddess and of Serapis, and also had temples erected to them.

213

The picture we have of the city under the Roman empire is supplemented by epigraphic evidence relating to the existence of slaves, freedmen, associations of citizens of a religious or professional nature, guilds and clubs. And also to the artistic achievements of the citizens, to religious ceremonies, and to the holding of gladiatorial combats between men, and between men and

212. Marble portrait head of a woman. 2nd century A.D. Beroia, Archaeological Museum.

213. Fragment of a funerary relief with a female bust, from Beroia (?). 1st century A.D. Beroia, Archaeological Museum.

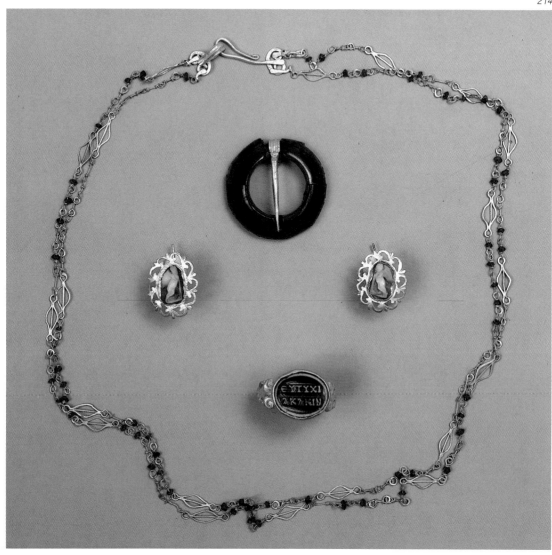

beasts, which obviously took place in amphitheatres and theatres, one of which may perhaps lie in the neighbourhood of the modern night-club, Elia.

The sporadic remains revealed by excavation speak of monumental building complexes and of a very carefully constructed road system: running beneath the modern Mitropoleos street, Venizelou street, and Akatamachitou street, and in the building plots bordering on Elia street, are paved streets 4 m. wide, with a subterranean drainage system and water-supply pipes to the right and left of the kerbstones - usually streets flanked by colonnades *(Viae Colonnatae)* - which are bordered by shops and blocks of houses. Public baths (balaneia) have been located in the modern Pindou street not far from Ayiou Antoniou

214. Gold jewellery from a cist grave. 3rd century A.D. Beroia, Archaeological Museum.

215. Gold niketerion, a coin-like medallion with a bust of Philip II from the find at Abukir in Egypt. 3rd century A.D. Paris, Bibliothèque Nationale.

Square, the centre of the ancient as well as the modern city, and a complex of shops has been excavated in building plots in Parodos Edessis street.

The cemeteries of this period, which extend alongside the exit routes from the city in the direction of Thessalonike (at Palaioforos), Kozani (near the Gymnasium), and Pieria, consist of

172

groups of pit graves, marble sarcophagi, some of them adorned with relief scenes and some without decoration, and tile-covered tombs. The small landowners on the outskirts (e.g. the modern district of Promitheas) chose for their final resting place some spot on their own lands.

The 3rd century A.D., which decisively stamped the history of the city - and indeed of Macedonia - bestowed honours and glory on Beroia. The imperial cult was combined with that of Alexander the Great, the games in honour of the earthly lords of the world were named the "Alexandreia Olympia" and the city, in order to cover the vast expenditure demanded by the organisa-

216. Two sides of a coin issued by the Macedonian Koinon. One side has the head of Alexander the Great, and the other temples associated with the imperial cult. 3rd century A.D. Athens, Numismatic Museum.

217. The so-called marble tower in the walls of Beroia, which is preserved at the north entrance to the city. It belongs to the period in the 3rd century A.D. when the defensive enceinte was reconstructed with architectural members taken from nearby buildings.

tion of all these events, issued bronze coins both in the name of the *Koinon ton Makedonon,* of which it was the headquarters, and in its own name (A.D. 242 onwards). To the same end, the famous *niketeria* circulated at this period, connected with the games as prizes for the winners; these were gold medallions in the form of coins with scenes relating to the career of the by now legendary Alexander the Great (one of these, from a find at Abukir in Egypt, is on display in Thessalonike Archaeological Museum). These final glimmerings however, were no more than a prelude to the events that were to follow. The barbarian tribes that had begun to trouble the Danubian regions and the eastern borders of the Roman Empire in the third quarter of the 3rd century A.D. seized the opportunity in the middle of the century to pour down into Greece, plundering and destroying: Carpi and Goths laid siege to Thessalonike and Sparta, and undoubtedly also to Beroia, which at this precise date was hastening to strengthen its defences by any means it could, repairing the fortifications with architectural material from nearby monuments, mainly from funerary structures of the late Hellenistic period, or rebuilding them with marble funerary altars of the 1st and 2nd centuries A.D.

Byzantine Period

At the end of the 3rd century A.D. the emperor Diocletian divided the Roman empire into 12 dioceses subdivided into provinces. Macedonia was a province of the diocese of Moesia. Beroia belonged to this province, the capital of which was Thessalonike. During the time of the Second Tetrarchy, the city, like the rest of Macedonia, fell within the sphere of authority of Licinius, but after 324 and the defeat of the latter by Constantine the Great at Chrysoupolis, Beroia came into the hands of the new lord of the world and first Christian emperor. A heavy price was laid by the church on the altar of faith in the martyrdom of the 40 virgins that took place at the time of the persecutions.

We do not know the fate of the city during the raids by the Goths and Huns at the end of the 4th and first half of the 5th centuries A.D. During the descent of the Ostrogoths, perhaps in A.D. 473, Beroia was ceded for a short time by treaty to the new conquerors.

Under Justinian I, in A.D. 535, the empire was divided into 2 prefectures (East and Illyricum) and 64 provinces with 435 cities. The prefecture of Illyricum included amongst its provinces one called *Makedonia Prima,* one of the 32 cities of which was Beroia. From this period, and even earlier, until the Fourth Crusade (A.D. 1204), the city and its region from time to time experienced all the horror of the wars conducted by the Byzantine state in the face of the attacks by barbarians of various origins, and witnessed of persecutions, ravaging and the enforced removal of its inhabitants to the ends of Syria and to the Danube. They also felt the terror of the destructive earthquakes that razed Beroia in A.D. 896, 904 and A.D. 985. Avars (A.D. 531) followed by Arabs (A.D. 904), Bulgars (985, 1040/41, 1286/7) and probably Normans (A.D. 1082) made themselves masters of the city, despite attempts to reinforce the fortification walls (e.g. A.D. 1016). On every occasion, however, the difficulties were overcome, adversities surpassed, and Beroia returned to the fold of the Byzantine state.

When the Franks of the Fourth Crusade dissolved the Byzantine Empire in 1204, Beroia was ceded to Boniface of Montferrat, lord of the Frankish kingdom of Thessalonike, and a Latin bishop was installed in the city. In 1220-24 the city shared the fate of the rest of Macedonia and came under the jurisdiction of the despot of Epirus, Theodore Komnenos Doukas Angelos. A few years earlier, however (1205), the rich plain that spread, and still spreads, before it was depopulated as a result of raids by Vlachobulgarians, under the leadership of their tzar Ioannis, who was called Skyloyannis by the Byzantines. The rapid changes of the situation on the political stage brought Beroia first within the kingdom of Nicaea, with Ioannis III Vatatzes and then, from 1261, into the bosom of the restored Byzantine Empire with Michael VIII Palaiologos, having previously, for a short interval in 1257, been attached to the "Despotate" of Epirus (Michael II Komnenos Doukas Angelos). The city's ordeal did not end at this point, however. Although it managed to avoid capture by the Catalans in 1309, it did not escape the misfortunes reserved for it by the dispute between the two Andronikoi, II and III Palaiologoi, in the period 1321-1328, nor the results of the feigned friendship between Ioannis VI Kantakouzenos and Ioannis V Palaiologos on the one side and the Serb kral Stephen Dušan on the other.

A certain amount of evidence is preserved from these last centuries of the city's life before its conquest by the Turks illuminating the public and private life of the inhabitants of the city: we know of a neighbourhood at the edge of Beroia called "Skoronychou" - possibly the modern

219

neighbourhood of Exo Panagia - and also a site called Elia, in the modern area of that name. The name "Basilikos" is securely attested for the river Tripotamos, as is the existence of a large indoor market. The castle was repaired and extended under Stephen Dušan (1331-1355), acquiring two acropoleis and a double row of oblique walls; of its gates, the names are known of "Opsikiani", "Basiliki" and "Anna Kapousi", possibly constructed by Anna Palaiologina, in the southern section. We also know that near the enceinte - clearly the eastern section - there was dense vegetation consisting of shrubs and bushes. According to one view, the semi-ruined tower now in the forecourt of the building of the Old Lawcourts (known as the Tower of Vergina), and the base of the Tower on which the city clock once stood in Orologiou Square, were part of Dušan's fortifications. At this period the Church of Beroia became the head of a metropolitan see and its importance as a centre with a religious tradition and as a place in which the artistic spirit prospered greatly is indicated by the large number of churches enclosed within its walls. Popular "historiographical writing" asserts that the large number of churches is due to the fact that the city was a place of exile for important persons, though this view remains unproven. It is a fact, however, that of the 72 churches that were preserved at the beginning of the 20th century - about 50 churches still survive today - many were the katholika of monasteries or private churches.

In Byzantine times, the plain before Beroia produced roughly the same crops as it does today, with the addition of rice, on account of its proximity to the marsh of Yanitsa. The area was

218. *The Virgin Glykophilousa. Icon from Beroia, probably by a Kastoria workshop. End of the 14th century.*

219. *Christ the Saviour. Middle leaf of a triptych, from the private iconostasis of a wealthy Beroian. Probably from a Thessalonike workshop.*

220. *Saints Georgios and Demetrios. Icon from Beroia, painted in a north Greek workshop. 17th century.*

220

Ο ἍΓ
ΓΕΩ

Ο ἍΓ
ΙΟς

Ο ἍΓ
ΑΗ

Μ

rich in forest products, and stock-raising, arboriculture, market-gardening, and particular viticulture seem to have been widely practised. Beekeeping and silk-making were also widespread. The nearby forests of Bermion offered rich game for the tables of the inhabitants.

There was an unprecedented number of water-mills, and Beroians were renowned throughout the kingdom as dyers and bleachers of cloth; these two industries flourished in the regions "Sarandovrysi" and "Lianovrochi" respectively. Large numbers were employed in the quarrying and working of marble, copper- and bronze-working, etc.

The Jewish element which had existed in the city since the Roman period and which was later enriched by those expelled from Spain in the 15th-16th centuries, was at this time one of the main driving forces in the growth of trade, both international and with Thessalonike and Constantinople.

With regard to the local administration of the city, Ioannis VI Kantakouzenos informs us that there were three main organs: the aristocracy (aristoi), the people (demos) and the clergy. The aristoi were the economically strong - the "powerful" - while the demos consisted of the lower and presumably also the middle classes. In addition to these groups, there was also the body of the "heads" of the city - that is, the executive organs.

Poor pit graves, mainly without offerings, normally in groups and rarely with plastered interiors, have been investigated in the area of the New Gymnasium (High School) in the south of Beroia (Kato Elia), and a few also on the way out of the city in the direction of Kozani. A small number has been located inside churches, presumably belonging to members of the clergy.

The Tourkokratia and Modern times

The capture of Kallipolis by the Turkish armies in 1354, and their rapid advance into the Balkans marked the beginning of a new period, characterized by gradual changes, both political and cultural, that had major consequences not only for the inhabitants of the region (Greeks, Bulgars, Serbs) but also for the states of central Europe. The capture of Serrhai (1383) was followed, during the siege of Thessalonike (1385/6) by that of Beroia, which the Turks made a tribute paying city (1387?). Its final incorporation into the Ottoman Empire, however, was accomplished under Bayezid I, in 1391. Documents in the notary archives of Venice make it clear that, in the period 1381-1388, and more specifically in the years 1383 and later 1387, many of those taken prisoner from Beroia were sold in Venice as slaves. It is to this period that the beginnings may be traced of a number of narratives invented by the popular muse and preserved to the present day: these are the "history" of "Queen Virginia or Vergina" who chose to commit suicide from her high tower in order to escape being taken prisoner, the legend of one Chatzikatvia, who betrayed Beroia to the Turks, facilitating their entry into the city through an unguarded gate in the south (the area is still called "Yola Geldi" - that is, "the road by which they came"), and finally, the narrative of Archbishop Arsenios, who was hanged from the plane tree next to the old cathedral. This same tradition has given rise to the false etymology of the name Karaferga (Kara Ferya = black Beroia) given by the Turks to Beroia because its capture caused them so much hardship.

The shock to the Ottoman state caused by the battle of Ankara (1402), internal disturbances, and the abnormal state of affairs checked the process of expansion by the new lords, albeit only temporarily. Liberation movements were suppressed, attempts to shake of the yoke were strangled at birth, and the situation was consolidated. Many fled to the mountains, others converted to Islam, but the majority remained and, under very harsh conditions of slavery, fought the good fight. The main task of the local archontes (nobles) was to protect the local institutions of the community, its religious freedoms, and the dignity of the inhabitants, particularly after the latest and final capture of Beroia by the Turks (1448/9), on the morrow of the defeat of the Hungarians at the Kossyphopedion (1448), and the loss of all hope of liberation.

Most of the churches were converted into mosques; others were abandoned and fell into ruins. The city was divided into two parts: the Greek element was concentrated in the north-east, while in the south-west were settled the Turks and the Jews fleeing persecution in Spain at the end of the 15th century. The latter were skilled craftsmen who brought a gift with them to their new country: the high art of weaving.

An important centre of trade and industry, Beroia had one of the first Greek schools in Macedonia, reared and promoted distinguished men, and found itself at the centre of the conqueror's interest. In 1519 it numbered 231 Moslim and 578 non-Moslim families. The 4000 inhabitants of the

16th century rose to 8000 by the 18th. At the time when it was visited by the Turkish traveller Evliya Çelebi (1668), Beroia had 600 shops, a *bezesten* (covered market), 15 *hans,* and 300 water-mills. It produced woollen clothes and specialized in bathing robes -products much in demand throughout the empire. It also exported silk. The rich plain in front of the city produced rice, cotton and cereals.

Alongside the things of this world, the Orthodox creeds of Christianity were cared for in the foothills of Bermion. A notable centre of monastic life, the region of Beroia produced men of great spirituality at this period: Hosios Antonios the younger, Hosios Dionysios, and Theophanes of Ioannina. It had monasteries as famous as that of Ioannis the Baptist on the river Haliakmon, and a vast number of churches were built, repaired or painted at this time, with funds supplied by wealthy citizens, and undoubtedly with the encouragement and under the protective aegis of personalities such as Patriarch Jeremiah II (1572-1595). At this time, the founding of schools became more general: Ioannikios (1721-23), Kyrillos (1771), Triandafyllos (1790) and Angelos (1817) were to teach at the Greek school of Beroia, founded in 1650 by the priest-monk Kallinikos Manios. Many, however, were educated at the teaching institutions of the Greek communities in Western Europe, and would bring honour to their country. Ioannis Kottounios (1572-1657), for example, that sage researcher and teacher at the University of Padua, left his fortune to the "Kottounianion Hellenomuseion" founded by him in 1653, providing in his will for eight scholarships for Greeks to study there.

There were also many who distinguished themselves in commerce and, having taken up residence in the great capitals of central Europe, at Budapest and Vienna, and also in the territories of Hungary, modern ex-Yugoslavia and Romania, kept alive the flame and consciousness of their duty towards the ideals of Hellenism and contributed in every way they could to the awakening of the nation: the families of Vikelas and Raktivan.

The wind of freedom that began to blow through the Balkan peninsula after the sea-battle of Lepanto (1571) stirred the desire of the Beroians to cast of the Turkish yoke. The ground had already been prepared by the oppression of the Greek element through repeated culls of children by the *paidomazoma,* by the wretched condition to which the countryside had been reduced, and by the humiliation, on the one hand,

and the harsh taxes and improprieties of the Turkish authorities towards their subjects on the other. Starting as early as the 16th century, organised bands of *armatoles* and *klephts* in the mountains around the city harassed the conquerors over the centuries that followed, and especially after the Orloff episode, though the effects of their raids were not of decisive significance, given that urban centres like Thessalonike and Larisa were not far away and housed strong military forces. The sentiments of rebellion that were aroused also by the sermons of enlightened missionaries preaching the ideal of independence - amongst them the indefatigable torchbearer of the Greek nation, Kosmas Aitolos, who visited Beroia in 1775 - were also fanned by the messages of the European Enlightenment.

This new spirit was the context for, and the regeneration of thought was channelled by the frenzy of building activity observable in both Beroia and the rest of Macedonia, with the erection of magnificent, frequently two-storey *archontika,* with their extensively painted interiors. Fine examples of the vernacular urban architecture of the 18th and 19th centuries, with their gilded wood-carved decoration and colourful wall-paintings, the *archontika* of Vikelas (1773), [sior] Manolakis, Raktivan, Tzintou, and Sapountzoglou (1850) vouch for the prosperity of their owners and are clear evidence for the change in mentality and way of life - undoubtedly an amalgam of central European models and local elements.

At the end of the 19th century, Beroia was a richly-watered city, in the lush foothills of Bermion, with 1200 families, of which 50 were Jewish, 30 Gypsies, and of the rest, half were Greek, and the other half Ottoman. It was divided into 12 neighbourhoods, had 15 houses of worship, 72 churches (several of which lay in ruins), 5 stone-built khania and 12 water-mills. It had a full town school with six grades, half a boy's school, a girl's school, and a number of nurseries. The "Melissa" guild had a library. Six water-powered factories (the cotton-mills owned by Sossidis, the Chatzinikolakis brothers and others), buildings of the beginning of the 20th century, and the first marble quarries marked the entry of the region into the period of industrialization. At the same time they prepared it for liberation and unification with the rest of Greece (October 1912).

221. Plan of modern Beroia with the sites of
architectural remains and destroyed Byzantine and
post-Byzantine churches marked on it.

222. View of the north-east section of the city walls.
Marble funerary altars and other architectural
members were hastily incorporated in the walls
during the barbarian invasions (3rd century A.D.).

THE MONUMENTS

THE WALLS

With sections going back to the Hellenistic period (isodomic masonry of dressed stone blocks/circular towers), the defensive enceinte of Beroia still encompasses, as far as its resistance to foes and friends alike has permitted, the plateau on which the modern city stands. Liberally sprinkled with marble funerary altars and other architectural members that were hastily incorporated in times of tribulation (3rd century A.D.), and repaired during the periods of respite (middle Byzantine period), and crowned with makeshift houses(Ottoman occupation), the walls now form a the litany of the city's history throughout the centuries. Guardians of memories and avenging angels.

THE BYZANTINE CHURCHES

Of the seventy-two (according to tradition) churches of Beroia, time, pagan conquerors. and unthinking Modern Greeks with their destructive urban designs, have left in the courtyards of the apartment buildings - which are not even properly speaking courtyards - a small number of ecclesiastical monuments, witnesses to the piety of members of wealthy families, important figures, exiled clerics and officials of the Byzantine court. Monuments that have seen the Komnenoi, the Palaiologoi, the Bulgarian tzars, the Serb krals, the Franks and the Turks. That were lit by the candles of anonymous believers. That were cared for by pious neighbours and now, having been incorporated into programmes of restoration, are looked after by some conscientious custodian of antiquities.

The Old Cathedral

The earliest church in Beroia, the Old Cathedral, dedicated to the apostles Peter and Paul, was erected on the ruins of an Early Christian church. A three-aisled, basilica with a tiled roof and an elevated central aisle, it is a work of the 12th century A.D., to which the Church Fathers on the apse also belong. The intrados of the arches in the colonnades were painted in the 14th century A.D. During the period of Turkish rule the church was converted into a mosque, named Hounkiar Cami. The south aisle was demolished at some undefined period. At present the interior of the building is inaccessible.

222

223. Saint Ioannis the Theologian. Wall-painting from the church of the same name in Beroia. 13th century.

224. "The Descent into Hades". Wall-painting in the church of the Christos(Resurrection of the Lord) in Beroia. Beginning of the 14th century. One of the masterpieces of Palaiologan painting.

Saint Ioannis the Theologian

Of the original building phase of the church - a structure of the beginning of the 13th century A.D. - only the west section is now preserved, with the sanctuary which was modified in places in the Ottoman occupation.

Saint Blasios

The aisleless church of Saint Blasios, with its tiled roof and austere, unaffected exterior, is a 13th century A.D. building that has undergone many alterations during the course of the centuries, which have altered its original form. The wall-paintings inside the church were probably the work of a specially gifted artist, and date from the transition from the 13th to the 14th centuries.

The Church of the Resurrection of the Lord (Church of Christ)

Directly related to the church of Saint Nikolaos Orphanos in Thessalonike, the Church of the Resurrection of Christ was decorated by the talented church painter Georgios Kalliergis in 1315 A.D. - according to the inscription - who

signs himself as "the best painter in the whole of Thettalia (i.e. Macedonia)". The scene of the Descent into Hades (Ressurection) is an exceptionally fine example of the art of the period and the sensitivity of the artist.

The church of Saints Kerykos and Ioulitta

With wall-paintings of the 13th century A.D., which were completed (and covered) three centuries later, the church dedicated to the memory of saint Kerykos and his mother saint Ioulitta, with its fine brickwork on the exterior of the apse, was probably founded by Bishop Makarios. The north and west annexes are later additions and alter the original shape of the church.

Of the post-Byzantine churches, some of which perhaps hide their Byzantine faces under the cloak of the Ottoman occupation, mention may be made of the Panagia Haviara and Saint Nikolaos in the parish of Saint Antonios. Sixteenth century painting is represented by the three-aisled basilica of Saint Georgios (parish of Saint Antonios) and the single-room church of Saint Nikolaos of Makariotissa, with its dark paint and ossified figures - dark as the years of slavery.

224

THE ARCHAEOLOGICAL MUSEUM

Looking out onto the plain that spreads in front of Beroia, the Archaeological Museum of the city, a building of the 1960s in the style of the "Macedonian house", standing on the edge of the plateau, could not have imagined the wealth of ancient treasures that would be bestowed liberally upon it in the ensuing decades by the earth of Bottiaia.

The three exhibition halls and the storage rooms house a suffocating quantity of discoveries from the prehistoric settlement at Nea Nikomedeia (Early Neolithic Period) and the Tumulus Cemetery at Vergina (Early Iron Age). Ceramic grave offerings (vases and figurines) of the Classical and Hellenistic periods jostle together (the iron sword with an ivory hilt, from the end of the 4th century B.C., is remarkable), along with sculptures and funerary stelai from Beroia and the surrounding area, Lefkadia and Vergina (the marble group of a huntsman and his dog from Aigai), table supports, portraits and the bust of the river god Olganos (middle of the 2nd century A.D.). A unique find is the "gymnasiarchal law", a text containing the internal regulations for the local Gymnasium.

In the Museum garden, the funerary and honorific altars (1st-3rd centuries A.D.) - many of which were incorporated into the city walls at times of tribulation - and a vast number of inscriptions inform the visitor about the "state and society" of the headquarters of the *Macedonian Koinon* (a not inconsiderable number of them - manumissions - come from the sanctuary of the Mother of the Gods outside Beroia in Pieria). The marble head of Medusa at the entrance to the Museum, a work of the 2nd century A.D. of impressive size, was once affixed to the east gate in the walls, where it discouraged the city's foes.

225

226

*225. Iron sword with an ivory handle decorated with
a gold Victory, from a cist grave at Beroia. End of
the 4th century B.C. Beroia, Archaeological Museum.*

*226. Bronze hydria/cinerary urn from the same cist
grave as the iron sword in fig. 225. 370-360 B.C.
Beroia, Archaeological Museum.*

*227. Detail of a painted stele with a depiction of a
female figure, from the earth deposits of the Great
Tumulus at Vergina. End of the 4th century B.C.
Beroia, Archaeological Museum.*

227

228. Marble table support with a relief scene of Zeus in the form of an eagle abducting Ganymede. 2nd century B.C. Beroia, Archaeological Museum.

229. Funerary stele of Paterinos, son of Antigonos. 100-80 B.C. Beroia, Archaeological Museum.

228

229

230

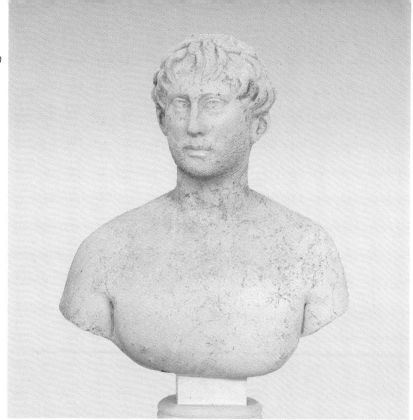

231

230. Roman portrait.
2nd century A.D.
Beroia, Archaeological
Museum.

231. Bust of the river
god Olganos, one of the
three children of Beres,
son of Makedon, about
150 A.D. His sisters,
Mieza and Beroia, gave
their names to the two
Macedonian cities of
those names. Beroia,
Archaeological
Museum.

186

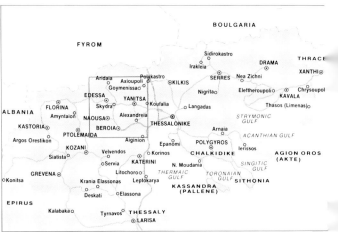

EDESSA
and its region

232

HISTORICAL REVIEW
AND ARCHAEOLOGICAL SITE

Edessa stands at the transition from the plains to the mountains of Macedonia, on a steep, imposing site, with an abundance of water and vegetation. Known from an inscription of Delphi (beginning of the 3rd century B.C.), the city is attested in Diodorus Siculus, Strabo, Appian and Livy. It has a composite articulation, spreading over two levels, the acropolis (in the east part of the modern city) and the main city (at Longos), and has some of the earliest indications of human settlement in the prehistoric period. A small rural settlement down to the 4th century B.C., it acquired the form of a town probably in the reign of Philip II, and was fortified with walls at the beginning of the 3rd century B.C., as part of an ambitious programme of fortification in the face of the uncertainty of the situation conceived in the period after Alexander the Great.

The acropolis has a wall 2.20 m. thick and is an isosceles triangle in plan, with an area of about 35,000 sq.m., enclosing the Council House, the temples of Zeus Hypsistos and Dionysos, and the other public buildings. The rushing waters of the river that enclosed it in two branches before falling foaming down to the plain gave it additional security.

The lower city, encircled by a wall about 3 m. thick, in the shape of a long, narrow parallelogram, occupied an area of 230,000 sq.m. The de-

232. The waterfalls of Edessa.

233

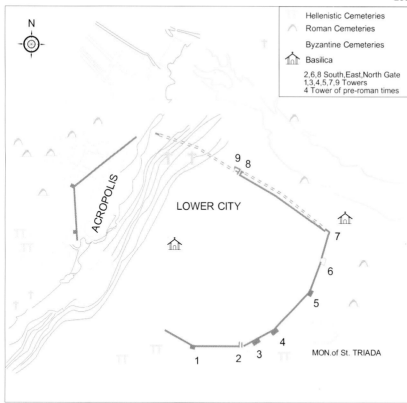

Hellenistic Cemeteries
Roman Cemeteries
Byzantine Cemeteries
Basilica
2,6,8 South,East,North Gate
1,3,4,5,7,9 Towers
4 Tower of pre-roman times

N

ACROPOLIS

LOWER CITY

9 8

7

6

5

4

1 2 3

MON.of St. TRIADA

233. Edessa. Plan of
the ancient city. [The
acropolis is at the top
left and the Lower City
(Longos), with the
defence wall in the
centre.]

234. Section of the city
walls from the south-
east.

235. The East Gate.

236. The South Gate.

234

235

236

239

fensive enceinte is given a monumental character by its well-built towers and gates, of which the most interesting is the south gate with the circular courtyard and the *Via Colonnata* (2nd century A.D.) leading to it; it is a work of about 1,300 m. in length and underwent repeated repairs and additions, reflecting the undiminished concern of the inhabitants over the centuries to safeguard the freedom of their city.

Like the other Macedonian cities, Edessa too had a council and *politarchs* in the Roman period. In addition to the Greeks, the city was inhabited by Italian colonists who exploited the fertile soil and the other productive potential of the region and, thanks to the Via Egnatia, developed significant commercial activity.

An important place in the local pantheon seems to have been occupied by the goddess Ma, in whose name many slaves were manumitted.

Cemeteries have been located both around the acropolis and along the perimeter of the lower city. They consist of groups of vaulted chamber tombs cut in the soft rock of the region, usually family tombs (middle and late Hellenistic periods), cist graves (early Imperial period) and single chamber tombs with painted interiors (early Byzantine period). The appearance of the barbarian hordes in Macedonia in the 3rd century A.D. obliged the Edessaeans to construct an outwork for the acropolis as hastily as possible and to reinforce the neglected walls of the lower city by demolishing monuments of earlier periods. Despite this, the fortifications were not strong enough in the following centuries to protect Edessa from the raids of the Avars and the Slavs: the city was captured and put to the torch. This may have been the occasion of the abandonment of the lower city and the confinement of the popula-

240

237. *Longos from the modern city of Edessa.*

238. *The street with the columns.*

239. *Relief stele with a pedimental finial which was made by Hermias and Paraskeve before they died. Roman period. Edessa, Archaeological Collection.*

240. *Funerary inscription of Secundus of Edessa and his wife Julia. Roman period. Edessa, Archaeological Collection.*

tion to the acropolis. A decisive role in this will undoubtedly have been played by the destructive action of the waters, which for centuries piled up sedimentary deposits at the site of Longos. The Fortress, as Edessa is called by Glykas and Kedrinos, the Vodena of the Greek-Bulgarian conflicts of the 11th century (Samuel, Basil II the Bulgar Slayer), was throughout Byzantine times and the period that followed (Ottoman occupation), the city on the rock. This is the city described by Kantakouzenos (1350 A.D.), captured by the Ottomans in 1380, and described again in 1669 by the Turkish traveller Evliya Çelebi.

In 1798, when Ali Pasha occupied Edessa, the city numbered 12,000 souls with 500 Greek and 1500 Moslim houses. It had six mosques, a cathedral and a bishop's residence built on the edge of the plateau on which the city stood, next to the cataracts, overlooking the rich plain with its fruit trees.

On the day of the weekly market - the bazaar - villagers from Sari-Yol, Arnisa and Florina flocked to Edessa to sell their farm produce and buy manufactured goods. The surrounding region had some beautiful countryside, with rich vegetation climbing the rocks, and the mud carried by the abundant waters that babbled at every step gave the region the blessing of the gods, covering, as the centuries passed, the walls, the streets and the houses of the ancient city, which once extended as far as Longos, concealing the Early Christian basilicas and tombs discovered in the neighbourhood of the modern monastery of Ayia Triada.

The prosperity of the inhabitants was matched by their achievements in the sphere of education: the private educational institutions were augmented in 1782 by a community school - the famous *Hellenomouseion* - which functioned without interruption until 1821.

The agitation of spirits at the news of the uprising of the nation in the Peloponnese, and the flame of freedom that consumed Chalkidike and Thasos, Olympos and Ossa, also spread as far as Central and Western Macedonia: at the beginning of 1822, Edessa was present at the monastery of Dobra, where military leaders from all parts of Western Macedonia assembled to plan the struggle. It was not absent from the victories, or, indeed, the defeats. It became familiar with the taking of slaves, the bestiality of the Turkish authorities and the pillaging of the Albanian bands of armed irregulars. On the peaks of mount Bermion, however, Macedonian *armatoles* - "the free besieged" - were to preserve the torch of the revolution unquenched, and many of them crossed into southern Greece to aid their brothers there.

241

241. Yeni Cami, a 19th century building in which the Archaeological Collection is housed.

242. The Old Cathedral, a Middle Byzantine church with wall-paintings of the 11th-14th centuries.

243. Street in Edessa with old houses.

242

243

THE ARCHAEOLOGICAL COLLECTION

The Archaeological Collection of Edessa (temporarily closed) is housed in the Yeni Cami, a 19th century building, and includes mainly the wealth of epigraphic material of the Hellenistic and Roman periods from Edessa and the surrounding region, and also material from excavations at Longos (mostly pottery of early Christian times).

244. Early Bronze Age blades and clay vases. Edessa, Archaeological Collection.

245. Black-glaze vases and alabastra. 4th century B.C. Edessa, Archaeological Collection.

244

245

*246. Glass vases. 2nd-4th centuries A.D. Edessa,
Archaeological Collection.*

246

247

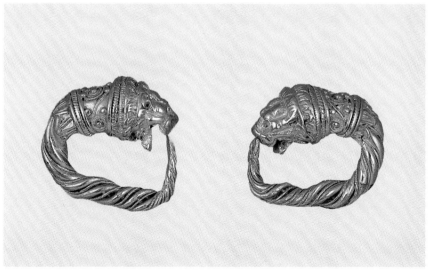

248

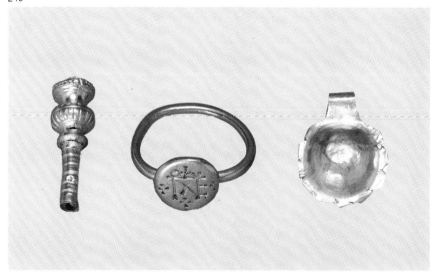

249

250

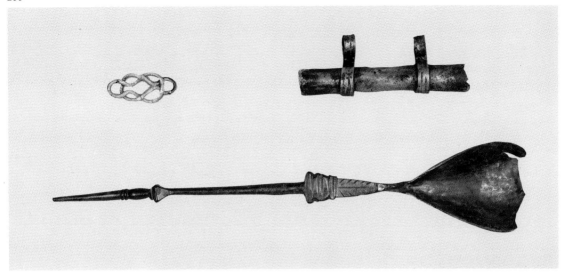

251

247. Gold earrings with lion's heads. 4th century B.C. Edessa, Archaeological Collection.

248. Gold objects (pin-head, inscribed finger ring and pendant). 3rd-6th centuries A.D. Edessa, Archaeological Collection.

249. Silver finger rings inscribed "Κύριε βοήθει τον φορούντα τούτο" ("Lord help the wearer of this"). Byzantine period (10th-11th centuries). Edessa, Archaeological Collection.

250. Magic amma"Knot" of Herakles, silver pendant and small silver spoon. 3rd-6th centuries A.D. Edessa, Archaeological Collection.

251. Early Christian inscription: "Παῦσε ὁ σύ, Ροδόπη ἄλοχε..." (Stop [crying] Rhodope my wife...). Edessa, Archaeological Collection.

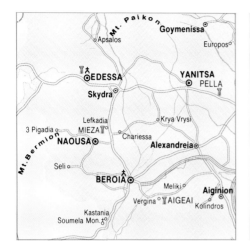

MIEZA
(Lefkadia near Naousa)
and its region

252

HISTORICAL REVIEW

In the foothills of Bermion, the land follows a gradual slope, moderated by a series of terraces, from the plateau on which Naousa stands today to the rich plain below. The soil is thick and soft, accumulated here centuries ago from the deposits carried by winter torrents.

Archaeological research adduces quite convincing arguments in support of the claim that the ancient city of Mieza, mother-city of Peukestas, one of the trierachs of Alexander the Great, should be placed in the notional triangle formed by Naousa, Kopanos and Lefkadia, an area that has from time to time yielded many portable finds, and above all remains of monumental buildings and tombs.

The theory is made more than attractive by the large building complex of the Hellenistic period in the area of Belovina, the extensive cemetery of rock-cut cist graves and pit graves of the 5th and 4th centuries B.C. at Kamara, the ruins and carvings at Isvoria, works of the 4th century B.C., the huge numbers of grave structures scattered over the fields of Kopanos and Lefkadia, and above all by the "Macedonian" tombs, four of which have been discovered to date.

In the early years of the Roman empire Mieza which, according to mythology, was so called af-

252. *The idyllic area of the Nymphaeum, the "shaded walks" of Plutarch, near the ancient city of Mieza. Set amidst luxuriant vegetation near babbling springs, this sanctuary dedicated to the water Nymphs was for three years the school at which Alexander, later conqueror of the world, learned how to "live well".*

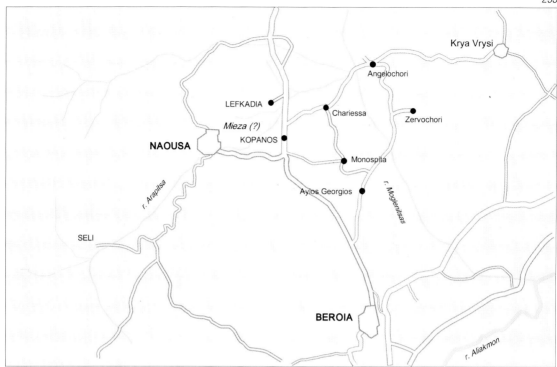

ter the daughter of king Beres of that name, probably retained its independence. There are very few Early Christian remains from the region.

THE ARCHAEOLOGICAL SITE

The archaeological site of Mieza, known sporadically already in the 19th century (Kinch, Delacoulonche) owes much to the tireless interest of Professor Ph. Petsas, who, continuing the excavations of Ch. Makaronas, Ephor of Antiquities, systematically investigated the area, successfully interpreting the archaeological finds and placing them in a historical context.

THE "MACEDONIAN" TOMBS

The Great Tomb of Lefkadia or **the Tomb of the Judgement.** The most important, and also the most imposing of the funerary monuments on the archaeological site of Lefkadia was found by chance in May 1954, during road-work on the widening of the country road to Chariessa, and was investigated by the then Ephor of Antiquities Ph. Petsas. The original height of the mound of earth that covered the tomb was no more than 1.50 m., while its diameter reached 10 m. The monument was constructed of poros and consists of two vaulted rooms - the main burial chamber and the antechamber. The grandiose,

imposing facade (height 8.60 m., width 8.68 m.) is articulated into two storeys, of which the lower has the doric order and the upper (actually a false storey) the ionic. Four "paintings" fill the spaces on the walls between the doric half-columns, and form the centre of interest. The theme of this four-figure scene is worthy of the monument it adorns: the deceased (to the left of the viewer), standing, and with his body turned, ready to set out on the great journey, is led by Hermes, the conductor of souls, to Hades. He is awaited by the judges of the Underworld, Aiakos and Rhadamanthys, one seated and the other leaning on his staff.

The raw material used for the relief frieze was stucco, often attached to the wall by means of nails. Its motif, a battle between cavalry and infantry - probably Macedonians and Persians - locked in a struggle of life or death.

The eleven metopes, three above the entrance and two over each intercolumniation, depict scenes from the mythical confrontation between the Centaurs and the Lapiths; painted with almost only a single colour, brownish-yellow, they were probably a preliminary study rather than a finished painting.

The antechamber, a parallelogram in plan (6.50 m. x 2.12 m.) with a greatest calculated height of 7.70 m., has not been completely excavated, for reasons of security. Apart from two re-

253. The region of the
notional triangle formed
by Naousa, Kopanos
and Lefkadia, in which
the ancient city of
Mieza is to be sought.
(Building complexes,
"Macedonian tombs", a
theatre, portable finds
and stoas have been
discovered in this area.)

254-255. Plan and
section of the Great
Tomb, or the Tomb of
the Judgement at
Lefkadia.

254

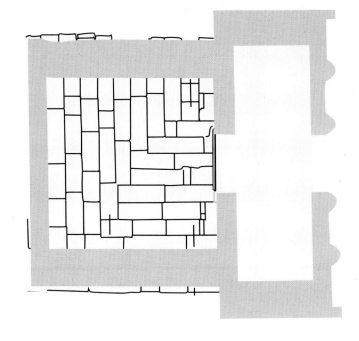

255

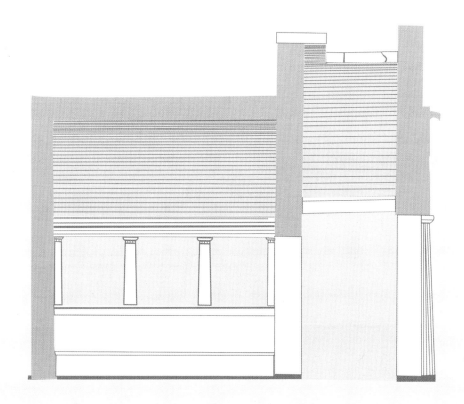

257-258. Two (the deceased and Rhadamanthys) of the four figures depicted in the main painted scene (the Judgement of the dead man) on the upper storey of the tomb.

256. The Great Tomb, or the Tomb of the Judgement at Lefkadia. Beginning of the 3rd century B.C.

256

257

258

lief circular shields (diameter 0.78 m.), one either side of the door in the dividing wall leading to the burial chamber, it has no decoration.

The burial chamber, an almost square room (4.80 m. x 4.72 m.), with a greatest height of 5.26 m., and a floor paved with poros slabs, is encircled by a podium on which stand pillars in the form of piers with an ionic architrave and a relief cornice.

The Great Tomb of Lefkadia, or Tomb of the Judgement belongs chronologically to the first half of the 3rd century B.C. Repairs and modifications, mainly to the facade, are undoubtedly due to its second and third use by the descendants of the first occupant.

The Tomb of the Palmettes. A hundred to a hundred and fifty metres to the north-east of the Tomb of the Judgement, near the country road leading to Chariessa, an attempted illegal excavation in 1971 lead to the investigation and excavation by the Ephor K. Rhomiopoulou of another "Macedonian" Tomb in the area around the ar-

chaeological site of Lefkadia. Covered with an earth tumulus, which had lost much of its height to the passage of time and to ploughing, and with a broad, descending *dromos,* or passageway, at right-angles to its plan, the monument has a facade in the form of a tetrastyle prostyle temple: four slender half-columns to right and left flank the wide opening-entrance of the facade, which was sealed by six large poros (corner stones) set one above the other (these were removed during the excavation). An architrave with two fasciae and a narrow frieze is surmounted by the pediment, which is crowned by freestanding palmette acroteria, two at the corners and one in the middle. The richly painted, fresh floral decoration of the frieze, alternating with the flashing white surfaces of the walls, the half-columns and the entablature, and a superbly composed reclining couple on the pediment, give the facade great brilliance and warmth. The harmonious dimensions of the monument (height 5.50 m., width 5.20 m. and length 8.10 m.) are matched by the frugal interior arrangement of the space: an ante-

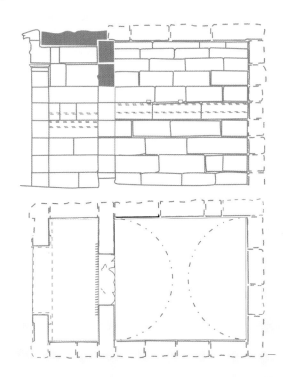
260

chamber with a plan in the shape of a parallelogram (dimensions 2 m. x 4.10 m.) leads, via a marble double door, of which even the mechanism of the lock is preserved, and which imitates a real wooden door, to the main burial chamber (dimensions 4.10 m. x 5.10 m.), the west side of which is occupied by a built throne. On the opposite side of the chamber, a square stone base decorated with finely painted olive branches, contained in antiquity the precious metal vase or chest with the bones of the deceased.

The austere black and red on the walls of the burial chamber contrasts with the soft pale yellow of the antechamber and the unique composition covering its vault: tall palmettes with slender stalks alternate with large open water-flowers in white and violet, against a dreamlike blue background that is perhaps a depiction, with artistic abstraction, of the landscape of the Underworld.

Although the grave-robbers who plundered the monument, gaining entry through the roof of the burial chamber, seem to have carried off all the grave offerings, careful investigation has produced from the floor of the tomb and the earth outside it dozens of small, precious ivory objects (limbs of male bodies, decorative motifs etc.), which belong to a relief frieze that adorned a wooden box containing the personal items of the deceased person, or perhaps to the funerary couch.

The monument is dated with a high degree of probability to the end of the 3rd century B.C.

Kinch's Tomb. On the modern road from Beroia to Edessa, a short distance away from the Tomb of the Judgement, an elegant two-chamber funerary monument was discovered in the early 1880s that was to become known by the name of

261

259. The uniquely beautiful composition adorning the vault over the antechamber of the Tomb of the Palmettes: at the top, on a dreamy sea-blue ground that may represent the Underworld, delicate palmettes alternate with white and violet open water-lilies.

260. Section and plan of Kinch's Tomb, ca. 300 B.C.

261. The facade of Kinch's Tomb, in the region of Lefkadia.

the Danish archaeologist K.F. Kinch, who studied it in the period between 1887 and 1892.

The facade, like the dividing walls and the ceilings of the two rooms, was covered with a thin layer of stucco. The outer doorway, which had no door but was sealed with large poros blocks, is defined by two pilasters surmounted by capitals and is crowned by a narrow architrave on which is supported a doric frieze with triglyphs and metopes.

The burial chamber is entered through the antechamber, a short, wide room (1.50 m. x 3.50 m.) with simple decoration. The door in the dividing wall, which is more carefully worked than that in the facade, has a threshold and is adorned with a relief doorframe. Of the painted decoration on the walls of the largest and most important room in the monument, only fragments now survive. We may, however, imagine the walls painted deep red up to a height of 1.70 m., and above this a narrow band with stylized floral decoration. On the drum of the rear, east wall, however, the multi-coloured depiction of a confrontation between a Macedonian horseman and a Persian fleeing in terror from the danger has been completely destroyed.

Kinch's Tomb probably dates from about 300 B.C., and is one of the few tombs of this type that had a *dromos,* a passageway affording access.

The Tomb of Lyson and Kallikles. Two hundred metres to the north of Kinch's tomb, a sign guides the visitor through a rich orchard to the Tomb of Lyson and Kallikles, sons of Aristophanes. The monument was discovered in the

262. The coloured scene depicting a conflict between a mounted Macedonian and a Persian fleeing in terror from the danger. From the tympanum of the east wall of Kinch's Tomb (now destroyed).

263-264. Detail of the painted decoration of the Tomb of Lyson and Kallikles. Depictions of Macedonian weapons: shields, helmets, swords, greaves and trophies. First quarter of the 2nd century B.C.

264

spring of 1942 and was investigated by the then Ephor of Antiquities, Ch. Makaronas, though it still remains half-buried; its articulation is simple, consisting of a vaulted burial chamber and an antechamber with a flat roof. Interest in the tomb is concentrated on the interiors of the rooms: both the antechamber and the burial chamber still preserve the painted decoration of their walls, with its vivid colours. The former has a perirrhanterion full of water with a small laurel shoot on the rim, and an altar with a snake (a chthonic symbol) climbing up it, which give the room an illusion of paradise. A low painted toichobate runs around all four sides of the room and supports the orthostates, which imitate coloured marble

revetment. On this false socle stand fourteen painted pilasters with ionic capitals, from which hangs a rich garland of flowers.

The vault of the main chamber is simply decorated in imitation of the battlements of fortification walls, and recalls designs on carpets and textiles. Above the entrance and on the rear wall of the room, the semi-circular drums (lunettes) are decorated in warm red and orange colours together with soft pale yellow and deep brown, with representations of cuirasses, helmets, swords and shields.

On the walls, three of the four sides have two rows of square niches, with dimensions of 0.36 m. x 0.36 m., originally sealed with mud bricks, which once contained the cinerary urns and the grave offerings of the deceased. The name of the dead person was written above each niche in deep red paint: the names of men at the top and of women at the bottom.

The tomb, whose construction may be dated to the end of the 3rd to the beginning of the 2nd centuries B.C., was also used by the descendants of the first occupants, down to the fourth generation.

265. The Nymphaion and the "School" of Aristotle housed in it, at Isvoria near the village of Kopanos. In the picture can be seen the foundations of a stoa at the bottom, and sockets cut in the smooth vertical surface of the rock to receive the roof supports.

265

THE NYMPHAION

Plutarch records that king Philip II, in order to remove his son from the influence of his mother Olympias, sent Alexander and his teacher, the philosopher Aristotle, to the idyllic site of the Nymphaion, near the city of Mieza. Set amidst thick vegetation and next to babbling springs, this sanctuary dedicated to the Nymphs of the waters was for three years the school in which the man who was to become conqueror of the world, learned how to "live well".

It is precisely to this "School", and to the Nym-phaion that was host to it, that (a theory of Ph. Petsas, its excavator) belong the ruins uncovered at the site of Isvoria (Kephalari) to the west of the village of Kopanos. The rich vegetation, numerous springs and the archaeological finds accord completely with this identification. The three natural caves with stalactites can be connected with statements by the Roman historian Pliny, and the stoa-like structure in the shape of the Greek letter Π, which is preserved up to its toichobate, the clay simas of which are preserved (in the Beroia Museum), is perhaps to be identified with the "shady walks" of Plutarch.

266

266. Clay sima from the Nymphaion. 4th century B.C. Beroia, Archaeological Museum.

267. Plan of the Nymphaion. The entrance to the Sanctuary can be seen, along with the natural caves and the Π shaped stoa.

267

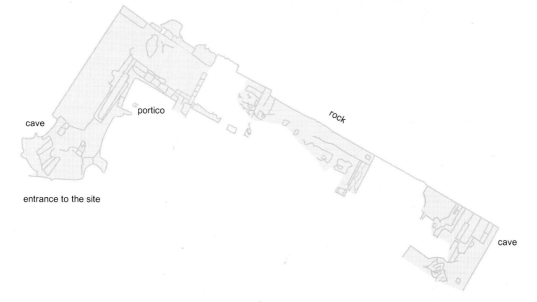

cave

portico

rock

entrance to the site

cave

210

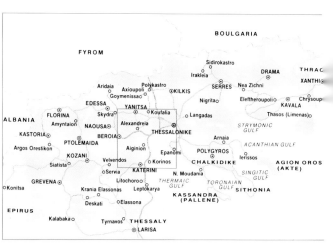

VERGINA [AIG(E)AI]
and its region

268

HISTORY OF THE EXCAVATIONS

Investigation of the site was begun in 1861 by the French archaeologist L. Heuzey who, together with the architect H. Daumet, excavated the eastern part of the famous Hellenistic palace of Vergina at the site at "Ayia Triada" and also a "Macedonian" tomb immediately to the west of the settlement of Palatitsa (the finds from the excavations were taken to the Louvre).

Excavation was resumed in 1938 by Constantinos Rhomaios, Professor of Archaeology at the then newly founded University of Thessalonike, who discovered a second "Macedonian" tomb near Vergina that proved to be one of the most elegant of these structures, with a marble throne in the burial chamber. This indefatigable and wise teacher continued the investigation of the site after the World War II with the assistance of the Ephor of Antiquities, Ch. Makaronas, (1954-1956) when other sections of the palace came to light.

After a break of two years the excavations were undertaken from 1959 to 1974 by the Professors of Archaeology, Georgios Bakalakis and Manolis Andronikos, with the support of the University of Thessaloniki. The destiny of Professor Andronikos had become bound up with the site of Vergina as early as 1937 when, still a student, he began to follow the excavations under the wing of his teacher C. Rhomaios, and he had the great fortune, after excavating the site of the Great Tumulus for many years, to discover the brilliant monumental tomb of king Philip II.

268. General view of the archaeological site of Vergina.

269

269. Bronze ornament in the form of a triple, two-headed axe, from a female burial in the Tumulus Cemetery at Vergina. Thessalonike, Archaeological Museum.

270. Protogeometric skyphos with typical decoration of concentric circles, ca. 900 B.C. Thessalonike, Archaeological Museum.

271. Part of the Tumulus Cemetery.

272. Bronze "crown" with punched decoration of circles and inscribed crosses forming the symbol of the sun, from a female burial in the Tumulus Cemetery at Vergina, ca. 900 B.C. Thessalonike, Archaeological Museum.

270

The excavation of the site, which continues to the present day under the aegis of the same university, has uncovered the entire area of the palace and has brought to light part of the ancient city of Aigai, with its fortifications, its theatre and sanctuaries dedicated to Eukleia and to Cybele, and also a number of other "Macedonian" tombs in the Royal Cemetery which is documented in this region. At the same time the university and the Archaeological Service have excavated sections of the prehistoric "Tumulus Cemetery" to the north of the city and north-east of the modern settlement.

THE ARCHAEOLOGICAL SITE

THE PREHISTORIC CEMETERY

The great size and the long life of the "Tumulus Cemetery" attest to the existence of a flourishing settlement, which was created about the end of the 11th century B.C. by colonists originating from Central Europe. Judging by the grave of-ferings found in the tombs, this settlement seems to have thrived particularly during the 9th century B.C. and to have enjoyed contacts with southern Greece. According to some scholars there are sound indications that the site of the settlement is to be identified with that of the city of the Classical period.

The original number of tumuli, of which only about one hundred have been investigated, is reckoned to have been roughly three hundred. Their diameter fluctuates between 14 and 16 m., while their height does not exceed 1.50 m.

Burials in the tumuli dating from the early Iron Age - for there were also later tombs, constructed in the Hellenistic period - were placed directly into the ground in rectangular pits, normally arranged radially: the offerings in the male graves were weapons and a few ritual vases, while female burials were accompanied by rich jewellery and large quantities of pottery.

Each tumulus probably belonged to a particular family, and the existence of groups of tumuli perhaps permits the hypothesis that these belonged to the same clan.

271

272

THE CITY

Archaeological investigation has located the city of Aigai in the area extending from the palace and the theatre as far as the Tomb of Rhomaios, though so far only small parts of the city have been excavated, mainly sanctuaries. The entire area of the settlement, which was enclosed by a defensive wall with an acropolis in the north-east foothills of the Pierian range, seems to have suffered badly from the beginning to the middle of the 2nd century B.C. The building complexes that have come to light, however, belong to the second half of the 4th century B.C.; they consist of the temenos of Eukleia and an edifice of monumental dimensions, probably a public building, that functioned until the end of the 1st century B.C. The sanctuary of Eukleia in the area of the

273

274

275

273. Marble base of a votive statue with the inscription ΕΥΡΥΔΙΚΑ ΣΙΡΡΑ ΕΥΚΛΕΙΑΙ ("Eurydike daughter of Sirrhas, to Eukleia"). Eurydike daughter of Sirrhas was the mother of Philip II. The base was found outside the Sanctuary of Eukleia at Vergina.

274. The temple of Eukleia at Vergina. Bases of votive statues can be seen at the left.

275-276. Marble portrait head of Eurydike (daughter of Sirrhas, wife of King Amyntas III, mother of Philip II and grandmother of Alexander the Great), originally set on the body of a marble statue of a woman wearing a peplos. The statue was erected on an inscribed base (276) and was dedicated in the sanctuary of the pan-Hellenic goddess Eukleia. It is one of the few original works of large-scale sculpture from the 4th century B.C. to have survived to the present day.

276

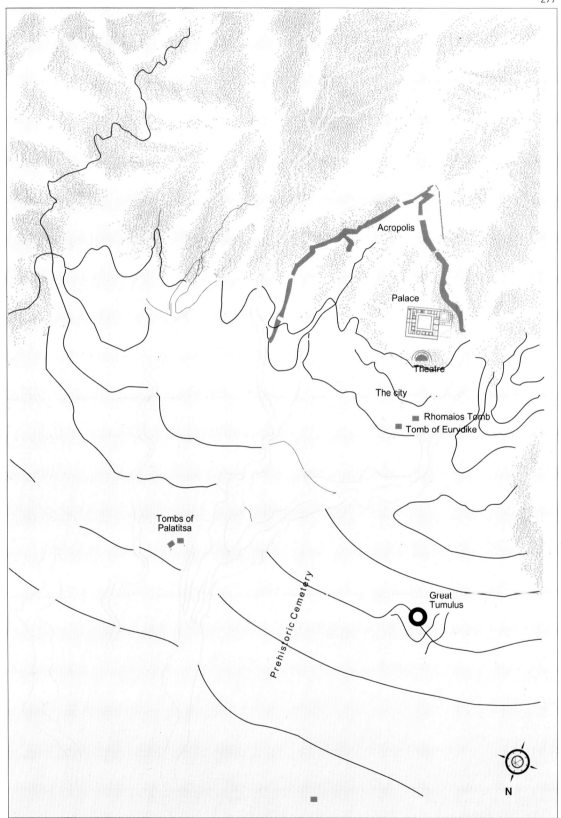

Acropolis

Palace

Theatre

The city

■ Rhomaios Tomb
■ Tomb of Eurydike

Tombs of
Palatitsa

Prehistoric Cemetery

Great
Tumulus

N

Agora is one of the most significant cult centres in the Macedonian kingdom; it consists of a temenos that includes a two-roomed *oecus* built of poros blocks (Hellenistic period), a structure in the form of a temple, a series of votive statue bases alongside the square and a street, and a stoa-like building. A marble snake was found in this area - possibly a depiction of Zeus Meilichios - and also a marble statue of Eurydike, daughter of Sirrhas, mother of Philip II and grandmother of Alexander the Great; this dates from the 4th century B.C., and is one of the few original portraits of large-scale sculpture to have survived from antiquity.

THE PALACE

The palace complex, on the "Ayia Triada" pla-

277. Plan of the archaeological site of Vergina.

278. Aerial photograph of the palace and theatre at Vergina.

teau, is the most imposing palace so far discovered in Macedonia. Built in an exceptionally fine position the northern foothills of the Pierian range, it dominates the plain of the river Haliakmon. Some scholars consider it to be a complex constructed exclusively for the holding of banquets, while others regard it as a country house (villa). Its identification with the royal residence, however, seems to be correct.

The palace is 104.50 m. long and 88.50 m. wide. The residential areas are arranged regularly around a central square courtyard (length of side 44.50 m.), the four sides of which are bordered by four stoas with doric columns of poros. A spacious, long veranda with a protective parapet made of poros, imitating a wooden parapet, was added to the exterior of the north facade of the complex which, in accordance with the original plan, overlooked the plain. The entire building was constructed of poros blocks, with only the thresholds of marble. The superstructure above the orthostates was of unbaked brick surfaced with lime-plaster in a variety of colours. The ar-

278

chitectural members were also plastered.

The entrance to the palace was on the east side which was probably two-storeyed and at ground floor level had an exterior doric stoa. Three contiguous antechambers, the first 10 m. wide and 6 m. deep, the second slightly smaller and the third measuring 10 m. x 10 m., led to the east portico of the peristyle of the inner courtyard.

The doorway between the second and the third room was divided into three parts by two imposing columns with ionic capitals. At this part of the complex, to the right and left of the entrance, there were large roofed areas that were perhaps used as barracks for the garrison or as storerooms. The east wing of the palace is believed to have been intended for cult purposes (an inscription, the only one so far from this area, was found here referring to Herakles Patroos) and for public life, and was connected with the public appearances of the leader of the state; to it belonged, to the left immediately inside the entrance, a tholos (a roofed area with a circular plan inscribed in a square), with four rooms to the south of it which were perhaps designed to house the archives or more probably the sacred vessels.

The disposition of the rooms on the south side, which is to be regarded as the most formal wing of the palace, is of particular interest: the ends were occupied by rooms square in plan with entrances looking onto the courtyard. Their pebble floors were undecorated. In the centre of this wing three imposing ionic double half-columns led from the south stoa to the *prostas* - a large hall that acted as an antechamber for the two finest rooms, one to the east of it, with an area of 82 sq. m., and another to the west. The mosaic floors decorating these rooms, particularly the composition with a floral motif in the centre flanked by four female figures holding baskets, confirm the identification of this wing with the "residence" proper of the palace. The south part of the west side is occupied by three rooms, a built conduit, which was probably connected with bathing installations and toilets, and three contiguous rooms which were the largest in the entire complex and had paved marble floors (probably banquet rooms). The dating of the palace to the third quarter of the 4th century B.C. may be regarded as certain.

Investigations in the 1970s have brought to light a structure of smaller dimensions and more

279

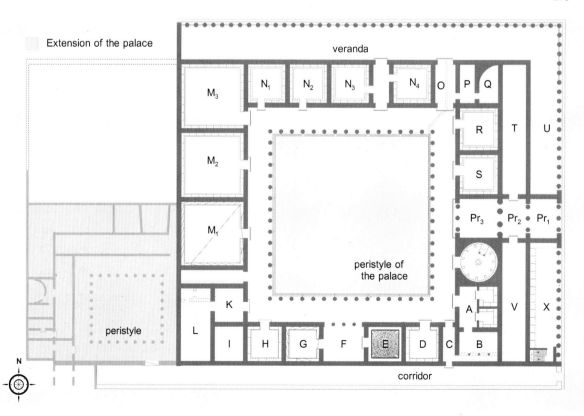

281

279. Plan of the Palace at Vergina

280-281. Drawing of the mosaic in room E of the Palace at Vergina. The core of the decorative motif is a large rosette from which spring eight pairs of shoots that intertwine and branch out towards the edge; the gaps left by them are filled with flowers, leaves and tendrils. The entire central motif is framed by a circular zone with a composite maeander and a spiral maeander. The triangles left in the four corners are filled with figures of female demons (Detail of the mosaic, below).

makeshift construction than the palace but having the same general plan, which was built as an extension to the west of and in contact with the palace itself. This structure, too, has a central, square courtyard (though the stoas on the four sides in this case had wooden columns, as may be deduced from the surviving bases), around which were arranged the residential areas, which are best preserved in the south-west corner. It has been suggested that this extension is probably contemporary with the large palace but a more probable view is that this is in fact an "emergency residence" which was erected immediately after the destruction of the palace complex (perhaps by an earthquake or a land slip), an event which certainly took place before the conquest of Macedonia by the Romans (168 B.C.).

THE THEATRE

The theatre of Aigai on the north side of the complex and separated from the palace by a mere 60 m., was probably closely connected with the latter and together with it formed a unified architectural group. Facing the fertile plain and the river Haliakmon, it gave the spectators the opportunity to enjoy the play amidst the tranquillity of a macedonian landscape. The only stone parts of the structure were the first row of seats, the drainage channel in front of them, the walls of the *parodoi* and the foundations of the stage. The absence of any other rows of seats and the gentle slope, which was clearly unsuitable for this kind of structure, lend credibility to the view that has been propounded that the *cavea* of the theatre consisted of wooden benches supported partly on scaffolding, also of wood. The *orchestra,* which has a diameter of 28.50 m. has stone base for the *thymele* in the centre, though this has not been found. Of the eight stone-paved aisles that divided the *cavea* radially into sections, the best preserved is the seventh from the west, which has a length of 20 m. and which allows us to estimate the original size of the horse-shoe of the *cavea*. The theatre was a work of the second half of the 4th century B.C., according to the excavational data - particularly

283

282. *The theatre at Vergina.*

283. *The clay female head (Cybele?) from the Sanctuary of the Mother of the Gods.*

the portable finds - and was probably abandoned in the second quarter of the 2nd century B.C.

The importance of the monument resides in the fact that it is connected with highly important events in ancient history: it was here that Philip II was assassinated in 336 B.C. while celebrating, with exceptional pomp and splendour, the marriage of his daughter Kleopatra to Alexander, king of Epirus.

A very important discovery near the theatre is the sanctuary of the Mother of the Gods, Cybele, in which a building has been excavated with two adjacent rooms, with hearths at their centre, cesspools, altars and holes for libations - evidently rooms in which the faithful were initiated. The building is dated by clay cult and votive objects to about the middle of the 2nd century B.C.

THE "MACEDONIAN" TOMBS

A. THE TOMBS OF THE GREAT TUMULUS

The Great Tumulus was an enormous mound that rose on the western edge of the "Tumulus Cemetery", and is completely without parallel anywhere else in Greece. Its diameter reached 110 m. and its average height exceeded 12 m. The excavation of it, which began in 1952, has brought to light the following three royal tombs.

The Tomb of Philip II

The Tomb of Philip II is one of the largest of this category of monuments so far excavated. It is made of poros, apart from the marble double doors of the entrance in the facade, and the dividing wall; about 10 m. in length and approximately 6 m. in width, it has two chambers and is vaulted. The dimensions of the antechamber are: length 3.66 m., width 4.46 m., and of the burial chamber: length 4.46 m. width 4.46 m. and height 5.30 m. The exterior of the vault had a thick layer of hydraulic plaster, while all the visible surfaces were covered with a thin white layer of plaster painted here and there in different colours to indicate or emphasise architectural details.

The doric facade was adorned with two half-columns and two antae at the ends. Above the entablature (epistyle and frieze of triglyphs and metopes) the pediment is replaced by a large frieze, 5.56 m. long and 1.16 m. high - unique in the whole of antiquity - whose superb colours and tonal gradations immortalize a hunt of lions, bears, antelopes and boars in a semi-forested landscape.

The walls of the antechamber were encircled by a broad, dark-red band, bordered by two narrower bands in white, one of which was decorated with rosettes. In about the middle of the left side of the antechamber, a marble ossuary enclosed a gold chest (dimensions 0.38 m. x 0.32 m. x 0.20 m.), which contained burnt bones wrapped in a gold and purple cloth, and a gold wreath. On the floor were found a gold *gorytos* (a combined bow-and-arrow-case), arrow-heads, greaves, the remains of organic substances, a gold wreath, alabastra, and gold roundels. The burial chamber, the walls of which were never given their final coating of plaster, contained a greater number of more luxurious finds. In an ossuary similar to that in the antechamber was found a second gold chest with bones inside it, originally wrapped in a purple cloth, and a precious gold wreath. On the floor had been placed about twenty silver vessels, an iron cuirass with gold decoration, bronze and ceramic vases, an iron helmet, a gold diadem, a sword with an ivory handle, a shield of exceptionally fine art and a vast number of small artifacts of ivory which came from the decoration of wooden furniture - probably of the funerary couch.

The dating of this tomb to the third-fourth quarter of the 4th century B.C. is a matter of investigation.

284

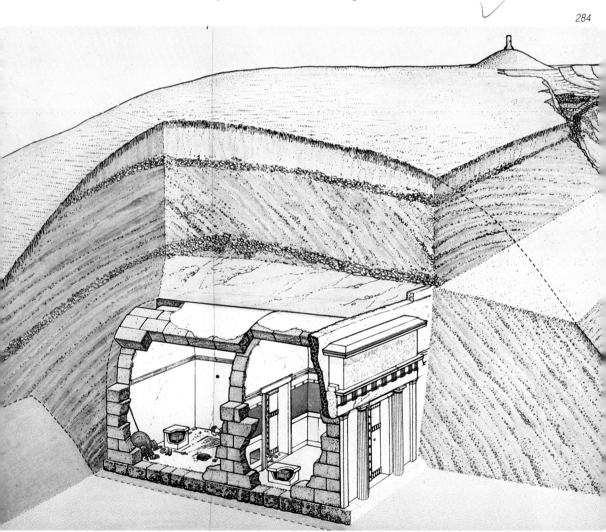

284. Drawing of the reconstructed tomb of Philip II.

285. The imposing facade of the tomb of Philip II.

285

224

287-288. Two pieces of purple material from the gold chest in the antechamber of the tomb of Philip II. Thessalonike, Archaeological Museum.

286. The gold chest from the antechamber in the tomb of Philip II. Thessalonike, Archaeological Museum.

286

289-290. *The gold diadem found in the gold chest in the antechamber of the tomb of Philip II. Thessalonike, Archaeological Museum.*

291. *The gold wreath of myrtle leaves and flowers from the antechamber of the tomb of Philip II. Thessalonike, Archaeological Museum.*

289

290

292. The inside of the gold chest from the main chamber of the tomb of Philip II. Thessalonike, Archaeological Museum.

293. The gold chest from the main chamber of the tomb of Philip II. Thessalonike, Archaeological Museum.

294. Ivory portrait head, probably of Olympias, the mother of Alexander the Great. It probably belonged to the decoration of the funerary couch. Thessalonike, Archaeological Museum.

295. Ivory head of a young man with a severe, reflective face. Thessalonike, Archaeological Museum.

296. Ivory head depicting a young man. This, like the two previous ones, probably belonged to the decoration of the funerary couch. Thessalonike, Archaeological Museum.

298

297. The gold and ivory shield
from the tomb of Philip II.
Thessalonike, Archaeological
Museum. (Drawing by
G. Miltsakakis).

298. The iron cuirass from the
tomb of Philip II. Thessalonike,
Archaeological Museum.

299. Bronze vases and iron
weapons, as they were found
in the south-west corner of the
main chamber of the tomb of
Philip II.

299

303

304

←
300-301. Two silver "amphoras" from the tomb of Philip II. Thessalonike, Archaeological Museum.

302. Bronze oinochoe from the tomb of Philip II. Thessalonike, Archaeological Museum.

303-304. Bronze bowl and bronze situla from the tomb of Philip II. Thessalonike, Archaeological Museum.

305. Bronze torch from the tomb of Philip II.
Thessalonike, Archaeological Museum.

306. Bronze tripod from the tomb of Philip II. It is
clear from the inscription around the rim that it was a
prize at the "Heraian" games held at Argos. It is
dated to before 430-420 B.C. Thessalonike,
Archaeological Museum.

305

306

The Tomb of the Prince

The Tomb of the Prince, a short distance to the north of the Tomb of Philip II, has several similarities with it. It has two chambers, is built of poros blocks, has a doric facade and marble door-leaves on the outer and inner doors, and it, too, is equipped with a large painted frieze above the entablature, though this has not survived, since the composition on it was apparently executed in a perishable material (leather?).

In contrast with the rich decoration of the antechamber, the characteristic feature of the burial chamber is its austere simplicity and severity. At a height of 2.20 m. above the floor, a plain band of dark blue encircled the four sides of the room, bordered above and below by an egg-and-dart and a leaf-and-dart pattern respectively. A built, roughly rectangular table, with a hollow in the centre, held a silver urn with a gold wreath on its shoulder. The decomposed remains of wooden furniture and decorative elements in silver and ivory, found on the floor, attest to the wealth of the deceased. Silver vessels and an iron lamp-holder in the north-west corner were accompanied by a further twenty-seven silver vases in the south-west corner.

In the antechamber, the walls of which were encircled by a band depicting a chariot race, were found the remains of precious gold embroidered clothing, bronze strigils, an iron ferrule (spear-butt), and part of a gilded spear.

In chronological terms, the Tomb of the Prince is probably somewhat later than the Tomb of Philip II.

307. The facade of the Tomb of the Prince.

308. Superb ivory relief from the couch in the Tomb of the Prince. At the left, goat-footed Pan is playing his pipes, accompanying with his music the couple who are following - a bearded man with a thyrsos and a young woman. Thessalonike, Archaeological Museum.

308

238

309. The poros "table" in the form of a pillar found near the west wall of the main chamber in the Tomb of the Prince, with the silver cinerary hydria in a hollow in the upper surface. Excavation photograph.

310. The silver funerary hydria with the gold wreath on its shoulder, from the Tomb of the Prince. Thessalonike, Archaeological Museum.

309

311

311. Small silver situla from the main chamber of the Tomb of the Prince. Thessalonike, Archaeological Museum.

312. Silver strainer for filtering wine, from the main chamber in the Tomb of the Prince. Thessalonike, Archaeological Museum.

313-314. Frieze with scenes of a chariot race, from the antechamber of the Tomb of the Prince.

312

313

314

The Tomb of Persephone

At the edge of the Great Tumulus, next to the foundations of a building dubbed the "Heroon" by the excavators, rises a roughly rectangular funerary monument constructed of poros, which has interior dimensions of 3.50 m. x 2.10 m. and a height of 3 m.: although it had been plundered by ancient grave-robbers when it was found, its rich decoration is a wonderful example of ancient Greek painting, in which the power and freedom of the drawing compete with the expressive tension of the colours; on three of the four plastered interior walls (the fourth, west wall was occupied by wooden "shelves" on which offerings were deposited), the gifted artist - the name of Nikomachos has been suggested, who worked with amazing speed, according to the ancient tradi-

315

tion - depicted the legend of the abduction of Persephone by Pluto in a wide frieze.

Opposite the three "Fates", who were fated to lose much of their original brilliance, and leaving behind Demeter all alone, seated on "the stone that does not smile", lost in bitter thought, startled and hesitating, the thickly bearded god of Underworld, holding the sceptre of his macabre authority, rushes madly in his four-horse chariot through the darkness of the centuries, holding tightly in his stout arms the precious object of his lust; the tragic figure of the young Persephone, whose breast is bare and who gestures in despair. The scene, which "stands" on a dark red podium crowned by a green-blue cornice with alternating frontal griffins and flowers, is counterbalanced by two figures, one centripetal and one centrifugal: swift-footed Hermes - the accomplice and treacherous guide of Pluto - and Kyane, the companion of the ill-fated Persephone, unable to help amidst the dizzying confusion of the abduction, and terrified at the miraculous, divine events happening all around her.

In contrast with other paintings and funerary monuments from this period at Vergina and Lefkadia, the wall-paintings in the tomb of Persephone make their presence felt not so much through the skilful variation of the colour of the volumes and the precision of the drawing, as through the power of the conception and the sparing use of a limited range of colours which, with swift vigorous brush-strokes, themselves acquire volume and movement.

To the north of these three tombs was discovered a fourth, with a free colonnade on its facade. Apart from the stylobate, the columns and a few stones from the walls, the rest of the building has been destroyed and quarried for building material.

These four royal tombs and the "Heroon" have been protected by a special roof since July 1993.

315. Kyane(?). Detail from the wall-painting of the Abduction of Persephone.

316. Detail from the superb wall-painting of the Abduction of Persephone. Part of the chariot is shown, with Pluto standing on it holding the reigns in his right hand and gripping Persephone tight with his left, while the latter attempts to escape. Behind the chariot, one of Persephone's friends (Kyane?) has collapsed on the ground in her astonishment and fear.

B. THE TOMBS TO THE NORTH OF THE PALACE

A second group of monumental tombs has been uncovered just to the north of the palace towards the plain, on the fringes of the ancient city and close to the houses on the edge of the village of Vergina.

The following tombs belong to this group.

The Rhomaios Tomb

The facade of this monument, whose conventional name derives from its excavator, Professor C. Rhomaios (1938), is emphasised by four ionic

half-columns, two to the right and two to the left of the entrance with its two-leaved marble door. An epistyle with two bands, a frieze (the decoration of which consists of a chain of repeated pairs of painted volutes), and an austere triangular pediment complete the architectural picture of the main facade of the tomb, behind which opens the long narrow antechamber (dimensions 4.50 m. x 2.50 m. x 4.3 m.).

The particularly interesting feature of this monument, however, is the existence of a superbly designed marble throne in contact with the south-east corner of the burial chamber, which is square in plan (dimensions 4.56 m. x 4.56 m.): this throne is 1.98 m. in height and has a separate foot-stool, sphinxes carved in the round on the arm-rests, and painted decoration on the side (griffins tearing a deer). This throne is one of the few examples of its type.

317. Reconstruction of the facade of the Tomb of Rhomaios, in the form of an ionic temple.

317

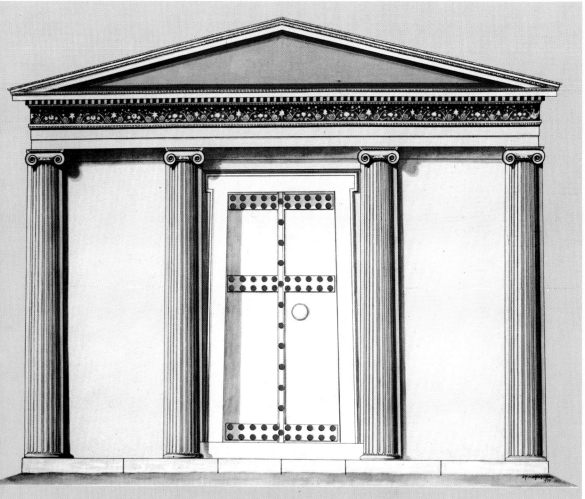

The Tomb of Eurydike

At a distance of a mere 4 m. to the east of the Rhomaios Tomb, archaeologists from the University of Thessalonike have in recent years uncovered the most distinctive of all the monumental funerary buildings of this kind: the "Macedonian" Tomb of Eurydike.

The tomb is a subterranean structure 10.70 m. in length and 7.50/7.90 m. in width, with two vaulted rooms - a burial chamber (5.51 m. x 4.49 m.) and an antechamber (2.50 m. x 4.49 m.) - the facade of which has not yet been uncovered. The special interest of this monument, however, the interior of which is simply coated with off-white plaster, lies in the brilliant architectural picture presented by the short wall at the back of the main chamber; the surface of this is coated with coloured plaster and articulated in the form of a false facade: beneath an undecorated semi-circular tympanum, four ionic half-columns flank a false door and two false windows and "support" an ionic epistyle with three bands and a blue frieze, which is embroidered with white palmettes. The entablature is crowned by a cornice with relief mutules. The marble throne with its foot-stool in front of the east intercolumniation (height of throne 2 m., width 1.18 m.) is a unique find. Both the throne and the footstool are richly decorated in the encaustic technique: the back-rest has a scene of a four-horse chariot depicted frontally with the rulers of the Underworld, Pluto

318. The main chamber of the Tomb of Eurydike, showing the shorter, back wall, articulated as a false facade, and the marble throne and footstool.

318

and Persephone, in the chariot, and at a lower level a double row of pillars forming openings in which are set relief sphinxes and "caryatids". The front of the throne and the foot-stool have bands/friezes with scenes of frontal griffins and winged lions as well as a stag being torn apart; executed in gold, blue, red, green and brown - warm colours, untouched by time - these scenes with their use of foreshortening and their inventive originality, are an enrichment of the gallery of ancient Greek large-scale painting.

The plundered marble chest stained by the purple colour of the cloth, which once contained the bones of the deceased - and possible also a gold wreath - mutely reflects upon the vast number of grave goods that accompanied the dead man, which were removed by profane hands in the past. The size and luxury of the tomb, its unusually careful construction and, finally, the unique, majestic throne, all lead to the conclusion that this was the final resting place of a member of the royal family. In the light of the chronological evidence, the most likely hypothesis relating to the identity of the dead woman - for the tomb is attributed to a woman - is, in the excavator's view, that this was the Tomb of Eurydike, the mother of Philip II, at least two dedications by whom in the city of Aigai are confirmed by the discovery of their inscribed bases.

C. THE TOMBS OF PALATITSA

A third group of tombs was excavated a short distance to the west of the village of Palatitsa. To it belong the following monuments:

The Tomb of Heuzey

Only the lower parts of the walls now survive of the tomb excavated to the west of Palatitsa in 1861 by L. Heuzey, who removed the marble doors to the Louvre.

The tomb is a monument with two chambers, with overall dimensions of 4.80 m. long by 3.85 m. wide, built of dressed poros and roofed with bar-rel vault over both the antechamber and the burial chamber. The plain facade was surmounted by a crowning member in the ionic style: an epistyle with three bands and a dentilated cornice, the ends of which rested on the impost blocks of pilasters - painted on the off-white plaster - and which covered the surface of the outer wall. The two-leaved marble entrance door was sealed by poros blocks piled on top of one another. The long narrow antechamber (1.45 m. deep) had plastered walls and led via a similar marble door to the wide burial chamber (dimensions 3.10 m. x 2.55 m.), in which two elegant marble couches, measuring about 2 m. x 1 m., on which the bodies will have been laid, were set symmetrically opposite each other against the long walls.

The tombs in the plot of land owned by the brothers Bella

Three "Macedonian" tombs, already plundered in antiquity, and a small unplundered cist tomb

320

319. The marble throne found in the main chamber of the Tomb of Eurydike.

320. The two-leaf marble outer door of Heuzey's Tomb. Paris, Musée du Louvre.

were investigated by the University of Thessalonike a short distance to the south-west of the Tomb of Heuzey, below a tumulus that before the excavation was 1 m. high and had a diameter of 45 m.

Tomb a. The largest of the three had its entrance facing south and had a built *dromos,* 7.80 m. in length, the end of which was flush with the sides of the facade of the monument. Four doric half-columns, two to the right and two to the left, flank the doorway, which before the excavation was sealed only by poros blocks. A plain epistyle, triglyphs and metopes, and a pediment with an unusually tall, hollow cornice, crown the main facade of the tomb, which was plastered with white stucco. The narrow antechamber (dimensions 1.20 m. x 3 m. approximately) has a horizontal roof imitating a timbered ceiling, and a frieze encircling all four walls at a height of 1.75 m. in which the predominant colours are red and white. This contrasts with the vaulted burial chamber which has a marble two-leaved door

321

322

321. The facade of Tomb a.

322. One end of the long side of the sarcophagus-couch found in the main chamber of Tomb a on the plot owned by the Bella brothers.

323

and is of much greater interest: in the north-west corner of the room, a funerary couch-sarcophagus, constructed of a large number of poros blocks, is carved and richly decorated with coloured plaster so as to imitate a real wooden bed; its lid is an imitation mattress.

The tomb is dated to the second half of the 3rd century B.C. by the study of the architectural members and the sherds from the pyre next to the *dromos.*

Tomb b. The second tomb has an entrance facing west and consists of a single chamber (3.50 m. x 3 m.), and its facade is not treated architecturally (dimensions of facade 3.87 m. x 4.95 m.); its most imposing feature is the painting above the lintel of the elegant door, which is austerely rendered, as though beyond time and place. The dead man is depicted in the centre of the scene, leaning with his raised right hand on his spear, hatless and with his gaze fixed in the distance; above his blue chiton he wears a cuirass, decorated by a gorgoneion. Some distance to right and left of him are two figures probably symbolizing Arete and Ares. The former, a richly dressed, motherly figure at the right of the composition, extending a gold wreath to him. The latter, resting on a shield which has an eagle as its "emblem" and touching the handle of his sword, is sitting on a pile of shields - presumably taken from defeated enemies.

On the east side of the burial chamber, a majestic marble throne, with its back-rest painted on the wall and with a separate foot-stool, was intended for use after death by the occupant of the monument, whose bones were placed in a metallic chest - today lost - which contained a poros casket. The tomb is dated by the excavators, with some probability, to the beginning of the 3rd century B.C.

Tomb c. The third and final tomb in the tumulus, which was plainer than the first two and was simply constructed, is to be dated towards the end of the same century. The only architectural feature on the facade is a small pediment rendered in low relief over the door. Two thirds of the interior of the single chamber (dimensions of the tomb approximately 2.50 m. x 2.30 m.) was occupied by an enormous sarcophagus set parallel with the south long wall.

323. The figure of the dead warrior from Tomb b in the plot owned by the Bella brothers.

250

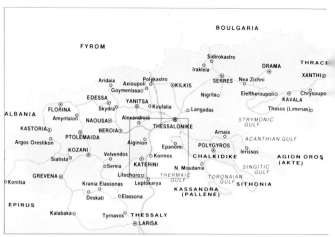

DION
and its region

324

HISTORICAL REVIEW

Dion stands in the northern foothills of Mount Olympos, and exercises complete control over the narrow defile leading from Macedonia to Thessaly. Formerly a distance of only 7 stades from the shores of the Thermaic Gulf, it was the most important sacred city of the Macedonians. Here it was that Archelaos I, at the end of the 5th century B.C., first held brilliant festivals at which sacrifices were offered to Olympian Zeus and the Pierian Muses, and introduced theatrical and gymnastic competitions - the "Olympia ta en Dion" - which were still celebrated about 100 B.C. Here it was that Philip II celebrated the capture of Olynthos, the capital of the Chalkidian League, and here Alexander the Great sought the aid of the king of the gods before setting out for the East. And it was in the sanctuary of Zeus, finally, that the famous group was erected depicting twenty-five of Alexander's companions who fell at the Granikos' battle, the work of the great Lysippos.

Dion's walls, however, were only 2,550 m. long, and its area was a mere 460,000 sq.m., and it never became more than a small township neither at the time of Thucydides, nor much later - in the early years of the Roman empire.

The first Roman colonists *(coloni)* possibly settled here in 43 B.C., perhaps as a result of the activities of Brutus; the mass transportation of Italians to the city and the foundation of the *colonia* was the work of Augustus, however, immedi-

324. Aerial view of the archaeological site of Dion.

ately after his victory in the battle of Actium (31 B.C.). Despite the fact that latin was the official language, the majority of the inscriptions are in Greek, attesting both to the predominance of the local element and to the swift hellenisation of the newcomers. The glory of Christianity is proclaimed by two basilicas built on the ruins of the ancient city and a third constructed outside the city walls. The bishop of Dion took part in the Synod of Serdike in the 4th century A.D. (343) and in the Synod of Ephesos in the 5th century A.D. (431). Dion fell victim to the invasions of the Ostrogoths and its wounds never healed. Flooding by the river Vaphyras, earthquakes and time would veil in oblivion the city that was admired and plundered by C. Caecilius Metellus after he had crushed the uprising of Andriskos (150-148 B.C.).

THE ARCHAEOLOGICAL SITE

THE WALLS

The regular shape (square) of the city was no doubt dictated by the flat plain in which it stands, but it is quite likely that, as has been suggested, both the town-plan and the fortifications of Dion called upon the experience gained by the city-builders of the time from the new cities founded by Alexander and his successors in the lands of Asia.

The enceinte, which is dated from excavational evidence to the first building phase about 300 B.C., was probably the work of Cassander. It had a solid *toichobate,* constructed of a single course of roughly dressed stones and one or two courses of finely dressed blocks, on which rested a wide wall made of unbaked bricks; at intervals the enceinte had square towers for more effective defence. The regular square plan was interrupted on the east side by a long narrow projection, which seems to have been designed to dam the flow of the river Vaphyras, which in antiquity was navigable, and which may have been due to the existence at this point of a harbour. The clas-

325

1. entrance to the archaeological site
2. thermae
3. basilica
4. luxurious dwellings
5. villa of Dionysos
6. r. Vaphyras
7. sanctuary of Isis
8. sanctuary of Demeter
9. temple in the Asklepios temenos
10. roman theatre
11. hellenistic theatre
12. basilica
13. macedonian tomb

326

325. Plan of the archaeological site of Dion (city, theatres, sanctuaries).

326. Section of the defence walls.

sical defences were probably destroyed in 220 B.C., when the macedonian sanctuary was plundered by the enemies of Philip V, the Aitolians, under their general Skopas.

They were obviously quickly repaired - presumably by the father of Perseus himself, and in an exemplary fashion - in view of the impression made by the defence works on the Romans when, in 169 B.C., shortly before the battle of Pydna, they entered the abandoned city. Down to A.D. 250, the walls of the Colonia Iulia Diensis do not appear to have attracted the interest of the Roman overlords. It was only at the beginning of the second half of the 3rd century A.D., when the barbarian Gothic tribes flooded into the Balkans, that concern was shown to fortify Dion. Building material taken from demolished structures of more glorious times, altars, marble statues and architectural members, now formed the raw material for this hasty construction.

The final phase of the defences, the work perhaps of the middle of the 4th century A.D., has characteristic masonry of rubble bound together with lime and framed with fragments of tile. The enceinte is distinctly smaller (length of walls 1,600 m., area of city 155,000 sq.m.) and included only a part of the formerly flourishing city. The final destruction of the city was not long in coming: as early as the middle of the 5th century A.D., Dion began to become a city of the past.

THE CITY

The majority of the finds yielded by excavations to date naturally belong to the Roman and the later Byzantine periods: the small depth of earth deposit and the continuous occupation of the site have, with very few exceptions, obliterated the remains of earlier periods. The main street, about 670 m. long, that traversed the city from north to south, was paved with large slabs of conglomerate in the imperial period, and was undoubtedly designed as part of the Classical-

Hellenistic urban tissue. The secondary streets at right angles and parallel to this main artery belonged to this same, possibly original grid, and were laid out on the "Hippodameian" town-planning system. Shops, luxury residences, public thermae (baths), workshops and vespasianae (public toilets) have been uncovered in the building blocks (insulae) formed by these streets. These are structures of the 2nd and 3rd centuries A.D., attesting to the wealth and prosperity of the inhabitants of the city, one of the earliest Roman colonies in Macedonia.

THE GREAT THERMAE

The Great Thermae, that is to say the public baths of Dion, located in the south of the city where they were protected from the north winds and communicated directly with the main avenue, welcomed the stranger who entered the city, as today, through the south gate. With a spacious atrium in the centre, and public toilets, shops and workshops around the periphery, the public baths were a complex in which one could pleasurably pass one's leisure hours. The main building was reached by crossing the open-air courtyard that connected it by means of a narrow flight of steps with the main road, passing the odeion on the right; it had swimming pools, dres-sing rooms, rooms with hot and cold water, relaxation rooms, sweating rooms and massage rooms. A complex water-supply and drainage network ran below the ground and a special system of hypocausts ensured a supply of warm air to the appropriate rooms. The north wing of the complex, where marble statues from the cycle of Asklepios have been found (they are on display in the local Museum), may have been intended for therapeutic purposes. The mosaic floors [marine (dionysiac) band], the marble inlays in the floors and the statues of deities and nymphs which once stood in decorative niches gave the rooms of the Great thermae a luxurious and monumental character.

THE "VILLA OF DIONYSOS"

The large "Villa of Dionysos", so called from the superb mosaic with the scene from the life of the god of wine adorning the floor of the main room, was built about A.D. 200 and is still one of the most impressive building complexes in ancient Dion. Behind a row of shops and workshops along one of the secondary streets in the east side of the city, next to a bath complex, the floors

327. Aerial photograph of the south-east sector of the city of ancient Dion. The main road traversing the city from north to south can be seen, with the shops and workshops on its west side, the thermae (public baths) and the Roman odeion.

329

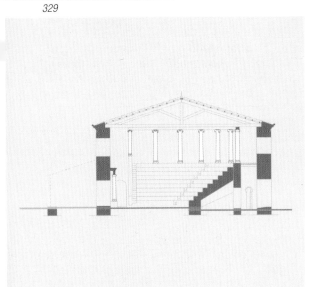

330

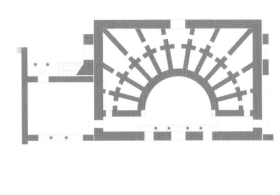

328. Part of the heating system (hypocausts) of the large public baths.

329-330. Section and plan of the Roman odeion.

of which are laid with large tesserae, was a courtyard with an ionic peristyle and a well that led to the east to the dining room of the large house, called *tablinum* by the Romans. This was followed by a number of smaller rooms, one of which, equipped with a semi-circular niche housing a statue of Dionysos with a horn in his left hand and a floor with tesserae laid in geometric shapes, was probably devoted to the cult of this god. The most brilliant room in the entire building complex, however, was a banqueting hall almost square in plan with an area of about 100 sq.m., the floor of which was covered by a multi-coloured mosaic with scenes from the Dionysiac cycle. The centre of the floor was occupied by a large panel flanked by three smaller ones above and below it. A band with a spiral-maeander design separates these "paintings" from a broad zone of chequer-board pattern around the walls, which formed the area in which the banqueting couches were placed. The main panel is given over to a striking, epic subject, rendered with a certain affectation, despite the painterly intent by which it is informed: the triumph of Dionysos. The god is depicted frontally, naked in a chariot pulled by sea panthers, holding a rhyton in his raised right hand, and a thyrsos in his left. Next to him stands an aged Silenos wearing a hairy chiton, stupefied with fear. The panthers are led on reins by two sea Centaurs, each of whom carries a large vase on his shoulders. The white colour of the tesserae of the background on which the scene unfolds contrasts with the violet/dark-blue of the waves to give the figures a relief quality and monumental size. The panels that flank the main scene in groups of three depict theatrical masks. A number of bronze couch attachments probably formed part of the original furnishings of the room. The general decoration of the house included statues of the imperial family, deities and also private individuals, which were found in the various rooms. Life in the villa came to a sudden end when a fire, possibly caused by an earthquake, swept through the building and reduced everything to ruins.

THE AREA OF THE SANCTUARIES

The sanctuary of Zeus and the Muses - that most venerable cult centre of the macedonian nation - has not yet been located, but it is almost certain that, as in the case of Olympia, Nemea and other sanctuaries, it lay outside the city, and perhaps in a grove, near the later Roman theatre.

The other sanctuaries of Dion have, indeed, been located outside and to the south of the city.

The sanctuary of Demeter

A complex of two-roomed buildings, measuring 11 m. x 7 m., just outside the south gate of the city, which faced east and were destroyed by fire, probably at the end of the 4th century B.C., has been identified with the sanctuary of Demeter, on the grounds that the finds from the excavation included a marble head of the goddess, a clay model of a piglet, kernoi and a cup with an incised inscription dedicating it to Demeter. In addition to these large buildings there were a large number of single roomed *oeci* in the area with foundations for a sacred altar and a cult icon. Excavation has shown that the life of this thesmophorion began as early as Archaic times, and that there were foundations of earlier structures below the 4th century buildings.

The sanctuary of Dionysos

The sanctuary of Dionysos was located very close to the Hellenistic theatre, as one would expect, and the epigraphic evidence and archaeological finds suggest that it enclosed a number of buildings in doric style. Amongst the dedications we may note some small marble altars, a marble sundial, a statuette of a Hermaphrodite, etc.

The sanctuary of Isis

The digging of a drainage channel in 1978 in an area that has been shown originally to have been devoted to the cult of Artemis Eileithyia, the goddess of childbirth, resulted in the uncovering of the temenos of Isis, the Egyptian goddess who was worshipped along with Serapis, Anubis and Harpokrates in Macedonia from the Hellenistic period until the end of the Roman Empire. Built in the period of the Severi (2nd-3rd centuries A.D.), the temenos consisted of four temples set side by side on the west side of a square, unroofed area enclosed by ancillary buildings. The largest temple, erected on a high podium with a monumental staircase, was a prostyle tetrastyle ionic temple (the columns were added later); it was dedicated to Isis Lochia and had a pronaos and a cella. The reverence felt by worshippers for this "listening" goddess is revealed, albeit in fragmentary fashion, by dedications standing on the steps of the staircase and around the built altar of the temple, to which a long corridor led from the east, main entrance to the precinct.

The temple to the north of the main one was devoted to Aphrodite Hypolympidia, and that to the south possibly to Eros. The former was a single-roomed building with a large doorway without door-leaves and housed the statue of the goddess, which stood on an inscribed base in a niche at the back. The close connection of Hypolympidia with the abundant, sacred waters of the highest mountain in Greece, at the foot of which Dion is located, is becoming more clear from the existence inside this temple of a large cistern which essentially replaces the floor. The fourth temple in the complex, a short distance from the

331. The statue of Aphrodite Hypolympidia. This stood on an inscribed base in a niche of a small temple dedicated to the goddess, which was included in the sanctuary of Isis. Dion, Archaeological Museum.

332. Aerial photograph of the sanctuary of Isis.

333. The Hellenistic theatre.

332

"temple of Eros", was probably built at a later period; it was dedicated to Amaltheia-Tyche, as is clear from the marble cult statue found in situ.

Earthquakes and repeated flooding seem to have put a relatively swift end to this charming sanctuary, which sank into oblivion in the marsh and water that were the source at once of its prominence and of its destruction.

THE HELLENISTIC THEATRE

The Hellenistic theatre of Dion was identified as early as the time of colonel Leake (beginning of the 19th century) to the south of the city and to the west of the area in which the sanctuary of Demeter was excavated; the theatre faces north-east and systematic excavation of it began in 1970.

The architect of the monument took advantage of the slopes of the low natural hill, and clearly followed the principles in force in the post-Classical period, though he re-modelled the area by removing soil and using artificial deposits, with the result that his work is a personal achievement, and indeed one of the most successful of its kind.

The *orchestra* has a diameter of about 26 m., is bounded by an uncovered stone drainage conduit and has a floor of beaten earth. On the axis of the theatre inside the orchestra, was an underground corridor with two chambers, one at either end, which is certainly to be identified with the "ladder of Charon" referred to by the ancients - that is the point at which actors playing characters from the Underworld made their ascent. The *cavea* had no retaining walls at its edges but took the form of pebble-strewn slopes that levelled out at the *parodoi,* and had benches made of mud-bricks, a feature unknown elsewhere. It is highly likely that during the Hellenistic period the top course of bricks was sheathed with marble.

In contrast with the *cavea,* the stage-building - *skene, proskenion* and *paraskenia* - was much more carefully constructed: the walls of the skene were made of marble from a certain height upwards, as was the proskenion which was roofed with a doric entablature. The tiles used were of laconian type. Excavational evidence leads to the conclusion that the theatre was probably abandoned after 168 B.C., though it continued to function in a primitive fashion down

333

to the early Imperial period. The construction of a Roman theatre in the area (see below) probably marked the final abandonment of the monument.

THE ROMAN THEATRE

The Roman theatre of Dion was probably built in the first half of the 2nd century A.D., to the south-east of the earlier Hellenistic theatre. Its form was akin to the Roman theatres of Corinth and Patrae, and it possessed a *cavea* (radius 16.45 m.) and *orchestra* (radius 10.70 m.), a *skene* and *proskenion,* and faced the east.

The *cavea* was divided into four wings by three narrow staircases, and its perimeter was surrounded by a tall, built, semi-circular wall. The seats rested on the roofs of eleven vaulted, radially arranged, wedge-shaped rooms which, with the exception of the two at the edges, which communicated with the parodoi, opened onto a

334. The dorian facade of "Macedonian" tomb I.

semi-circular corridor running around the inside of the perimeter wall. The theatre probably had twenty-four rows of seats, though very few of these survive today. The stage-building was once decorated with coloured marble revetment and sculptural decoration and was independent of the cavea; the bigger part of it has now been destroyed by the bubbling waters.

Repairs dated by coins to the last quarter of the 4th century A.D. were made to at least four points of the cavea and the skene. They were perhaps due to the destruction of parts of the theatre as a result of earthquakes, or to a partial change in its function.

THE CEMETERIES

The finds from the cemeteries of Dion, which are located to the north and west of the city, cover the period from about the middle of the 5th century B.C. to the beginning of the 5th century A.D. "Hut" tombs, set in enclosures of dry-stone walls, relief stelai, and funerary altars all attest to the concern of the inhabitants about their deceased. The most imposing of the funerary

334

335

335. Gold finger ring from a burial in front of the threshold of "Macedonian" tomb IV. Second half of the 4th century B.C. Dion, Archaeological Museum.

336. Gold bracelet from the cist grave found beneath the tumulus of "Macedonian" tomb IV. Second half of the 4th century B.C. Dion, Archaeological Museum.

336

structures, however, are the "Macedonian" tombs, which have occasionally come to light - most frequently plundered - from 1929 onwards.

"Macedonian" tomb I

This is a two-chamber tomb, with a doric facade, the doorway of which was sealed by five well-dressed blocks of poros placed one on top of the other, an ionic antechamber with a flat roof, and a vaulted burial chamber, in which there was a large marble funerary couch painted with geometric motifs, palmettes and a scene of a cavalry battle. Lavishly decorated in antiquity, it has suffered badly at the hands of grave robbers and time. It was excavated by Professor G. Sotiriades at the end of the 1920s and is located a short distance away from the west wall.

"Macedonian" tomb II

Discovered in 1953 to the north of the city, this is a single-chamber subterranean building with a plastered facade and has the door-frame at the entrance and the pediment above it carved in relief. Inside the tomb, the floor of which consisted of multi-coloured pebbles, was a stone funerary couch along the short side at the back, on which was found the skeleton of a young girl, accompanied by few grave offerings.

The room was once adorned by garlands of flowers suspended from the walls by nails, ribbons and rich garments, of which today only fragmentary traces remain.

"Macedonian" tomb III

The doorway to this single-chamber funerary monument, discovered in 1955 not far from "Macedonian" tomb I, had an enormous lintel and was sealed by three stone blocks placed one above the other. Inside the tomb was a built couch to which were later added three pedestals of various sizes. The painted decoration consisted of coloured bands.

"Macedonian" tomb IV

The single-chamber tomb excavated in 1980 to the west of Karitsa, below an artificial earth tumulus, had a distinctive feature found mainly in similar monuments in Eastern Macedonia and Thrace: a built *dromos*. The plastered facade had a pediment, beneath which the door leaves of the entrance, of greyish marble, led to the burial chamber, where the evidence suggests that the wooden funerary couch was adorned with relief ivory scenes. The monument was plundered in antiquity and was probably constructed about 200 B.C.

THE ARCHAEOLOGICAL MUSEUM

The Museum of Dion acts as the museum for the archaeological site and at the same time a place in which objects from the wider region of the county of Pieria are exhibited. It houses a vast number of finds that are an eloquent commentary on the history and artistic achievements of the residents of the sacred city of the Macedonians and its surrounding area down to the Byzantine period: vases, bronze jewellery and iron weapons, grave offerings found in Early Iron Age (1000-700 B.C.) tombs covered by tumuli in the foothills of Mount Olympos. Funerary stelai of the 5th century B.C., with superb relief scenes or plain ones adorned only with the name of the deceased (from Dion and Pydna). Marble dedications and cult statuettes of gods, goddesses and the Muses dating from the 4th and the 2nd centuries B.C. found in the *oeci* of Demeter, Asklepios, and other gods. Epigraphic texts (votive inscrip-tions, treaties, alliances etc.). Finds from "Macedonian" tomb IV at Dion (ivories - 3rd century B.C.). Groups of statues depicting the sons and daughters of Asklepios (from the public baths of Dion - the products of a late Attic workshop). Portraits of the 2nd century A.D. (of philosophers and emperors). Tools.

337. Clay skyphos from the tumulus cemetery in the region of Dion, on Mount Olympos. Iron Age. Dion, Archaeological Museum.

338. Funerary stele of a mother and child, from the cemetery at Pydna. Masterpiece by a north-Greek workshop. Second half of the 5th century B.C. Dion, Archaeological Museum.

337

339. Detail of a funerary stele of a young girl from Dion. Middle of the 5th century B.C. Thessalonike, Archaeological Museum.

340. Statue of a Muse, probably Terpsichore, holding a lyre made from a tortoise shell and standing on a rock. Late Hellenistic period. Dion, Archaeological Museum.

341. Statue of Podaleirios, son of Asklepios, with inscribed plinth. Part of a sculptural ensemble depicting the family of Asklepios. From the public baths, ca. A.D. 200. Dion, Archaeological Museum.

340

341

344

345

342. Silver kalyx with repoussé and incised decoration on the outside, and a relief bust of a Maenad at the bottom of the inside. Last quarter of the 4th century B.C. From a tomb in the Pappas tumulus at Sevasti, near Dion. Dion, Archaeological Museum.

343. Silver kalyx with repoussé and incised decoration on the outside, and a relief bust of a young satyr on the bottom of the inside. Last quarter of the 4th century B.C. Found in the same tomb as the previous vase, in the Pappas tumulus at Sevasti, near Dion. Dion, Archaeological Museum.

344. The bottom of the inside of the silver kalyx in fig. 342, with the bust of a Maenad.

345. The bottom of the inside of the silver kalyx in fig. 343, with the bust of a young satyr.

346. Gold wreath of ivy leaves and berries, from a tomb in the Pappas tumulus at Sevasti, near Dion. About the middle of the 4th century B.C. Dion, Archaeological Museum.   →

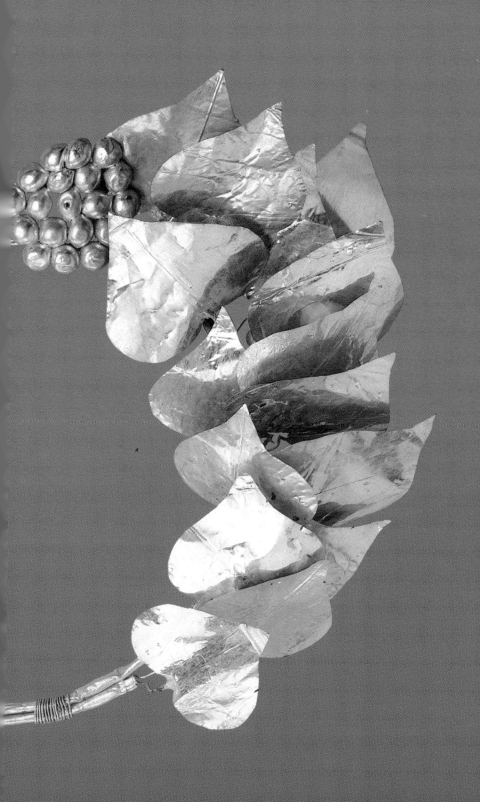

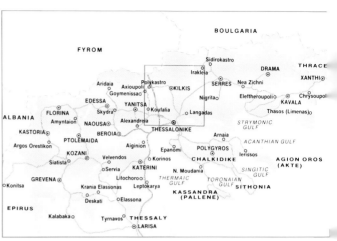

KILKIS
and its region

HISTORICAL REVIEW

The region to the north of Bottiaia is the home of cities like Idomene (Marvinci), Europos, Gortynia, Allante, Morrylos (Ano Apostoloi), Bragylos (Metallikon), Klitai and others, and is divided by the river Axios (whence its name in antiquity, Amphaxitis); over the centuries it has made use of the rich gifts offered up by this giant amongst rivers to create some interesting cultural achievements.

The prehistoric settlements of Polykastro, Limnotopos and Axiochori, from the 3rd and 2nd millennia B.C., and the later Iron Age settlements have yielded original architectural solutions to the problems of residence facing the inhabitants - mostly farmers and stock-breeders - though they also reveal contacts with the Mycenaeans of the South in the Late Helladic period, as attested by imported potsherds. Bronze jewellery and pottery have been discovered on sites such as those excavated at Tsaousitsa, Axioupolis and Gynaikokastro (cemetery).

At the dawn of historical times, Crestonia and Paionia (to the east and north of Amphaxitis) were still occupied by Thracian tribes. With the rise of Argead power, Amphaxitis passed under the control of the macedonian kingdom, and later the restless personality of Philip II carried the spear of the "Macedonians" as far as the area of Lake Doirani.

To the archaeological remains are now to be added the Late Archaic kouros from Europos, the "Macedonian" tomb at Toumba in Paionia (4th century B.C.), a number of decrees, boun-

347. General view of Kilkis.

dary stones, votive and funerary inscriptions from Morrylos, and also cult statue types of marble votives to Asklepios and his family from the sanctuary of this god in the same city (Hellenistic period); these were followed in the Roman period, when the entire region (the majority of which is today the area of the modern county of Kilkis)

348

was part of the third meris and thereafter formed part of the *Provincia Macedonia* (146 B.C. onwards), by honorific inscriptions to emperors (Bragylos), grave offerings and statues from the early Roman period (Pege), monumental heroon with marble decoration carved in the round dating from A.D. 100, etc.

The region of the lower Axios saw all the hordes of those who from time to time entertained designs against the integrity of Macedonia and the wealth of its cities and land pass by, as the wheel of time turned, on the main road axis from North to South: Ostrogoths and Slavs, Bulgars and Serbs successively attempted from the 5th to the 14th centuries A.D. to reach the coveted Aegean and Thessalonike. Just before the Turkish conquest, the fortress at Gynaikokastro, built by Andronikos III Palaiologos, was called upon to defend the vital pass leading into the heart of the Balkans.

The Yürüks, who occupied the territory of Central Macedonia directly after the capitulation of Hellenism to the Ottoman Turks, expanded to the area around Kilkis, and Avret Kisar, with its famous market, became a *timar* of Hasan Man(i)asi, who had converted to Islam.

Under the heavy cloak of Turkish rule, the *kaza* of Kilkis remained in the rearguard of events and the only disturbance of the stagnant waters arose from local confrontations between the state authorities and Albanian irregulars. Nevertheless, it was in this land, where in the past the Roman proconsul M. Minucius Rufus had been honoured for his victories over the Scordisci and the Thracians in 119 B.C. (inscriptions from Europos), that the most significant military events of the Balkan Wars were to take place (Battle of Kilkis: the checking of the advance on Thessalonike of the Bulgarian army in June 1913; Battle of Skra-Ravine: the victory of the Greek army over the Germans and Bulgarians in May 1918), consolidating the freedom of the birthplace of the Macedonians after four hundred years of subjection to foreign rule. The small museum housing souvenirs of the bloody confrontations, and the hill next to the city of Kilkis with the monument to the fallen, today contemplate the past, lighthouses of support and torches of endurance for the future. Unsullied repositories of the history of the nation.

348. The kouros from Europos. Probably from a local workshop with strong ionian influence. End of the 6th century B.C. Kilkis, Archaeological Museum.

THE ARCHAEOLOGICAL MUSEUM

The building of the Archaeological Museum of Kilkis stands in the foothills of the hill of Ayios Georgios, next to the Prefecture. Since 1971 its two rooms have housed chance finds and discoveries from excavations in the county. Amongst the fragments of Roman marble sarcophagi, objects from the Early Iron Age, statuettes, and assorted clay vases, we may note the well-known late Archaic *kouros* from Europos, the product of a local workshop with pronounced ionic influence, a number of funerary stelai, the decree of the city of Morrylos, and the honorific base of the city of the Europaioi. There is an impressive group of four statues dating from the time of Trajan, from the heroon at Palatiano.

349-350. A heroon was discovered at Palatiano near Kilkis, dating from ca. A.D. 100. Four statues stood on a high pedestal, depicting four members of the same family. The two illustrated are those of Alexandros son of Patraos and Ammia daughter of Menandros, according to the inscriptions. These statues of the deceased, portrayed in heroised style, were probably produced in a local workshop by a Macedonian artist. Kilkis, Archaeological Museum.

349

350

CHALKIDIKE

At the dawn of historical times the Pelasgoi and the Edonoi of the Chalkidike peninsula were joined by Bottiaioi, and were later driven out by the Temenids and colonists from southern Greece (Eretrians, Chalkidians) who were seeking new homes and new fortunes in this region (8th-7th centuries B.C.). The cities created both in the hinterland and in the coastal regions of the three tongues of land, Pallene (the peninsula of Kassandra), Sithonia and Akte (Mount Athos), rarely advanced beyond the level of township. Towns with charming scenes advanced on their superb coins. Towns for which the archaeologist's spade has only in recent decades begun to attempt to reconstruct the past, as assiduously as conditions allow: Potidaia/Kassandreia, Aphytis, Skione, Mende, Sane on Pallene; Torone, Sarte, Sidone, Parthenopolis, Physkella - on Sithonia; Dion, Olophyxos, Akrothoroi, Charadrous, Thyssos - on Akte; Stageira, Akanthos, Sermylia, Olynthos - on the main body of the peninsula.

Despite the fact that the majority of these cities never advanced beyond the level of townships, they experienced periods of great prosperity and entered into commercial exchanges with the east and south, acted as middlemen for the macedonian kingdom and enjoyed the goods bestowed upon them by their privileged position, which at the same time, however, made them the objective of intrigue and ambition.

They were adorned with brilliant temples, like Aphytis, founded trading-posts like Mekyverna, built forts and harbours like Torone, and had town-plans that were pioneering for their period and wealthy private residences, like Olynthos.

Swept away in the maelstrom of the confrontation between the naval empire of the Athenians and the aggressive king of the Macedonians, Philip II, and powerless before the rapid development of events, those that resisted the victor gave way to ruins (348 B.C., Olynthos). Those that capitulated were annexed by the Argead kings to their state, though preserving a shadowy independence. The country had to wait for the epigoni (Successors) before it again experienced times of prosperity: the town-planning programme inaugurated by Cassander for reasons of dynastic propaganda and continued by Antigonos II Gonatas, Demetrios II Poliorketes and Philip V, led to the construction of Kassandreia (316 B.C.) on the site of the earlier Potidaia, Ouranoupolis (founded by Alexarchos the brother of Cassander) at the head of the Akte peninsula, Antigoneia (founded by Antigonos Gonatas) near the settlement of Ayios Pavlos, Stratonikeia (founded by Demetrios Poliorketes and named after his daughter Stratonike) in the Singitic Gulf.

As part of the "second meris", in the period after the Roman Conquest (168 B.C.), Chalkidike lived in the rearguard of developments, on the margin of the events that marked the Roman presence in the Balkan peninsula. Of the list of settlements mentioned in Thucydides, Herodotus and Xenophon and in the fragments of other, later historians, very few have resisted the encroachment of time. Scattered archaeological and literary evidence gives life to Akanthos, Stratonikeia and Aphytis down to the 5th century of the Christian era, and Kassandreia is an exceptional case, having been settled with Roman colonists as early as 43 or 42 B.C., initially by the proconsul G. Ortesius Ortalus and subsequently by Augustus (Colonia Iulia Augusta Cassandrensis), later becoming in Livy's eyes one of the two (the other was Thessalonike) celeberrimae urbes (famous cities) of the "second meris" of Macedonia. With a territory that included those of ancient Potidaia, Sani, Skione, Mende and Aphytis to the south and Olynthos to the north, Cassandreia repelled the Goths in A.D. 268 but did not escape capture by the Kutrigurs in A.D. 540. Justinian I rebuilt the city and endowed it with stout walls.

Chalkidike was part of the "diocese" of Macedonia within the prefecture of Illyrikon during the 4th century A.D., and belonged to the "theme" of Thessalonike during the 8th to 9th centuries A.D., playing host to a large number of monks and hermits from the East. In accordance with imperial policy, these new inhabitants of the Athos Peninsula, who had fled from their homes in the face of the appearance and expansion of the Arab invaders, re-settled the abandoned townships and villages and founded the most important centre of Orthodox monasticism, which in A.D. 885 received official recognition and support in the chrysobull of Basil I the Macedonian.

During the 11th century, Chalkidike was part of the administrative district of Thessalonike-Strymon-Voleros, and after the dissolution of the Byzantine Empire by the crusaders of the Fourth Crusade (1204) it was included in the Frankish kingdom of Thessalonike.

Having returned to the bosom of the Byzantine Empire in A.D. 1261, it experienced the difficult years that marked the 14th century and felt the might of the plundering Catalans (A.D. 1307/08), the greed of the Turkish pirates (A.D. 1334), and heard the distant echoes of the Zealot uprising (A.D. 1342) and the Serb invasion. Shortly before the first siege of Thessalonike (A.D. 1385/86), freedom became a thing of the past for Chalkidike: the Ottomans burst violently into European space and made themselves master of the peninsula and, despite the ephemeral successes of the Byzantines and the Venetians, exercised undisputed control over it from about A.D. 1430.

Cut off from the main body of Macedonia, forested and mountainous, the peninsula was an asylum for the hunted and a last refuge of the persecuted from the very beginning of the Turkish occupation; at the same time it was a safe bastion for its population and, thanks to the nature of the terrain preserved the purity of the race, far from foreign intermingling. Tranquillity was not slow to bring development in its train and the exploitation of the forests and mines swiftly bore fruit for the inhabitants. Chalkidike prospered at the time of Mehmed II (A.D. 1451-1481) and later that of Süleyman I the Magnificent (A.D. 1520-1566), when special decrees were issued relating to the organisation of the exploitation of the silver beds at Madem Lakko; and a group of Jewish refugees from Germany, expert in new techniques for extracting and purifying the metal, settled in the region at the beginning of the 16th century. The prosperity of Chalkidike is clear in the descriptions of the European travellers of the period.

During the 18th and the beginning of the 19th centuries, building materials and fire-wood were shipped from the bays and harbours of the peninsula (Rentina/Orthanos) for Thessalonike, Crete and Egypt. Carpets were shipped to European Turkey from Arnea (Liaringovi). From Siderokapsa, a co-operative of the villagers from twelve communities (the Mademochoria), which worked the silver mines of mount Cholomon, supplied the imperial mint with precious metal and furnished the Sultan with the lead that was exported after the metal had been processed locally. Wheat, cotton, excellent honey, wax and wonderful silks were produced and made by the Hasikochoria (or hass-villages, villages belonged to the sultana's hass) - a co-operative of fifteen villages, whose land stretched from the Toronaic to the Thermaic Gulf - while the twelve villages of the Kassandra peninsula, centred on Valta, made their living on the fruit so liberally supplied by the sea.

The situation created at the beginning of the Russo-Turkish War and the Serbian liberation movements (end of the 18th-beginning of the 19th centuries A.D.) rekindled the dreams of throwing off the Turkish yoke entertained by the Macedonians of Chalkidike. In 1807, Stavros, at the head of the Strymonian Gulf lived through the impulsive vision of Nikotsaras and his comrades and, under the inspired leadership of Emmanuel Papas, the "Leader and Defender of Macedonia" as he was proclaimed by the general assembly of officials of the monasteries of Mount Athos and the sailors of Psara island, Polygyros, Kassandra, Ormylia, Nikiti and Parthenonas raised the torch of freedom and armed their faith with the weapon of daring.

Enthusiasm and self-denial, however, were accompanied by lack of discipline in the Chalkidike of 1821, and lack of munitions and charismatic leaders rendered the measures taken ineffective and the defence weak. Against the repeating weapons and the fully armed military corps hastily despatched by the administration of Thessalonike and the *Sublime Porte,* the few dozens of youths at Sykia outside Vasilika, the irregulars at Rentina, the ailing women and children at Polygyros and the noble defenders of Ayios Mamas could hold out only their breasts, and their perseverance in the struggle; all they had to counter with was the smoking ruins of their homes. Many converted to Islam, others were led off to Benghazi, bound in chains and thinking nostalgically of the unredeemed fatherland; the majority, with their eyes turned backwards, took refuge in the Sporades and from there the Cyclades and the Peloponnese. The monks of Mount Athos, the last refuge of so many refugees, finally submitted and were obliged to pay a heavy price to pasha Mehmed Emin for the friendly attitude they had adopted towards the insurrectionaries. In roadsteads and passes, misery and hunger now roamed at large. Oppression, piracy and poverty kept company with despair. The smoke of the ruins was the only memory taken with him by Emmanuel Papas on his last journey to Hydra.

Time, that forgets and remembers, heals all wounds, however, and life gradually resumed its course. The inhabitants returned and began to cultivate their fields again, planting the seeds of their visions deep in the soil. The appointment of a Greek consul to Thessalonike, after the normalisation of relations between the Ottoman Empire and the newly created Kingdom of Athens, brought Greece closer, and put flesh and bones on hope. Despite the fact that Tsamis Karatasos of Naousa played a major role in re-settling the refugees on the other side of the borders, and despite the moving contribution of Makriyannis, the time was not ripe. Voices were strangled and movements were suppressed, often with the assistance of the representatives of the Great Powers -allies of Turkey in the Crimean War (1853-1856). The descent on Mount Athos (1853) met with no response and the failure of the enterprise of Eugenios Voulgaris with Captain Georgakis at Ormylia (1866) together with the Russian penetration of the monastic community on Mount Athos, turned the Greek nation to the rewards of intellectual endeavour and the search for its identity. After the Treaty of San Stefano (1877) and the Congress of Berlin (1878), and especially after the annexation of Eastern Roumeli by the Bulgarians (1885), no-one doubted any longer that the liberation of Macedonia was a matter for the inhabitants of the region and of the free Greek state.

351

351. View of the inside of the cave of Petralona, in which the fossilised skull of Archanthropus and animal skeletons were found.

352. The Petralona skull is the oldest evidence for the presence of humans in Greece during the Palaeolithic period. It probably belonged to a woman who lived about 750,000 years ago.

THE PETRALONA CAVE

Good fortune, in the form of a simple shepherd, led to the discovery and gradual investigation at various periods since 1959 of the Petralona cave, one kilometre to the east of the community of Petralona in Chalkidike, in the foothills of Mount Katsika, at a height of 300-350 m. above sea level. The cave is 1,500 m. long and known to the international bibliography on account of the skull of Archanthropus it contained (about 750,000 years B.C.), along with remains of human activity in this distant epoch (bone and stone tools). Petrified leaves of holm-oak and oak, along with bones of rhinoceros, elephant, deer, lions and equines are evidence for the flora and fauna of the place at the dawn of the human presence in what was still an inhospitable land. The cave has been converted into a museum and may be visited. The skull is housed in the University of Thessalonike.

352

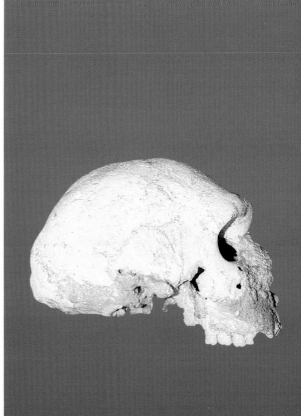

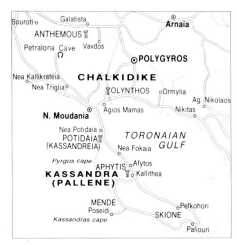

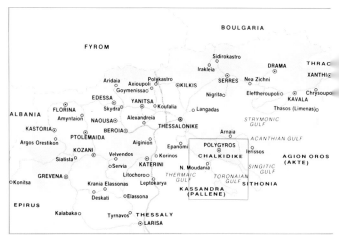

OLYNTHOS
and its region

HISTORICAL REVIEW

Olynthos, capital of the Chalkidian League, and famous from the fiery Philippic orations of Demosthenes, was created just before the beginning of the Peloponnesian War by the transfer of the population of a large number of coastal cities. Laid out according to the "Hippodameian" plan on a site next to the winter torrent Sandanos on which there are remains from the Late Neolithic period (3,000-2,500 B.C.), it is for scholars one of the finest examples of town-planning and urban architecture surviving from Classical antiquity. At the same time, thanks to its systematic excavation by the American Professor D. Robinson in the period between the World Wars, Olynthos has enriched our knowledge of the daily life of the ancient Greeks in the Late Classical period.

Located sixty stades from Potidaia and twenty from Mekyverna, with a harbour at the head of the Toronaic Gulf, the city, whose pre-Greek name means "wild fig tree", according to the most common tradition at least, owed its foundation to Olynthos, son of the river god Strymon. Herodotus, however, reports that the "hero builders" of Olynthos were the Bottiaioi who dwelt near the river Axios who, having been expelled by the Macedonians about the middle of the 7th century B.C., migrated to Chalkidike. This first settlement was destroyed in 479 B.C. by the Persians, returning to Asia after their defeat at Plataea, and was handed over, together with its "territory", to the Chalkidians, who had gone over to the Persian side.

353. The ruins of ancient Olynthos.

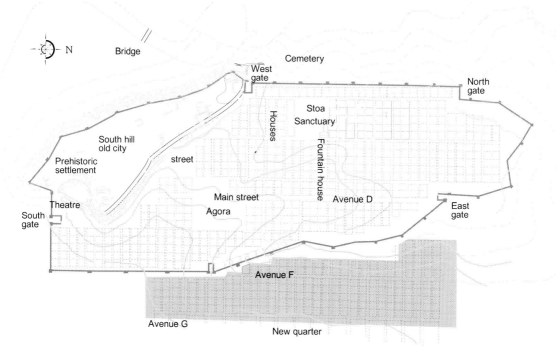

N

Bridge

Cemetery

West gate

North gate

Houses

Stoa
Sanctuary

South hill
old city

street

Prehistoric
settlement

Fountain house

Main street

Avenue D

Agora

Theatre

East gate

South gate

Avenue F

Avenue G

New quarter

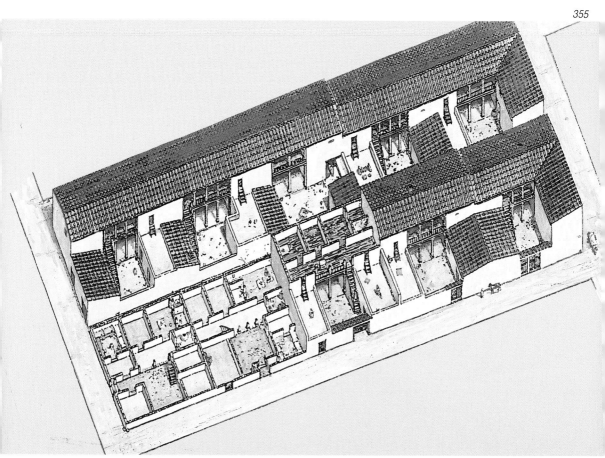

Classical Olynthos was a member of the first Athenian Confederacy though it deserted its tyrannical protectors in 440 B.C. and within a few years became the most populous and the richest city in the region, receiving waves of settlers from Potidaia (429 B.C.), Mende (423 B.C.) and Singos (before 422 B.C.), who were forcibly expelled from their homes during the maelstrom of the Peloponnesian War.

The strength of the city brought it into confrontation with Amyntas III of Macedonia (393-370 B.C.), whose capital, Pella, it captured for a brief interval. It also came into conflict with the Spartans (382-379 B.C.) who laid siege to the city and obliged it to surrender. Olynthos revived during the time of the Theban hegemony and broke with Athens (368-358 B.C.) over the question of Amphipolis; Philip II sought to take advantage of this circumstance in 356 B.C. by offering the city of Potidaia and the territory of Anthemous as a reward for Olynthian friendship. The ring was tightening dangerously around Olynthos, however, and as the institution of the city-state entered upon its decline, the rising power of the Macedonian kingdom, which had other visions and other aims, razed the bastion of the resistance of the Chalkidian League in 348 B.C. and sold its inhabitants into slavery.

THE CITY

Olynthos was created by the transfer of existing coastal settlements in 432 B.C. and had a population of 6,000 inhabitants a few years later, rising to 10,000 by the middle of the 4th century B.C.; the city spread over two plateaux, of which the one to the south was the first to be occupied, and was built according to a free plan that fol-

lowed the configuration of the terrain. This, the Archaic city, was burned by the Persians and was abandoned almost entirely, giving way to the Classical settlement, built on the adjacent northern plateau and covering an area measuring 600 m. x 300 m. The city was divided into sixty-four insulae (dimensions approximately 87 m. x 36 m.) by two sets of parallel streets intersecting each other at right angles, some of which, running from north-south, are 7 m. wide and have appropriately been dubbed "avenues". Each insula had ten square building plots, with five residences on each of the long sides; these were two-storey on the north side and had a paved courtyard, the *pastas,* on the south.

With the sun to warm them on winter days and the shade to cool them throughout the hot summers, the inhabitants of the astutely oriented houses of Olynthos entertained their guests to banquets in the "andron" (banqueting room for men) on the ground floor, reclining on couches and admiring the mosaic compositions that spread at their feet, created of river pebbles with floral or multi-figural compositions: the Nereids,

356

354. Plan of Olynthos, showing the two plateaux on which the city was built the insulae and the rectilinear street grid, the avenues and the defence wall. The south plateau (top left in the illustration) was the first to be inhabited, during the Archaic period.

355. Reconstruction of one of the insulae, which contained ten two-storey houses.(Figures 354 and 355 are from the book "Haus und Stadt im Klassischen Griechenland" by W. Hoepfner and L. Schwander, who have kindly allowed us to reproduce them).

356. Silver tetradrachm of the Chalkidian League, with the head of Apollo on one side and the lyre on the other. First half of the 4th century B.C. Athens, Numismatic Museum.

sea-horses, Bellerophon slaying the Chimaera, griffins tearing apart deer, spiral-maeanders and double maeanders. They passed the hours of their day in the "diaiteterion", dined in the "oikos", cooked in the "optanion" and attended to their ablutions in the "balaneion" with its clay basins. On the upper floor, which was reached by a wooden internal staircase from the courtyard, married couples relaxed in the arms of desire in the "thalamos", and the women of the household sought the isolation of their sex in the "gynaikon-ites" (womens' gallery).

The public areas of the city included the Ago-ra, which was located to south of the residential area on a rectangular plot of land four houses wide and six houses long. It also included the public Fountain and probably the local public Te-menos, in an area to the west; and the Theatre, which is thought to have been located in a de-pression in the south side of the southern pla-teau.

Despite the fact that no remains of the fortifi-cations of the Archaic city have been found and the very few sections of defence walls that have been located on the northern plateau are not particularly revealing, scholars believe that the Classical city was defended by an enceinte made of unbaked brick that enclosed both pla-teaux. This fortification was obliterated in 348 B.C. by Philip II, when he razed the capital of his hated foe, the Chalkidian League.

Amongst the first victims of the military con-frontation between the Macedonians and the Olynthians were presumably the wealthy houses in the unwalled aristocratic suburb of the city im-mediately to the east of the northern plateau; this

357. Bronze arrow-head found at Olynthos. The cylindrical shaft bears the relief inscription ΦΙΛΙΠΠΟ ("of Philip"). Polygyros, Archaeological Museum.

358. Mosaic floor of a private luxury residence at Olynthos, headquarters of the Chalkidian League. The mosaic depicts Bellerophon astride Pegasos, killing the Chimaira, and is one of the earliest mosaics of the historical period discovered in Greece. First half of the 4th century B.C.

suburb was also built according to the "Hippoda-meian" system in the years after 379 B.C., when the region was particularly prosperous. Some of the finest residences in ancient world have been excavated here; they have been dubbed villas and are known by conventional names: the villa of Good Fortune, the villa of the Comedian, the villa of the Twin Erotes.

To the east of the modern settlement of the same name, 80 km from Thessalonike and 25 km from Polygyros, Olynthos, its eyes filled with de-struction and smoke, and the screams of the wounded and the wailing of prisoners of war in its ears, contemplated the centuries as they repli-cated its urban grid in the Hellenistic cities built by the *epigoni* in the East. Untended and aban-doned, with the earth deposited after the exca-vations concealing and protecting the mosaics in its houses, it rejoices from afar in the brilliant portable finds from its cemeteries and houses, now in the Archaeological Museum of Thessalo-nike and that of Polygyros. In the face of history - and itself history - it lives with its memories. As do its visitors.

358

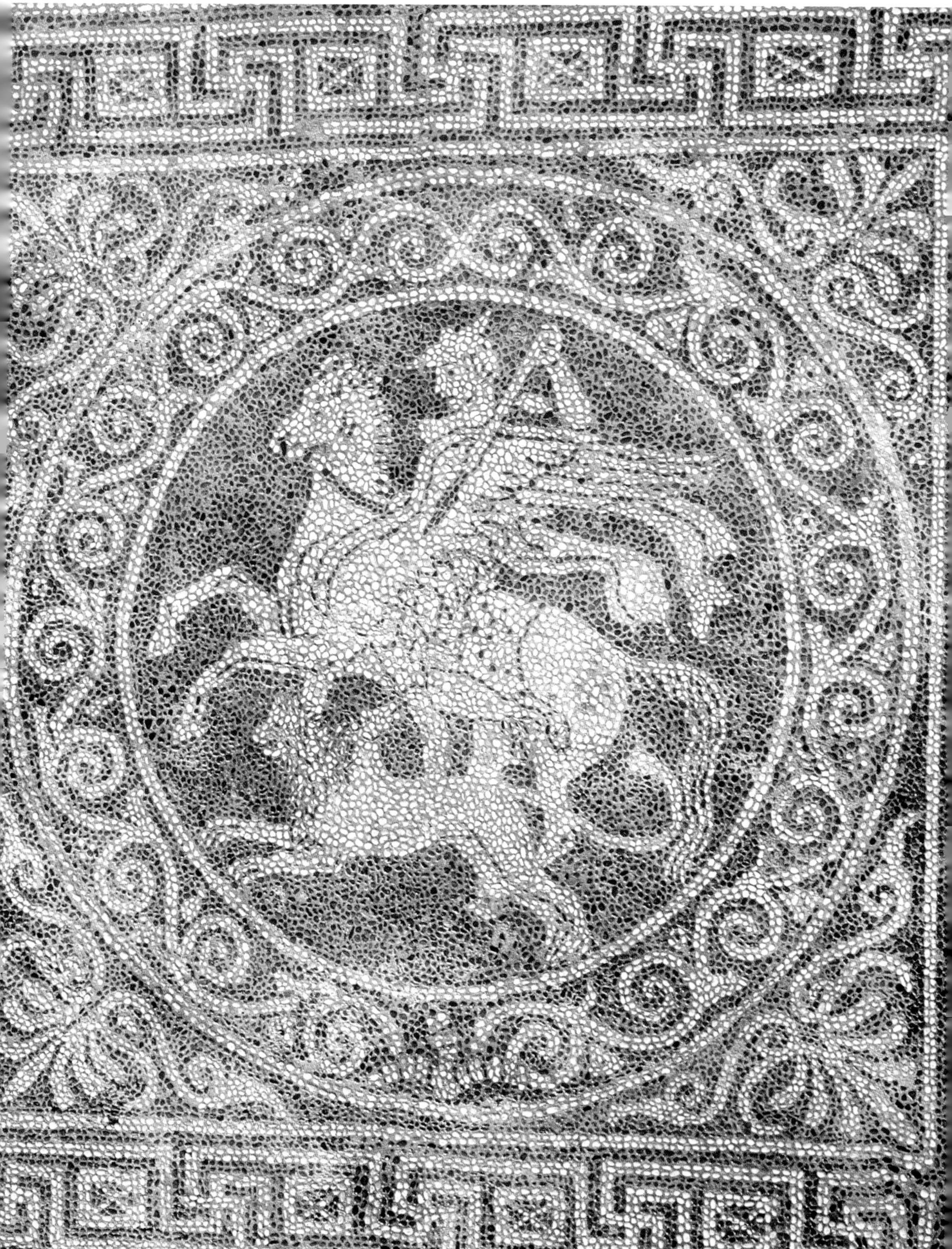

284

359. Bronze door-knocker in the form of a relief lion's head, from the door of a house at Olynthos. Polygyros, Archaeological Museum.

360. Embossed copper sheet from Olynthos, with relief figures of a naked youth (a Greek) at the left and a bearded ruler holding a sceptre and a characteristic Phrygian head-cover at the right. First half of the 4th century B.C. Thessalonike, Archaeological Museum.

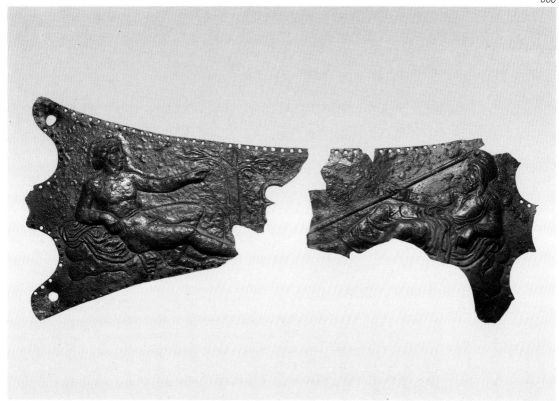

361

362

361. Clay female bust from the "House of the Comedian" at Olynthos. 5th century B.C. Polygyros, Archaeological Museum.

362. Plastic clay vase in the shape of a head of Dionysos, from a house at Olynthos, ca. 400 B.C. Polygyros, Archaeological Museum.

363-364

363-364. Clay mould of
a bust of Cybele, a
Phrygian goddess of
motherhood and
vegetation, and a
modern plaster cast
made from it. Found in
the commercial centre
of Olynthos. Beginning
of the 4th century B.C.
Polygyros,
Archaeological
Museum.

365. Attic red-figure
hydria with an
Amazonomachy scene,
from the West
cemetery at Olynthos,
ca. 370 B.C.
Polygyros,
Archaeological
Museum.

288

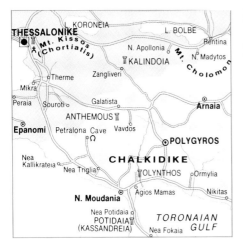

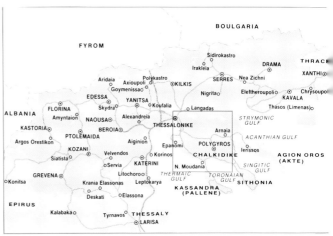

POLYGYROS
and its region

366

HISTORICAL REVIEW

The town of Polygyros, to the south of mount Cholomon, was the seat of an aga, and originally numbered 600 families (beginning of the 19th century A.D.). Capital of the Hasikochoria, it was the meeting place for the representatives of the surrounding communities who assembled for the purpose of distributing the taxes, and for deciding other matters of communal interest.

The wealth of the place is apparent from the description of the English traveller Urquhart, whose account is full of praise for the brilliant silken dresses worn by the women.

The families of Papayannakis and Kotsaras were members of the Philike Hetairia, and will certainly have inspired the restless youths of Polygyros to revolt during the prelude to the uprising in southern Greece (1821). Despite some temporary successes, however, the insurrection led to the slaughter of the notables and the destruction of the settlement. Like Naousa, Polygyros, at the mercy of the inexperience of its inhabitants and the superior training of the much larger Turkish armies, had to wait over half a century before it gazed upon the blue and white colour of freedom.

366. General view of Polygyros.

THE ARCHAEOLOGICAL MUSEUM

The two tastefully arranged rooms of the Archaeological Museum of Polygyros, with their explanatory texts, maps, photographs of excavations and other information, give the visitor the opportunity to browse amongst ancient finds from various sites of Chalkidike prehistoric finds (vases, tools, spindle-whorls) from Olynthos, Agios Mamas and Molybdopyrgos and rich grave offerings from the Archaic-Classical cemetery of Ierissos (ancient Akanthos), amongst them figurines, clay female busts, clay and glass vases of Phoenician type, clay actor's masks, bronze coins and a richly decorated clay sarcophagus of Clazomenian type, dating from the end of the 6th century B.C.; the very beautiful laurel, ivy and oak wreaths, with lead circlets, gilded bronze leaves and stalks, and gilded clay berries and flowers, dating from the end of the 4th and the beginning of the 3rd centuries B.C.; everyday and cult objects from Olynthos, offering a picture of the life of a 4th century B.C. city (clay female busts, figurines, a kernos and a censer, a clay mould of a horse,clay tablets with representations of gods, clay sphinxes, figurines of animals from a child burial, a bronze frying-pan, bronze arrow-heads bearing the embossed inscription Philip, and a shield); a marble head of Dionysos from the sanctuary of the god at Aphytis, mentioned by Xenophon in the Hellenika, pottery from the altar and temple of Zeus Ammon,that where constructed in the sanctuary of Aphytis at the end of the 5th and in the second half of the 4th centuries B.C. respectively, grave offerings from stone chests from the end of the 6th century B.C. and the tombs at Kastri, near Polygyros and at Neos Marmaras; Early Bronze Age and proto-geometric vases from the cemetery at Torone; a funerary amphora from Mekyberna and a column krater from the workshop of Lydos, from Vrasta; small marbre statues from Potidaia and two large (a male and a female), dating from the 1st century B.C. from Stratoni (ancient Stratonikeia); inscribed funerary stelai from various places in Chalkidike, male marble heads and ones (sales contracts) relating to houses and vineyards from Olynthos and Vrasta. The visitor has the opportunity to become acquainted with the magnificent achievents of the colonists from cities and areas of southern Greece, who sought fame and fortune on the verant coasts of the North Aegean.

367

368

367-368. Clay figurines from houses at Olynthos, connected with the household cult. 5th century B.C. Polygyros, Archaeological Museum.

369. Marble head of Dionysos from ancient Aphytis. 4th century B.C. Polygyros, Archaeological Museum.

370

372

370. *Red-figure pelike with a depiction of the birth of Aphrodite, ca. 370 B.C. Polygyros, Archaeological Museum.*

371. *Attic red-figure column-krater by the Florence painter, with a scene of a departing warrior. From the cemetery by the river at Olynthos. Early Classical period. Polygyros, Archaeological Museum.*

372. *Black-figure skyphos with an Amazonomachy scene, between Sphinxes. Found inside a stone chest in the area of Aphytis. About 500 B.C. Polygyros, Archaeological Museum.*

373. *Black-figure column krater from the workshop of Lydos, from Vrasta in Chalkidike. Third quarter of the 6th century B.C. Polygyros, Archaeological Museum.*

373

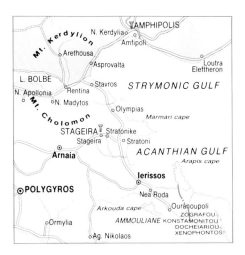

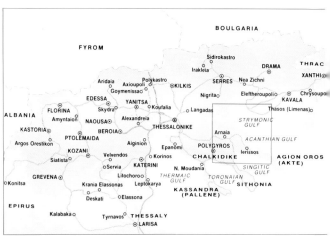

OURANOUPOLIS

374

HISTORICAL REVIEW

The fore-fathers of the modern inhabitants of Ouranoupolis were refugees from the sacred soil of Asia Minor, who carried the bitterness of persecution in their baggage, and embraced the Byzantine tower that awaited them at the head of the Singitic Gulf. Between 1923 and 1927 they built the settlement of Prosphorion, whose name was changed to Ouranoupolis by the omniscience of learning, and which was converted into an architecturally colourless settlement by newcomers - farmers, bee-keepers and workers during the first years of the settlement, and superficial beggars and exploiters of Zeus Xenios (the god of hospitality) in the years after the war. Blind to the messages of the cultural ark of Christianity transmitted despairingly by neighbouring Mount Athos, and blind to the beauties of verdant nature.

374. View of the coast and tower of Ouranoupolis.

THE CHRISTIAN MUSEUM

375

The tower of Ouranoupolis - known in the sources as the tower of Prosphorion - was built in the 14th century A.D. to protect a *metochion* (dependency) of the Vatopedi Monastery at the head of the Mount Athos peninsula. Today, after a recent successful remodelling of the interior of both the tower and the two-storey boat-house attached to it, the tower houses an interesting collection of Christian monuments almost exclusively drawn from archaeological sites and churches in Chalkidike: lamps of the 5th century A.D. from Torone; marble architectural members from an early Christian basilica at Nikiti; a hoard of folleis of Leo VI the Wise from Nea Syllata; grave-offerings (jewellery) from Palaiokastro and Hierissos (10th century A.D.); a cross from Sykia (11th-12th centuries A.D.); vases and other objects from Kassandreia (12th-14th centuries A.D.); a gold embroidered *epitaphios* from Ormylia (14th century A.D.); wall-paintings of the 17th century A.D. detached from Ayia Triada, a *metochion* of the monastery of Ayia Athanasia; post-Byzantine devotional icons (16th-19th centuries A.D.) from the workshops of Galatista and Mount Athos and also of Asia Minor.

376

377

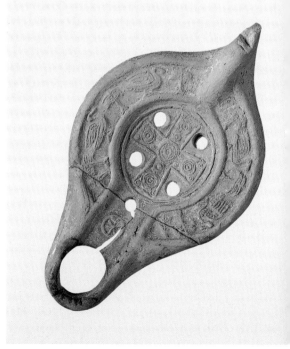

378

375. View of the tower from the south-east.

376. Column with waving acanthus leaves, from the Early Christian basilica of Sophronios at Nikiti. 5th century A.D. Ouranoupolis, Christian Museum.

377. Lamp with a relief cross on the disk, from an early Christian basilica at Torone. 5th century. Ouranoupolis, Christian Museum.

378. Silver earrings from the medieval cemetery at Ierissos. Ouranoupolis, Christian Museum.

379. Hoard of folleis of Leon VI the Wise (886-912) from Nea Syllata. Ouranoupolis, Christian Museum.

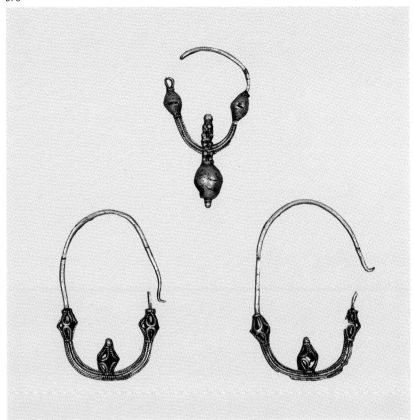

379

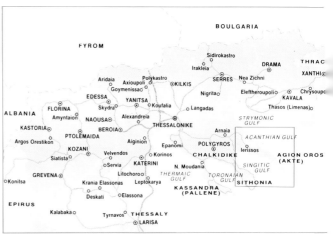

MOUNT ATHOS

HISTORICAL REVIEW

On the fringes of the Aegean, on the fringes of Macedonia, a rocky land with no hospitable harbours, covered with dense, wild vegetation, hostile to the human presence, shut in by restless, foaming waters, cut off from the rest of the mainland, cut off from the transience of daily routine and the things of this world.

On the fringes of history - and itself history - a land travelling through the centuries like an Ark. Indestructible, contemplating the still-born regenerations and the chained revolutions of the times. Young and fine and so old. Wise and yet so child-like. Lonely and alone.

On the fringes of the conscience, the Holy Mountain, the Garden of the Virgin. Five to ten kilometres wide and about fifteen long, touching, at two thousand metres, the boundless heavens, in direct communion with the divine. An earthly paradise, dedicated to the glory of the Son of Man, nestling in the arms of the Mother of God, a place to exercise the body and the soul, a piece preserved unsullied from the time of Creation.

The beginnings of monastic life on Mount Athos belong to the sphere of myth. Although some of the sources - the "Patria" or "Proskynetaria" - date this phenomenon to the reign of Constantine the Great and his mother Saint Helen,

380. Kafsokalyvia, a scete of the Great Lavra Monastery.

the first hermits seem to have come to Athos in the 7th century A.D., having been displaced from Egypt and the East, which at that period were being seized by the Arabs. It is a historically attested fact, however, that the peninsula was first designated a place of Quietism by a chrysobull of Basil I in A.D. 885. The founder of coenobitic monastic life there is thought to have been Saint Athanasios of Trebizond who, with the support of his friend the emperor Nikephoros Phokas (A.D. 963-969), founded the Great Lavra, the first monastery on the peninsula (A.D. 962/963).

A few years later in A.D. 971/72, at the instigation of the emperor Ioannis Tzimiskes (A.D. 969-976), Euthymios, the Abbot of the Studite monastery in Constantinople, composed the first *typikon* (a charter governing the organisation and administration of the Athonite State). This text, known as the Tragos (because it was written on a parchment of a goatskin, *tragos*=goat), and now housed at Protaton (the *katholikon* at

Karyes, the capital of the Athonite State), formed the basis for the later *typika* and the subsequent development of all the monasteries on Mount Athos. It has been claimed that the intervention of the state in the creation of a monastic polity was dictated mainly by the spiritual need for the Byzantine Empire to become more involved in the Balkans, with a view to defending and strengthening the Orthodox Church after the conversion to Christianity of the South Slavs and the Bulgars (A.D. 864/65), and in response to attempts by the Roman Catholic Church to penetrate the spheres of influence of the Eastern Church. The eminent men of the cloth who took an active part in the enterprise, the personal interest shown by members of the imperial family, and the fact that from as early as the 10th and the beginning of the 11th centuries A.D. Iberians (A.D. 965 ff.), Amalpheni (A.D. 981), Slavs, Russians and Bulgars flocked to Athos to man the new monasteries, were all factors leading to the place acquiring an ecumenical character and becoming a crusading centre for the True Belief.

These were the years of "Romiosyni" and the establishment of a Greek-Orthodox conscious-

381. The peninsula of Mount Athos.

381

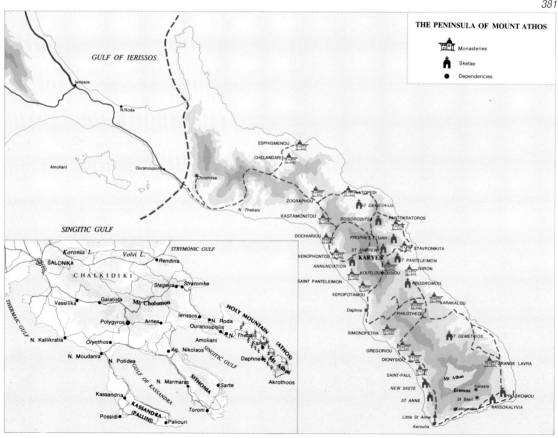

ness, during which the great monasteries were founded (the Great Lavra, the monastery of Vatopedi and that of Iveron), and the foundations were laid for other, smaller monasteries (those of Docheiariou, Xenophontos and Philotheou). From these times, and from the period of generous royal gifts of huge landed estates, of domes decorated with gold, of richly adorned *katholika* and of echoing cells - multi-storey, fortress-like defensive structures - down to the enslavement of the nation by the Turks, Mount Athos knew moments of grandeur and of decline. Periods during which monasticism thrived and new monasteries and annexes were built (11th/12th and second half of the 14th centuries), and difficult times of abandonment and pillaging (13th and beginning of the 14th centuries), during which the undefiled mother of endurance - the immaculate Mother of God - enfolded the inner sanctum of her house in love and tenderness.

Mount Athos became acquainted with the Franks of the Fourth Crusade, the oppression of Michael VIII Palaiologos, a fervent supporter of the Unification of the Churches, and the plundering invasions of the Catalan pirates. It was also the object of the active interest of the emperors of Trebizond and the kings of Serbia.

Faced with a "fait accompli", the monks were reconciled with the Ottoman conqueror and during the first half century or so that followed their subjection to the Sultan, they retained the privileges they had been granted by the Byzantine emperors. One indication of their prosperity was the renovation, at about the middle of the 16th century, of the Monastery of Stavronikita (1536) and the decoration of a large number of *katholika,* refectories and chapels by named painters of the period (Theophanes the Cretan, Tzortzes and Frangos Katelanos).

Fresh buffetings, however, lay in wait for the ship of the Orthodox faith in the stormy ocean of the three centuries that remained before liberation: swingeing taxes and confiscations of estates led to the abandonment of monasteries, to the replacement of the coenobitic way of life by the "idiorrhythmic" and to the foundation of *scetes,* and spiritual unity was undermined by religious strife. Even in these moments of adversity, however, the spirit succeeded in achieving great things and producing a host of scholars and wise men of the stature of Nikodemos of Naxos, Eugenios Voulgaris, Kosmas Aitolos, Athanasios of Paros - all teachers and pupils at the famous "Athonite School".

The territory of the Athos Peninsula is now an integral part of the Greek State, though it is self-governing, on the basis of a special charter (Treaty of Lausanne, 1923), and is distributed between the twenty sovereign monasteries, which follow a traditional hierarchy based on their imperial titles and other privileges. Monasteries to which the centuries have bequeathed rare examples of illustrated manuscripts and codices, brilliant wall-paintings, silver-clad icons of saints, and clerical vestments studded with precious stones, endowing them with imperial gifts, imposing buildings, shipyards and scetes, old peoples' homes, hospitals, *kathismata* (a kind of monastic building), and hermitages. Beacons and bastions, safe harbours, refuges of the soul and the spirit.

For Greeks, Mount Athos is the cradle of their national traditions and a part of Greece that for over a thousand years has preserved their Greek-Christian traditions, literature and authen-

382. A monk of the Monastery of Simonopetra ringing the bell on one of the outer balconies of the monastery.

382

383

384

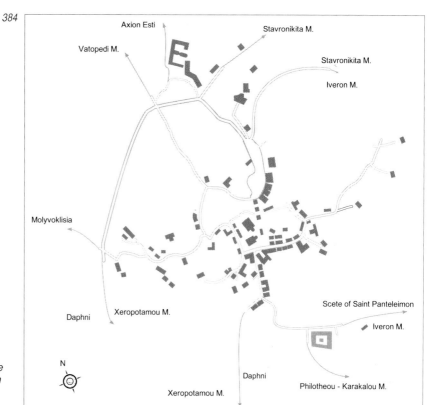

383. General view of
Karyes, from above.

384. Plan of Karyes.

385. View of the
Protaton with the
campanile, from the
east. The building of the
Sacred Community can
be seen in the
background.

Axion Esti

Vatopedi M.

Stavronikita M.

Stavronikita M.

Iveron M.

Molyvoklisia

Daphni

Xeropotamou M.

N

Scete of Saint Panteleimon

Iveron M.

Daphni

Xeropotamou M.

Philotheou - Karakalou M.

tic Byzantine worship. It is a sacred repository housing still unknown sources for scholars investigating theology, philosophy, history, Byzantine and post-Byzantine art and eastern mysticism, and a boundless museum containing invaluable treasures and heirlooms of the Orthodox tradition.

KARYES

The small town of Karyes, in roughly the centre of the sacred peninsula, has a plan corresponding to that of idiorrhythmic *scete,* and acts as the seat of the *Protos* (primate), the spiritual leader of the monasteries, who is chosen for life from amongst the body of abbots (hegoumenoi).

The town followed the fluctuations of the au-

thority of the president of the Athonite State and found itself sometimes confronted with the power acquired by the three large monasteries - the Great Lavra, Vatopedi and Iveron - and at other times strengthened by imperial chrysobulls and patriarchal sigils. It is home to monuments of outstanding importance for ecclesiastical art (Church of Protaton, dating from the first half of the 10th century, and dedicated to the Dormition of the Virgin, painted by Emmanuel Panselinos at the beginning of the 14th century A.D.) and also a great number of portable vessels and objects of worship (miracle-working icon of *"Axion Estin").*

Karyes is the headquarters not only of the *Protos* and the Sacred Community but also of the civil governor of Mount Athos, who is attached to the Ministry of the Exterior.

386. *The warrior saint Theodore. Wall-painting of the beginning of the 14th century in the Protaton at Karyes, by the famous painter Manuel Panselinos, the most important representative of the Macedonian School.*

THE MONASTERIES
GREAT LAVRA

The Great Lavra is first in the hierarchy of monasteries and dedicated to the Dormition of hosios Athanasios, the wise monk and friend of the emperor Nikephoros II Phokas, who in A.D. 963 founded the first *lavra* (small group of hermits with a common superior and a central house of prayer) on Mount Athos at a site probably previously occupied by the ancient township of Akrothooi.

The monastery, a model of the coenobitic life and an example for those that followed, received generous gifts from Nikephoros II Phokas, his successor Ioannis Tzimiskes, and Basil II the Bulgar Slayer, and experienced moments of glory and grandeur down to the end of the 14th century. It was rescued from decline - the result of destructions and raids by pirates (15th-16th centuries) - by the patriarch Dionysios III (A.D. 1655), who gave his entire fortune to it. It was later rescued both by the Russian tzars and by the princes of the Danubian principalities. The great Cretan painter Theophanes and Frangos Katelanos both worked in the Great Lavra - the former in A.D. 1535 and the latter in A.D. 1560.

387. The Great Lavra. Part of the inside of the monastery.

387

306

388

389

390

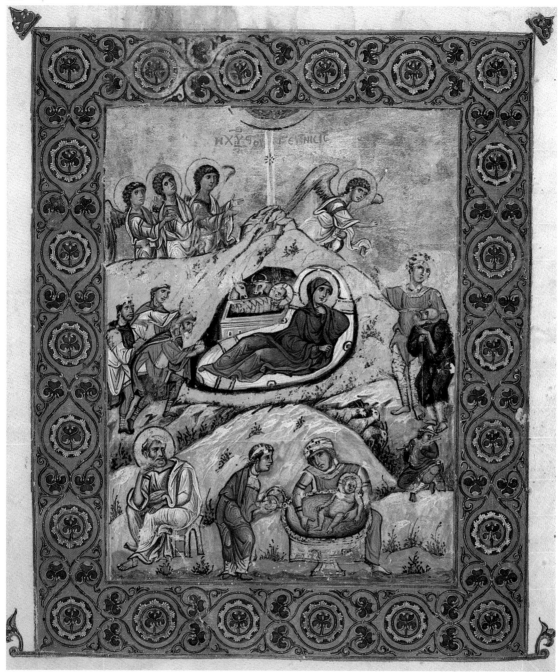

388. *The Great Lavra. The consecration font.*

389. *The Great Lavra. The katholikon from the east.*

390. *Gospel book. The so-called "Gospel of Nikephoros Phokas" with a scene of the Birth of Christ, in the sacristy of the Great Lavra Monastery.*

391. *"Praise the Lord", wall-painting from the chapel of Koukouzelissa.18th century. The Monastery of the Great Lavra.* →

ἄρι ν ϑ

ΑΙΝΕΙΤΕΙΟΝ ΕΝ ΨΑΛΤΗΡΙΩ ΚΑΘΑΡΩ ΑΙΝΕΙΤΟΝ ΕΝ ΧΟΡΔΑΙϹ

Κ ΥΜΒΑΛ ΟΙϹ

ΜΑΝΑΗΛΙΟΝ   ΕΙϹΙΩΝ   ΘΕΟΔΟΛΟϹ   Ο ΑΓΙΟϹ ΧΑΡΑΛΟϹ   Ο ΑΓΙ

ΧϹ   Ο ΑΓ ΚΟϹΜΑϹ

THE MONASTERY OF VATOPEDI

The monastery was founded shortly after A.D. 972, possibly on the site of the ancient town of Dion, by Athanasios, Nikolaos and Antonios of Adrianoupolis. The monastery owes its name to the flora of the surrounding area which consists of dense groups of shrubs *(vatos* = shrub, *pedion* = plain, ground). It celebrates the feast of the Annunciation and is the second ranking monastery of the Athonite State. It was here, close by the monastery, in 1743, that the "Athonite School" was established, at which taught enlightened teachers of the Nation. The mosaic icons on the walls of the *katholikon* of the monastery (Annunciation - Saint Nikolaos) convey the spiritual and artistic regeneration of the Palaiologoi as formulated in Constantinople, while parts of the painted decoration of the exonarthex of the same church, untouched by later hands, reflect the form that regeneration took in Thessalonike (Panselinos School).

THE MONASTERY OF IVERON

Dedicated to the Dormition of the Virgin, this monastery, the third in the hierarchy, was founded by Ioannis Tornikios and the Iberians (Georgians) Georgios and Euthymios in the last quarter of the 10th century A.D. The Palaiologoi, the princes of Iberia and the Serb kral Stephen Dušan all endowed the monastery with new buildings. It was also given support by many of the patriarchs, mainly during the Ottoman occupation.

392. *View of the large Monastery of Vatopedi from the sea.*

393. *General view of the Monastery of Iveron from the sea.*

394. *The Virgin and Child between the archangels Michael and Gabriel, in the Monastery of Vatopedi (cod. 762, fol. 17a).*

395. *The miracle-working icon of the Virgin Portaitissa in the Monastery of Iveron.*

THE MONASTERY OF CHELANDARI

Dedicated to the Presentation of the Virgin in the Temple, and fourth in the hierarchy, the monastery was founded, as a result of a chrysobull issued by Alexios III Komnenos (A.D. 1198), on the ruins of an earlier monastery of the same name which existed here already before A.D. 1015.

Its founder was saint Sabbas (secular name Rastko) with the support of his father the King of Serbia, Stefan Nemanja, the later monk Symeon. The monastery received fabulous wealth and gifts from the Serb rulers in the 14th century and from the Russian tzars and the voivods of the Danubian principalities under the Ottoman occupation. It made a great contribution to the spiritual awakening of the Serbian people. The high quality of the wall-paintings in the katholikon of the monastery links them with the artistic production of Thessalonike during the first decades of the 14th century and particularly - according to one view - with the activity of the anonymous painter who worked on the church of Saint Nikolaos Orphanos in Thessalonike.

THE MONASTERY OF DIONYSIOU

This, the fifth monastery in the hierarchy, is dedicated to the Birth of Ioannis the Baptist. It was founded by saint Dionysios from Koresos near Kastoria in the period A.D. 1370-74. The great Alexios III Komnenos, Emperor of Trebizond, made large sums of money available to bring the building works to completion. The monastery was enlarged through grants by the Palaiologoi and, after the fall of Constantinople, by various rulers of the Danubian principalities.

396. *View of the interior of the Monastery of Chelandari, with the katholikon and the font.*

397. *View of the Monastery of Dionysiou from the south-west.*

398. *Christ Pantokrator. 13th century icon in the sacristy of the Monastery of Chelandari.*

399. *Chrysobull of the emperor Alexios III Komnenos, in the Monastery of Dionysiou.*

402

400. *Interior of the Monastery of Koutloumousiou with the font and part of the katholikon and the altar.*

401. *View of the Monastery of the Pantokrator from the sea to the north.*

402. *Sixteenth century icon with a scene of the Transfiguration of Christ, from the Monastery of the Pantokrator.*

THE MONASTERY OF KOUTLOUMOUSIOU

Dedicated to the Transfiguration of the Saviour, this monastery, the sixth in the hierarchy, was probably erected in the first half of the 12th century A.D., according to a document dating from A.D. 1169. Its founder was probably a monk from Africa *(koutloumous* = the saint from Ethiopia). Decimated by the raids of the Catalans, it found a fervent supporter and generous patron in the person of Ioannis Vladislav, Prince of Hungro-Wallachia (second half of the 14th century). The monastery acquired prestige and power through its designation as a patriarchal establishment (A.D. 1393), its annexation of the Monastery of Alypios (A.D. 1428) and gifts from many emperors.

In A.D. 1497 it was destroyed by a great fire, and again in A.D. 1767 and A.D. 1870. It was supported in its times of trial by laymen and clerics from many parts of the Orthodox Christian world who made generous contributions.

THE MONASTERY OF PANTOKRATOR

Seventh in rank, and dedicated to the Transfiguration of the Saviour, the monastery was founded by the brothers Ioannis and Alexios Strategopoulous. The latter served as the "great camp-commander" of Michael VIII Palaiologos and helped to recapture Constantinople in A.D. 1261. Amongst those who made bequests and donations to the monastery are mentioned Ioannis V Palaiologos, Katherine II of Russia and the princes of the Danubian principalities. It suffered extensive damage from the fires of A.D. 1773 and 1948.

THE MONASTERY OF XEROPOTAMOU

The monastery is dedicated to the memory of the Forty Martyrs and is eighth in the hierarchy. According to tradition it was founded by the empress Pulcheria (A.D. 450-457). It is more likely however that it was founded by hosios Pavlos Xeropotamenos, a rival of saint Athanasios, shortly after monks first came to the Great Lavra. Amongst the benefactors of the monastery were the Palaiologoi and the kings of Serbia and, during the Tourkokratia, sultan Selim I. The monastery suffered badly from raids and fires in the 16th and 17th centuries A.D., and modern times have not been particularly kind to it.

THE MONASTERY OF ZOGRAPHOU

According to tradition the founders of this monastery, which is ninth in the hierarchy and is dedicated to saint Georgios, were the brothers Ioannis, Moses and Aaron from Ochrid (in the time of Leon VI the Wise, A.D. 880-912). However, the text of the *First Typikon* makes it clear that the monastery already existed in the 10th century A.D. Concern for its well-being was shown by the Palaiologoi (Michael VIII, Andronikos II and Ioannis V) and by many of the rulers of Hungro-Wallachia.

406

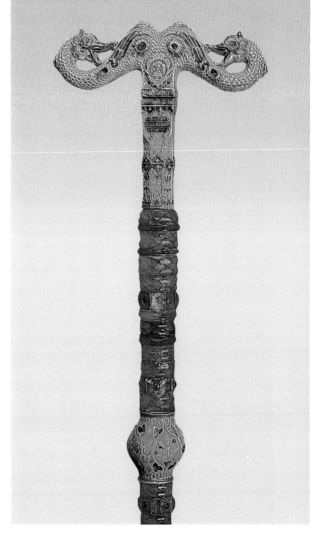

403. *View of the Monastery of Xeropotamou from the south-west.*

404. *Exterior view of the Monastery of Zographou.*

405. *One of the many archbishop's mitres preserved in the sacristies of the monasteries on Mount Athos.*

406. *Archbishop's crozier of electrum, one of the treasures in the Monastery of Xeropotamou.*

THE MONASTERY OF DOCHEIARIOU

Dedicated originally to saint Nikolaos Myron, and later to the Archangels Michael and Gabriel, the monastery, which is tenth in the hierarchy, was founded, according to tradition, in the second half of the 10th century A.D. by saint Euthymios, fellow-monk and pupil of saint Athanasios. In times of hardship, it was supported by Ioannis V Palaiologos and the king of Serbia Stefan IV. Gifts were bestowed upon it in later periods by the princes of Moldavia and Wallachia. In 1821 the monastery was abandoned and lost almost all its property.

THE MONASTERY OF KARAKALOU

According to the generally accepted view, a small monastery, founded by a monk named Karakalas at the beginning of the 11th century A.D. probably formed the basis for the later building complex on the site. The monastery is dedicated to the memory of the Apostles Peter and Paul, and occupies eleventh place in the hierarchy. Like the majority of the monasteries on Mount Athos, this one too has known difficult times (piratical raids, plundering by Latin soldiers, the expropriation of its estates by the Turks) though it has also experienced periods of prosperity (gifts by emperors and patriarchs, the princes of Wallachia and the kings of Iberia). The monastery played a leading role in the Greek struggle for liberation and supported the chieftain Tsamis Karatasos (A.D. 1854).

407. Exterior view of the Monastery of Docheiariou.

408. Exterior view of the Monastery of Karakalou.

409. The famous lavra of saint Savvas in Palestine, illuminated capital K. From the Proskynetarion (book of pilgrimage) of the Holy Land in the library of the Monastery of Docheiariou.

410. Saint Mark the Evangelist (cod. 272, fol. 206b), from the Monastery of Karakalou, 18th century.

412

THE MONASTERY OF PHILOTHEOU

The monastery is twelfth in hierarchy and dedicated to the Annunciation. According to tradition it was founded on the site of an ancient Asklepieion, and is mentioned for the first time in a document of A.D. 1015. However, it seems to have been built (end of the 10th century) by hosios Philotheos, a contemporary of saint Athanasios. The monastery received benefactions from the Emperor Nikephoros Botaneiates (A.D. 1078-1081), the two Andronikoi Palaiologoi and the Serbian kral Stephen Dušan. During the period of the Ottoman occupation it was aided by the tzar of Russia Michael (A.D. 1641) and the princes of Wallachia (Gregore Gikas A.D. 1734, etc.). The great fire of A.D. 1871 is one of the natural disasters that have befallen the monastery, while the sojourn there of Kosmas Aitolos is regarded as a high-point in the history of monasticism.

THE MONASTERY OF SAINT PAUL

Now dedicated to the Presentation of Christ, the monastery earlier honoured the Saviour, the Virgin and saint Georgios. Ranking fourteenth in the hierarchy, it owes its foundation, to the 8th/9th centuries A.D., according to tradition. The monastery is probably, however, a foundation of Pavlos Xeropotamenos in the second half of the 10th century A.D. The monastery of Saint Paul only acquired a permanent place amongst the other Athonite monasteries after A.D. 1370, thanks to the intervention of the Serb monks Gerasimos Radonia and Antonios Pegases. Early in the 14th century the Palaiologoi and the kings of Serbia extended the complex, and after the Fall of the Byzantine Empire, the Christian sultana Mara, Greek and Romanian princes of the Danubian principalities made funds available for renovation and additional building. It was deserted at the time of the War of Independence but finally recovered, thanks to donations by the Russian tzars.

411. The katholikon of the Monastery of Philotheou with the consecration font.

412. General view of the Monastery of Saint Paul in the foothills of Mount Athos.

413. Wooden cross decorated with miniatures, in the Monastery of Saint Paul. 13th century.

414. Scene of Christ Enthroned with the Virgin and Saint John the Evangelist. Stained glass in the Monastery of Saint Paul. 13th-14th centuries.

413

414

416

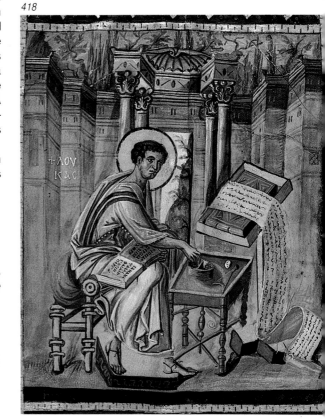

THE MONASTERY OF SIMONOPETRA

The foundation of the monastery, which is dedicated to the Birth of Christ, is owed to hosios Simon, a hermit on the Holy Mountain in the middle of the 14th century A.D. The monastery owes its name to its founder and to the rocky area in which the seven-storey complex rises *(petra-rock)*. The site received benefactions and gifts from the Serb kral Ioannis Ugliesa (A.D. 1364) and also from the entire community of active monks, who used the money that they collected to mitigate the effects of adversity (fires of 1580, 1626 and 1891) and to repair damages and losses. The monastery occupies thirteenth position in the hierarchy.

THE MONASTERY OF STAVRONIKITA

The monastery was presumably built in the 10th century A.D. and was one of the first to be founded in the early years of organised monastic life on Athos. It owes its name, according to one version, to the combination of the names of the monks Stavros and Niketas, who had previously lived as hermits in the area. The monastery followed the historical fluctuations of Mount Athos and suffered badly during the period of Frankish rule, to the extent that it was abandoned and razed to the ground by a series of destructive fires (A.D. 1607, 1741, 1864, 1874, 1879); it was also, however, the object of benefactions and a wide variety of gifts by patriarchs, elders of the communities, princes of Wallachia and others. A decisive role in the general renewal of the monastery was played by Gregorios Giromereiatis (first half of the 16th century A.D.).

The monastery occupies fifteenth position in the hierarchy. The Cretan painter Theophanes worked there (A.D. 1546).

415. *View of the Monastery of Simonopetra from the west. The summit of Mount Athos can be seen in the background.*

416. *View of the Monastery of Stavronikita from the east.*

417. *The Virgin and the Anapeson (cod. 45, fol. 12a) in the Monastery of Stavronikita. 14th century.*

418. *Saint Luke the Evangelist (cod. 43, fol. 12b)in the Monastery of Stavronikita. 10th century.*

419

420

THE MONASTERY OF XENOPHONTOS

Ranking sixteenth, the monastery was founded in the 10th century by hosios Xenophon, according to tradition. It is mentioned in a document of A.D. 1083. As with the other monasteries on Mount Athos, attempts were made to repair the effects of plundering, piratical raids, fires, and ravaging by Franks, Catalans and Turks, first by the Byzantine emperors, and then by the princes of the Danubian principalities, archimandrites, archbishops and abbots. The monastery honours saint Georgios.

THE MONASTERY OF GREGORIOU

Dedicated to the memory of saint Nikolaos, the monastery was founded during the 14th century (in the time of Ioannis Palaiologos 1341-1391) by saint Gregorios the Younger or by his namesake and teacher Gregorios Sinaitis.

It occupies seventeenth place in the hierarchy. During the 15th and 16th centuries A.D. it was destroyed by raids, and in the following century (A.D. 1761) by fire. Amongst its benefactors and restorers may be counted the princes of Moldavia, a large number of Phanariotes, archbishops of Hungro-Wallachia, and even Sultans.

421

422

419. View of the Monastery of Xenophontos from the sea.

420. View of the Monastery of Gregoriou from the south-west.

421. Miniature icon of steatite with a scene of the Transfiguration of Christ, in the Monastery of Xenophontos. 12th century.

422. Saint Matthew the Evangelist (cod. 2m, fol. 8b), from the Monastery of Gregoriou. 13th century.

423

424

THE MONASTERY OF ESPHIGMENOU

Eighteenth in the hierarchy, the monastery is dedicated to the Ascension of the Lord. It is mentioned officially for the first time in a document of A.D. 1016, though tradition has it that it was a foundation of Pulcheria, sister of the emperor Theodosius II. The name derives either from a founder monk, who was girded "with a tight rope" *(schoinioi sphinktoi)* or from the site on which the monastery is built ("shut in amongst three small mountains by the shore"). Contributions were made to the prosperity of the monastery by Ioannis V Palaiologos, the king of Serbia Stefan IV and, after the capture of Byzantine Empire, the tzar of Russia Alexios, the archbishops of Melenikon and Thessalonike, and the princes of Moldavia and Wallachia.

THE MONASTERY OF SAINT PANTELEIMON

Nineteenth in the hierarchy, the monastery honours the name of saint Panteleimon of Thessalonike. It dates from A.D. 1765 on its present site and owes its construction to contributions by Skarlatos Kallimaches, the prince of Moldo-Wallachia. It earlier stood on a site that is still called "Paliomonastero", ("Old Monastery"), founded in the 11th century by monks who came to the Holy Mountain from Russia.

THE MONASTERY OF KONSTAMONITOU OR KASTAMONITOU

Tradition has it that the monastery was a foundation of the 4th century A.D., and indeed one by Constantine the Great - whence its name. Another version records as its founder a monk from Kastamoni in Asia Minor. The first mention of the monastery, however, occurs in an 11th century A.D. document. Amongst its benefactors and donors may be counted the Serb prince Georgios Brancowicz and Princess Anna Philanthropini. Aid was also provided in the form of considerable sums of money to help it in the troubles that came with subjection to the Turks by Vasiliki, wife of Ali Pasha of Ioannina.

423. General view of the Monastery of Esphigmenou from the west.

424. Exterior view of the Monastery of Saint Panteleimon with its multi-storey annexes by the sea.

425. Exterior view of part of the Monastery of Konstamonitou.

425

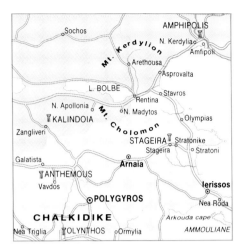

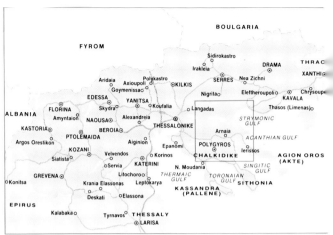

RENTINA
and its region

426

HISTORICAL REVIEW
AND ARCHAEOLOGICAL SITE

For several years the Polytechnic School of the University of Thessalonike, in the person of the indefatigable Professor N. Moutsopoulos, has been bringing to light the ruins of an imposing fortress and the surrounding settlement on the site of Rentina. The fortress is located not far from where research locates ancient Arethousa, the Mygdonian city in which king Archelaos entertained Euripides, and occupies a site perfectly placed to control the Via Egnatia before this wanders off amongst the green, rocky passes that link lake Bolbe with the gulf of the Strymon river. The site - the Macedonian Tempe, as it has well been called - has remains dating from the Stone Age, though it enters the stage of history in the period of Justinian I, with a thracian past, and sherds of ancient Greek vases dating from the Classical, Hellenistic and Roman periods behind it. Behind it, too, the blonde princesses of legend, sometimes committing suicide by flinging themselves from the highest tower so as to avoid fall-

426. The medieval castle at Rentina.

330

427. Landscape
at Rentina.

ing into the hands of some pagan despot, and sometimes escaping dishonour by means of a secret underground passage; behind it, too, a temple in the name of Artemis (Artemision) and a fortification work probably of late Roman date.

With the river Richios flowing at the bottom of the hill and the Via Egnatia and its predecessor a short distance away to transport enemies and friends alike, the fortress - Pyrgoudia in popular parlance - probably had, at its zenith, more than 400 houses (some of which were two-storey), three temples, a stout, defensive enceinte with towers, subterranean cisterns, and bath-houses.

From about the beginning of the 10th century A.D., when the seat of the bishopric of Lete was transferred here and called "Lete and Rentine" the *mutatio Peripidis* (a station for changing (horses) of Euripides?) of the *tabula Peutingeria-*

na (a 13th century portolano) seems to have thrived as a centre of the carrying trade, as a township offering security, and as a staging post between Thessalonike and Constantinople and also Mount Athos. Its prosperity is attested by the rich grave offerings in the tombs, the ecclesiastical and secular buildings, the strengthening of the fortifications, and the testimony of the written sources in the monastic archives - from the middle-Byzantine to the Palaiologan periods.

The Turks do not seem to have captured the fortress in their furious advance, for no traces of destruction have been observed. Forgotten by time, and emptied of its inhabitants, who gradually abandoned it, the site filled with oak trees. Became a forest. Became a myth. A legend for the travellers. Until the archaeologist's spade came to restore history to its cradle.

EAST MACEDONIA

East Macedonia, between the southern reaches of the Strymon and the Nestos, has remains of habitation dating from the Middle Neolithic Period (Dikili-Tas, Sitagroi, the region of Serrhai) and the Bronze Age (Pentapolis near Serrhai, the settlement of Skala Soteros on Thasos, the mouth of the Strymon, Potamoi and Exochi near Drama, Kastri on Thasos), and of cemeteries and settlements dating from the Iron Age (Drama industrial zone, Amphipolis, Stathmos of Angista, Toumba at Nikisiani), entered the historical period as the promised land for the Greeks of the South. During the period of the great migrations and of colonisation (8th century B.C.), the gold-bearing heights of mount Pangaion, the rich plains of the Strymon, and the enchanting shores of the northern Aegean welcomed, admittedly not always in a friendly fashion, the ships of the Andrians and the Parians - and in the Classical period those of the Athenians - and were filled with bustling trading-posts and flourishing colonies: Thasos, Argilos, Eion, Oisyme, Krenides, Neapolis, Galepsos and Amphipolis, bastions of Hellenism on the fringes of the thracian world. Cities that evolved into dynamic cultural centres, commercially active in the productive and retail sectors.

After the turbulent events of the Peloponnesian War, which brought the confrontation between Athens and Sparta to the gates of Amphipolis (422 B.C.), and after a long period of uncertainty, the region passed into the hands of the forceful king of Macedonia, Philip II (357 B.C.) and was incorporated into the state of the Temenids, whose destiny it followed thereafter. Amphipolis evolved into one of the most vital ports in the area throughout the whole of the Hellenistic period, and Krenides was reinforced with colonists and its name changed to Philippoi. These two developments, combined with the generally intense and continuous relations between the royal dynasty (Temenids and Antigonids) and the area, contributed to the general development of East Macedonia (Amphipolis, Nikisiani, Philippoi, Drama, Angista), where the wealth of finds from settlements, organised cemeteries and isolated funerary monuments rivals that of Lower Macedonia. With the passage of time the local population - the Bisaltai, the Sintoi,

the Odomantes and the Edonoi - despite the stout resistance they offered to the Macedonians, were assimilated and Hellenised. In 168-167 B.C., after Roman arms had prevailed, this part of Macedonia formed the first of the four administrative-geographical divisions *(merides)* into which the country was divided.

Under the Roman republic Lower Macedonia had to wait for the sole rule of Augustus before it saw the longed-for *pax Romana,* of which it was deprived by barbarian raids from the north (Skordiskoi, Bessoi - 110 B.C.), the invasion of the armies of Mithridates VI, king of Pontus (93-87 B.C.), and above all by the confrontation at Philippoi (42 B.C.) between Brutus and Octavian and Mark Antony. Meanwhile, under the new state of affairs, the situation in East Macedonia remained the same on general lines, though the economic, demographic and cultural development of the area was affected by the construction of the Via Egnatia and the settlement of Roman colonists (Philippoi) and Italian merchants (Amphipolis). Many ancient cities and institutions and the names of their inhabitants strongly reflected the Hellenistic tradition [Serrhai/Sirra, Skotousa (Siderokastro?), Gazoros, Paroikopolis (Sandanski), Herakleia Sintike (Neo Petritsi?), Verge] and others, that either now make their first appearance in the sources or appear for the first time with the status of city, retained their Greek speech and their national identity even under Roman suzerainty, eventually becoming repositories of the Greek spirit in a primarily thracian-dominated region. The cities of East Macedonia assimilated and, through their superior strength, at the same time Hellenised the heterogeneous cultural elements and alien religious dogmas that they welcomed into their ranks (Thracian substratum, Roman customs and morals, Christian/Judaic theosophy, Egyptian mysticism), and faced the early Christian centuries, after the administrative reforms of Diocletian and Constantine the Great, in fear of Gothic raids (A.D. 473-483) and in terror of the plundering invasions by hordes of Huns (A.D. 540). It was now that Philippoi - the first Christian centre on European soil -came under threat. Now it was, too, that Paroikopolis was struck down. It was in these troubled years (6th-7th centuries A.D.) that the Rynchinoi settled in the region between lake Bolbe and the Strymonic gulf and the Strymonites near the Strymon river and devoted themselves to piratical raids.

The Byzantine intervention, however, was as effective as it was decisive: military enterprises throughout the entire 7th century A.D. were confined to the region of the Strymon, and were designed to secure the road network between Constantinople and Thessalonike. Particularly at a time when, with the creation in A.D. 680-681 of an independent state, the Bulgars appeared on the scene in a manner very threatening for the affairs of the Byzantine Empire. Events unfolded with great speed - A.D. 789 murder of the *strategos* of Thrace, A.D. 809 attack on consignment of money in the region of the Strymon - and, despite a brief peace, led to a decisive breach between tsar Samuel and Basil II - a breach that bathed both kingdoms in blood (A.D. 989-1014). The region between the Strymon and the Nestos river, however, did not for long enjoy the peace promised to it by the military successes of the Byzantines: revolts by eminent militarians (G. Maniakes: A.D. 1042), invasions by western armies (Normans: A.D. 1185), and the mobilisation and invasions of the Bulgars (A.D. 1195) all threatened the region of Amphipolis, desolated Serrhai and threw mount Pangaion into turmoil.

The Fourth Crusade, which radically transformed the Balkans (A.D. 1204), assigned East Macedonia to the Frankish Kingdom of Thessalonike, only to convert it almost immediately after the conquest, along with Thrace, into a battle field between the Franks, the Bulgarians and the Byzantines. In the maelstrom of events, Serrhai passed within a few years from the hands of the Latins into the power of the Bulgarian tzar Ioannitzes (A.D. 1205), and was then freed by Theodore Komnenos Doukas Angelos (A.D. 1221), after which it was captured by Ioannis Asen II (A.D. 1230). Finally, in A.D. 1246, it reverted to the empire of Nicaea under Ioannis III Vatatzes.

The Turks, who crossed to the shores of Europe (A.D. 1355) had no difficulty in advancing to the west and implementing their ambitious designs: completely devastated by the war between the two Andronikoi Palaiologoi, the invasion of the Serbs and the dynastic confrontation between Ioannis Kantakouzenos and Ioannis V Palaiologos, the country was easy prey for the bellicose conqueror. After A.D. 1389, a large number of Yürüks, mainly farmers and shepherds, settled in the rich region of Serrhai, which had first seen the crescent moon only six years earlier. In A.D. 1391, Christoupolis (Kavala) fell, to be plunged almost immediately into the lamentation for the *paidomazoma* (child-levy), while Thasos, a possession of the Gattilusi of Genoa, was given by sultan Mehmed II as a fief to his father-in-law Demetrios Palaiologos, the former despot of the Peloponnese (A.D. 1460). Angiottelo, who travelled through the country as a prisoner of war in A.D. 1470 and describes with naive wonderment the ancient ruins at Philippoi - vigilant witnesses of the past - extols the ruins of Christoupolis with its once beautiful orchards of fruit trees - now the lair of fearsome robbers and corsairs.

The situation following the shock of the conquest, however, improved in time, as possessions were consolidated, time healed wounds and life adjusted to its destiny. In the middle of the 16th century A.D., Serrhai was a flourishing city with a significant community of Jewish merchants, settled there by Süleyman I the Magnificent (A.D.1520-1566), who brought them from Buda and Pest. Kavala (Christoupolis) was now founded (A.D. 1527 or 1528) by disenchanted Greeks, who deserted the inhospitable mountains - a refuge during the early years of slavery - and swiftly developed into an important port. Nigrita and Syrpa were now created. Ships from Ragusa, Chios, Venice and Egypt sailed up the Strymon and made their merchandise available to the local inhabitants, taking cargoes of wheat, hides and wool on the return voyage. Bulgarian reapers and builders met the increased demands of production in farming and building in the countryside around Kavala and on Thasos. Inns and warehouses of merchandise in the cities, lead-roofed mosques and *imaretia* (poor-houses), *mendresedes* (church-schools), monumental aqueducts, fortresses and *archontika* (mansions) reveal the economic prosperity characteristic of the second half of the 16th century, a prosperity surveyed with a fierce eye by the Janissaries and exploited through heavy taxes by the central authority.

In the ruins of Philippoi - known to the Turks as Philippoijik - amongst which roamed the legend of Alexander, in the name of Kavala, which the false etymology of popular wisdom connected with Boukephala, and in the debris of fortresses and churches, the past daily revived memories that stained the recollection with blood and made slavery unbearable. Slavery, which wealthy *Romioi* (Greeks) such as the "hyper-wealthy" Patroulas of Serrhai (A.D. 1598), or anonymous laymen and clerics - new martyrs of the nation -, were called upon to pay for with their lives and their properties; slavery which Greeks in exile in Vienna, Brasov, Buda and Pest, attempted to mitigate by gifts and contributions,supporting schools,establishing libraries, giving support to communities and caring for the victims of injustice.

And as the 16th century, with its persecutions and piratical raids reaching as far as the hinterland of Kavala, gave way to the 17th - a century marked both by desolation and by attempts at reconstruction - Drama, thanks to its fertile plain, was transformed into a dynamic centre of cotton-production, of the weaving of linen cloths and of rice. Serrhai, with its Byzantine fort, its fine inns, its bezesten, its poor-houses and its rich gardens, became an exclusive supplier to Arabia and Persia of kerchiefs and bath-wraps made by Christian women. At Orphani -a modern settlement on the site of Chrysoupolis, next to the Strymon - merchant vessels loaded the fruits of the labour of the inhabitants of the region (mainly wheat). The consuls and vice-consuls of the Great Powers who settled in Kavala or, with their base in Thessalonike, travelled throughout East Macedonia in the 18th and the beginning of the 19th centuries A.D., describe the bazaar at Nigrita with its dyer's workshops, and gold- and bronze-smiths; refer to the superb quality cotton of Zichna, which, spun into thread, travelled to Hungary and Poland; speak with admiration of Kavala, where commercial establishments organised the export of tobacco and oil and state functionaries oversaw the enshipment of iron bullets made in Pravista; allude, finally, to Melenikon with its thirty tanneries, its Greek press and its notable library. At the end of the 18th century, Thasos possessed vast tracts of olive-trees, and produced excellent honey, and its dense forests were famous for their timber for ship-building, while thasian marble travelled to the mainland opposite, where it embellished the *archontika* (mansions) of the rising nobility.

The Serbian uprising at the beginning of the 19th century rekindled Macedonian dreams of freedom. What matter if out of fear of rebellion, the Greeks of Serrhai were disarmed: Nikotsaras, a fiery armatole and daring ideologue, carried the torch of national regeneration to Achinos and Zichna (A.D. 1807), and the Turks were driven forcibly back on Potos on Thasos (A.D. 1821). What matter if Albanian raiders devastated the region around Serrhai, taking advantage of the revolutionary ferment, and plundered the *kaza* of Petric and that of Siderokastro (A.D. 1829): the

foundation of the independent modern Greek state (A.D. 1830) and the appointment of a Greek consul to Thessalonike (A.D. 1835) and consular residences at Kavala and on Thasos strengthened the hopes of the enslaved Greeks and put flesh on the yearnings of those in exile and refugees. Yearnings that remained unfulfilled for at least half a century. The undiscriminating romanticism of the policy of Athens during the decade 1840 to 1850, with its painful consequences for Greek affairs, the pro-Slav position adopted by the Russians on the morrow of the Crimean War, and the emergence of Bulgarian nationalism and the attempts to penetrate and settle Slav elements in Greek-speaking areas (Melenikon, Nevrokop, Stromnitsa) were all obstacles to any attempts at intervention by free Greece, strangling at birth any movement towards insurrection, and disarming courage. The Macedonians, faced with Turkish oppression, unprotected in the face of Bulgarian expansionism and Serbian vacillation, enlisted, with the support of the Greek Government the oldest ally of Hellenism, education, and erected monuments of an immortal civilization in villages and cities-primary schools, "boys" and girls" secondary schools and other educational institutions. They studied in the secret schools of communication and moral resistance. To pass, after the first unsuccessful attempts (1897), from the waiting room into the first line of events, hand in hand with the military corps of Cretans and Peloponnesians. The Greek armies that pressed forward victoriously to Drama, Serrhai and Kavala, defeating the Turkish forces and the Bulgarian battalions, which were superior in strength and weaponry, bought East Macedonia back into the bosom of Hellenism at the end of the Balkan Wars (1912-13). And in person brought the prize of the "Macedonian Struggle" to the sorely tried inhabitants. The Treaty of Bucharest (1913) completed a great circle in the history of Macedonia that had opened in the 14th century A.D. with the conquest of the area by the Turks, and the country now moved on to new achievements.

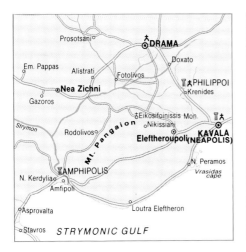

AMPHIPOLIS
and its region

428

HISTORICAL REVIEW

Founded by the Athenians in 437 B.C., under the leadership of Hagnon, son of Nikias, Amphipolis developed into one of the most important cities of the Macedonian north. Built on the site of the thracian township of Ennea Hodoi ("Nine Ways") whose past reached back to the prehistoric period, it quickly became the most populous centre in the area, standing as it did at the intersections of basic road arteries and controlling the navigable Strymon and the nearby gold mines of mount Pangaion, from which it also exploited timber for ship-building.

The city had a heterogenous population, with Ionians from the neighbouring regions, Thracians, and other foreigners swiftly being added to the Athenian colonists; it was a rich city standing on a strategic site and played a very important role during the fierce confrontation between its mother city, Athens, and the Spartans (422 B.C.). In 357 B.C. it passed into the hands of Philip II and became one of the most powerful and sensitive centres in his kingdom, with many Macedonians settling there: it was from Amphipolis that the army of Alexander III the Great set forth for the Asian miracle and it was here that his wife Roxane and son Alexander IV were exiled. It was at this city, finally, that Philip V died.

At Amphipolis, after the battle of Pydna (168 B.C.), Aemilius Paulus, proclaimed the new re-

428. The Gymnasium complex from the east.

gime for Macedonia, according to which the city was made capital of the first of the four administrative-economic units *(merides),* into which the old kingdom was divided. Granted the status of *Civitas libera* (free city) on the morrow of the victory by the triumvirate at Philippoi (42 B.C.), it enjoyed all the privileges - autonomy etc. - allowed to it by Roman sovereignty, and indeed issued coins commemorating the event. Half a century earlier (87/86 B.C.), the city had been captured by Taxilles, general of Mithridates VI, in the attempt by the King of Pontus to outflank the forces of Sulla. Pompey had also taken refuge there after the defeat at Pharsalos (48 B.C.) in his despairing efforts to secure resources to continue his struggle against Julius Caesar. Later too, before the naval battle at Actium (31 B.C.), Mark Antony turned to Amphipolis as the base for his fleet for the impending clash with Octavian.

Between roughly the beginning and the middle of the 1st century B.C., the city appears to have been destroyed by revolted Thracian tribes, though not completely, since in A.D. 50, it was visited by saint Paul the Apostle. With Augustus on the throne of the Roman empire, Am-

phipolis experienced a new period of prosperity, which continued throughout the three first centuries of the Christian era and is attested not only by the rich coinage of the city, but also by inscriptions and building activity.

THE ARCHAEOLOGICAL SITE

THE WALLS

There were two defensive enceintes in the Classical period, an outer one - the "long wall" - about 7,500 m. long, and an inner one 2,200 m. long, the first enclosing the broader area of the city and the second the main urban centre. Square and round towers, gates, bastions built with very careful masonry of local poros, and an ingeniously conceived drainage system to lead. off the rain water give this defensive structure, which in some places is still preserved to height of 7-8 m., a monumental character. The locating of the wooden infrastructure (stakes) of the bridge over the Strymon river, known from the period of Thucydides, is a unique discovery.

THE CITY

There are considerable gaps in our knowledge of the town-plan of the city, for the picture offered by those ruins that have been excavated is still a fragmentary one. It is enriched, however, by detailed observations of the street network (paved streets) and the decoration of the buildings (wall-paintings, mosaic floors), and also by the study of the plans of the houses; these are of the familiar type with rooms arranged around an open, square courtyard with a well and a water-supply system (house of the 4th century B.C. at the west edge of the acropolis, house in the south part of the city, dating from the 2nd century B.C.).

429

429. The two sides of a tetradrachm issued by Amphipolis. On the obverse Apollo and on the reverse a torch, ca. 390-357 B.C. Berlin, Münzkabinett.

430. Part of the city fortifications.

431. Plan of the Gymnasium complex at Amphipolis.

431

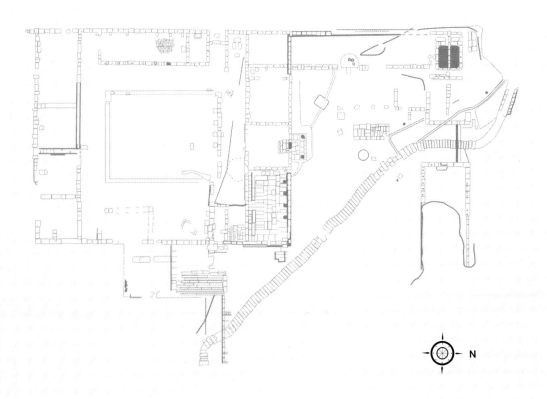

 N

433

THE SANCTUARIES

A number of sanctuaries have been located at various points of the vast area occupied by Amphipolis, with no apparent relation between them; they include the small sanctuary of the Muse Clio (first half of the 4th century B.C.) and sanctuaries devoted to the cult of the eastern and Egyptian deities, Cybele and Attis. The large number of inscriptions and the literary sources afford evidence for the existence of sanctuaries in honour of Asklepios, Athena, the Dioskouroi, and Herakles. A special place amongst the gods worshipped was occupied by Artemis Tauropolos and the river Strymon, depictions of which appear on the coins of the city from as early as the Hellenistic period. A rectangular building outside the north section of the wall, with a well, a large number of vases (hydriai and kernoi) and ceramic figurines, mainly of women, has been considered a Thesmophorion, though it may also be a Nymphaion.

THE GYMNASIUM

Excavations in recent years have brought to light the Gymnasium of the city to the south-east of the hill of the acropolis and within the defensive enceinte, which was built of poros blocks, with careful opus reticulatum in some places and isodomic masonry in others, perhaps at the same time as the east wall. The building, which is rectangular in plan and measures 46.80 m. x 36.10 m., appears to have been destroyed by fire at the beginning of the 1st century B.C., presumably a victim of the upheavals that beset Macedonia at this period (raids by Thracian tribes, invasion by the armies of Mithridates VI).

Repaired at the beginning of the Roman Empire or perhaps a little earlier, it again educated

432. The Gymnasium complex from the north.

433. The large north-east bathing room of the palaestra.

434. The interior courtyard of the palaestra from the north, Roman propylon.

434

the youth of Amphipolis in "the fine and the good" though it did not function beyond the middle of the 1st century A.D. In its ruins have been found some very important inscriptions, including an "ephebic law", equal in importance to the "gymnasiarchal law" of Beroia.

The Gymnasium of Amphipolis, built on the model of the Classical/Hellenistic house, is articulated around a central peristyle courtyard (dimensions 20.60 m. x 15.40 m.), on the four sides of which are stoas and other, hypostyle rooms to meet the needs of the athletes (palaestra).

The entrance to the Gymnasium, which is 3 m. wide, has been identified in the east wing of the building, beneath later additions, and the west wing diametrically opposite has a tiled semi-circular floor; the function of these wings has not yet been adequately explained, though the suggestion that they should be identified with the Ephebeion is perhaps not improbable.

The overall plan of the rooms in the north and south wings is the same - though the areas are disposed differently: in both cases the largest of the four rooms (the north-east is the best preserved), each of which was equipped with a system of water-supply and drainage, acted as a bathroom for the complex.

435. Wall decoration of a hellenistic house at Amphipolis, with an interesting imitation of pseudo-isodomic masonry.

436. The stone "Lion of Amphipolis", one of the most imposing funerary monuments of the last quarter of the 4th century B.C., stands on a conventionally restored pedestal, on the precise spot where the scattered pieces of it were found (west bank of the Strymon). It has been described by some as a funerary monument for some illustrious personage, though others regard it as a "sema" of military virtue in honour of a distinguished son of Amphipolis. In the latter case, the names have been suggested of Nearchos, Alexander the Great's admiral, Androsthenes and Laomedon.

THE CEMETERY

The majority of the 400 tombs excavated in the area of the cemetery - rock-cut, chamber, and "hut" tombs etc. - have enriched the Kavala Museum with some fine examples of vase-painting, miniature art and gold-work. They have also enriched the history of funerary art with a number of charming grave stelai, several of which have relief scenes.

THE ARCHAEOLOGICAL MUSEUM

The local Museum has been built at the entrance to the modern village of Amphipolis, which is also the entrance to the ancient city. It houses an interesting collection of finds from the excavations of ancient, Early Christian and Byzantine Amphipolis. In keeping with the programme of the Ephorate of Prehistoric and Classical Antiquities of Kavala, the aim of display in the museum is to offer a sketch of the personality of Amphipolis and its region over the time, rather than simply to set out the artistic and other achievements of its inhabitans throughout the centuries.

The gallery on the ground floor has a selection of finds (pottery, weapons and jewellery) from the Prehistoric period of the city followed by an exhibition of finds from Amphipolis in historical times. Sculptures, figurines, pottery, coins, tools, weapons, jewellery, inscriptions - all of them finds from excavations of the public and private buildings of the city and its cemeteries - describe the public and private life of the city. They are accompanied by maps, photographs and reconstructions of monuments, which help visitors to gain a complete picture of the importance of the site.

The elevated mezzanine floor is devoted to occasional special exhibitions relating to particular themes in cultural history of ancient, Early Christian and Byzantine Amphipolis.

437. Clay model of a tragic mask of a woman, from a tomb at Amphipolis. Second half of the 4th century B.C. Amphipolis, Archaeological Museum.

438. Clay female bust, probably of a goddess, from a tomb at Amphipolis. Middle of the 4th century B.C. Amphipolis, Archaeological Museum.

437

439. *Silver ossuary with the gold wreath of olive leaves found inside it. 4th century B.C. Amphipolis, Archaeological Museum.*

441

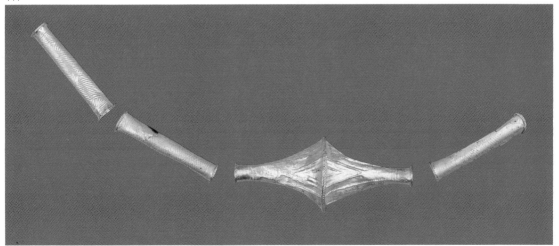

440. Gold wreath of olive leaves from Amphipolis.
4th-3rd centuries B.C. Amphipolis, Archaeological
Museum.

441. Four gold necklace beads. Early 5th century
B.C. Chance find from Ennea Hodoi. Amphipolis,
Archaeological Museum.

442

442. Clay plastic vase:
figurine of a small Eros
asleep on a circular
pedestal, leaning
against an amphora
and holding a torch in
his right hand. From the
cemetery at Amphipolis.
2nd-1st centuries B.C.
Amphipolis,
Archaeological
Museum.

443. Clay figurines of
actors playing the parts
of slaves, from tombs at
Amphipolis. Second half
of the 4th century B.C.
and second half of the
2nd century B.C.
Amphipolis,
Archaeological
Museum.

443

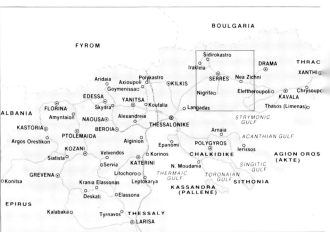

SERRHAI
and its region

444

HISTORICAL REVIEW
AND ARCHAEOLOGICAL SITE

Known from the 4th century B.C. in the literary sources (a reference in the 20th book of the *Philippics* of Theopompos) and from 3rd century B.C. inscriptions, Sirra or Sirai - modern Serrhai - is an excellent example of a Macedonian city with an unbroken life from antiquity to the present day.

Serrhai was a member of the *Macedonian Koinon,* with councillors and agoranomoi, and at the time of Septimius Severus (A.D. 192-211) it occupied an important position amongst the five cities of Odomantike (Verge, Gazoros, Adrianoupolis, Skimbertioi and Sirra) that had organised themselves into a confederacy. Situated on the route from Herakleia Sintike to Amphipolis, the city channelled the products of its plain to the north Aegean via Eion, the port of the largest urban settlement in the area. It was an independent city in late antiquity and is described as the seat of a bishop (5th century A.D.).

A "stout city", "large and wondrous town", "large and rich" and a bastion of the Byzantine Empire in the face of the incursions by the Slavs, Serrhai was reinforced by Nikephoros II Phokas

444. Serrhai, view from the acropolis.

446

445. Small inscription on the west side of the tower of Orestes.

446. Large inscription on the west side of the tower of Orestes.

447. The south side of the old Cathedral at Serrhai.

and was an apple of strife between the Franks of the Fourth Crusade, the Bulgarians, the Serbs and the Turks. The "excellent" city repelled its besiegers (A.D. 976 - Basil II the Bulgar Slayer), was razed to the foundations (A.D. 1206 - the Bulgar tzar Ioannitzes) and came under the control of its implacable foes (1230-45 the Bulgarian tzar Ivan II Asen). It was reduced to an insignificant village by repeated ravaging and destruction before its capture by the Turks (1383), it suffered badly during the confrontation between the Palaiologoi and was occupied by the Serb kral Stephen Dušan (1345-71), to whom was due the erection of the "Tower of Orestes" on the acropolis, known from an inscription.

Evliya Çelebi, who visited the city in the 17th century A.D., when the upheavals caused by the advent of the Ottomans had subsided, describes the walls of Serrhai - already demolished in his time - and registered the population inside and outside the fortress. It is to him and to Cousinéry that are owed the first references to the church of Saint Nikolaos of the castle, a work of the first half of the 14th century restored by private individuals in 1937 though in a way that does not reflect the original plan of the monument.

At the time of the all-powerful rule of Ismael bey (17th to 18th centuries) Serrhai was a not inconsiderable centre: with about 30,000 inhabitants, half of whom were Turks, it stood at the cross-roads of commercial routes linking it with Thessalonike and Kavala, Melenikon and Stromnitsa, and Ano Nevrokop. It belonged administratively to Monastir (Bitola). The city was divided into the old town (Varosi), in which dwelt the Christians and a few Jews, and the new. Wheat, cotton and tobacco brought Serrhai prosperity and economic well-being.

The majority of the thirty-one churches that adorned the city were completely destroyed or left in ruins by the fires of 1949, which reduced three quarters of the old quarter and the main agora to ashes, and of 1913. Today the Archaeological Service has restored to its former glory the "most beautiful of all" cathedral of Saints Theodoroi, built in the end of the 11th and the beginning of the 12th centuries and dedicated by Theodore Komnenos Doukas Angelos despot of Epirus in thanks for the dissolution of the Frankish kingdom of Thessalonike.

Of those monuments devoted to the worship of Allah, mention may be made of the mosque of Ahmet Pasha (1492), of Kotza Mustafa Pasha (1519), and Tzintzirli Mosque.

THE ARCHAEOLOGICAL COLLECTION

The Archaeological Service has housed the portable antiquities, dating from Hellenistic to Byzantine times, of all the sites in the county of Serrhai in the city Bezesten, a spacious, single-storey building of the 15th century A.D. They consist of sculptures and inscriptions, statues and funerary reliefs from Aidonochori (ancient Tragilos), Daphnoudi, Siderokastro, Metalla and Toumba, votive reliefs from Serrhai, a marble couch and marble double-leaf door from a "Macedonian" tomb at Kerdylia, vases, figurines, lamps and strigils from Argilos, Tragilos and Verge, a mosaic portrayal of the Apostle Andrew, dating from the 12th century, and a relief marble icon of Christ Euergetes, dating from the 12th-13th centuries, from the Old Cathedral in Serrhai.

448. Clay figurine of Leda from ancient Tragilos (Aidonochori, near Serrhai). End of the 4th-beginning of the 3rd centuries B.C. Serrhai, Archaeological Museum.
449. The Bezesten (indoor market) of Serrhai, now the home of the Archaeological Museum.

450

450. Votive stele to Artemis Bendis, from Serrhai.
2nd century A.D. Serrhai. Archaeological Museum.

451. Inscribed honorific stele: the city of Siris (?)
honours Tiberius Claudius Flavius, agonothetes at
the festival held in honour of the Roman emperor.
2nd century A.D. Serrhai, Archaeological Museum.

452. Inscribed funerary relief with a male and a
female bust and a Thracian horseman at the top and
two male and a female bust at the bottom, from
Serrhai. 2nd century A.D. Serrhai, Archaeological
Museum.

451

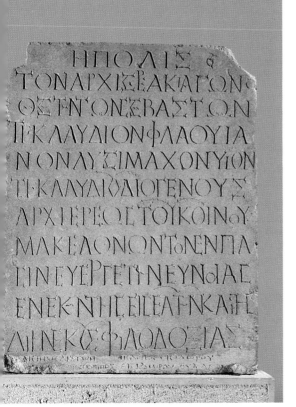

452

454. Part of a mosaic scene with the Apostle Andrew, from the old Cathedral at Serrhai. 12th century. Serrhai, Archaeological Museum.

453. Relief icon of Christ Euergetes, from the old Cathedral at Serrhai. 12th-13th centuries. Serrhai, Archaeological Museum.

453

454

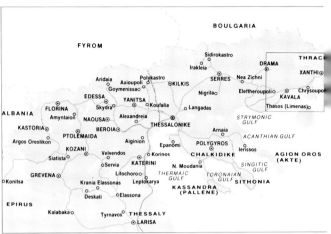

KAVALA (NEAPOLIS)
and its region

455

HISTORICAL REVIEW
AND ARCHAEOLOGICAL SITE

The literary sources reveal neither the name of the mother city of Neapolis nor the year in which the foundation occurred. Modern research however inclines to the view that Neapolis - modern Kavala - was founded about the middle of the 7th century B.C. by residents of Thasos, along with new settlers from Paros, in an attempt to establish themselves on the mainland opposite the island and to repel Thracian raids. A long narrow peninsula projecting from mount Symbolon, the low mountain range at the foot of mount Pangaion - the site of the modern quarter of Panagia - was the strong point from which the new inhabitants contemplated their island, though with their eyes at the same time turned towards the interior of the hostile mainland.

The city swiftly acquired a fortification and an importance that derived from its privileged position on the road leading East, on the one hand and, to its gold-bearing hinterland. The brilliant marble late Roman temple of Parthenos - a Hellenised form of the Thracian god Bendis - standing at the centre of a precinct which has an enclosure wall of large blocks of granite, has an ionic sensitivity and elegant decoration which, together with the numerous dedications from all parts of Aegean world, are irrefutable evidence of the prosperity of the city in the years around 500 B.C. A prosperity also attested by the rich

455. View of Kavala.

358

456. Silver stater of Neapolis with a gorgoneion on the obverse, from Pontolivado, near Kavala. 520-500 B.C. Kavala, Archaeological Museum.

456

458

457. Detail of a clay figurine of a kore, from the sanctuary of Parthenos at Neapolis (modern Kavala). Third quarter of the 6th century B.C. Kavala, Archaeological Museum.

458. Ionic capital from the Late Roman temple of Parthenos at Neapolis (modern Kavala). Kavala, Archaeological Museum.

459. Clay lid of a black-figure lekanis from the sanctuary of Parthenos at Neapolis (modern Kavala). End of the 6th century B.C. Kavala, Archaeological Museum.

460. Decree of the Athenians for the citizens of Neapolis, 356/5 B.C. Depiction of Athena and Parthenos, the patron goddess of Neapolis. Kavala, Archaeological Museum.

coinage of Neapolis with its silver staters and their subdivisions.

After the battle of Plataea and the withdrawal of the Persians, the city became a member of the first Athenian Confederacy and from 454/53 B.C. onwards contributed 1000 drachmas annually to the common treasury. In the Athenian Tribute Lists it is recorded as Neapolis in Thrace. Faithful to the city of Pallas, it resisted the expansionist designs of the Thasians on the Thracian Peraea and patiently endured a siege by the Spartans in 411-410 B.C. A member, too, of the second Athenian Confederacy, it had recourse to the support of the Athenians in the face of the new danger threatening it after the capture of Amphipolis by Philip II. The assistance offered was not effective, however, and the end of its dependence was not long in coming.

About 340 B.C. the city was converted into the port of Philippoi and followed the destiny of the Macedonian kingdom. In the following centuries, its name is mentioned only occasionally: in 189 B.C. the city was visited by the Roman legions who had been dispatched to Asia Minor to face Antiochus III. The harbour of Neapolis was used by the republicans Brutus and Cassius as a base for their fleet before the battle of Philippoi (42 B.C.) and it was here that saint Paul, the Apostle of the Nations, disembarked (A.D. 49/50) on the start of his european journey to proclaim the new message.

The new name of the city, Christoupolis (the City of Christ) is first mentioned at the beginning of the 9th century A.D. When the Byzantine Epire was organised into "themes", the city became part of the "theme of the Strymon" and was invariably the last stronghold against the raids of the Slavs. In the 12th century A.D. it was admired by the Arab geographer Idrisi as a strongly fortified site with a commercial harbour. Its prosperity did not last long however; in A.D. 1185 the Normans, having already captured Thessalonike, put it to the torch and razed it to the ground. The internecine conflicts between the Franks after 1204 were followed by the reacquisition of the territories of east Macedonia by the Byzantines under Ioannis III Vatatzes. The unsuccessful manoeuvres by the Catalans at the beginning of the 14th century A.D. in front of the "long wall" built to defend the city by Andronikos II Palaiologos were succeeded by the disturbances arising out of the military confrontation between the forces of the two Andronikoi. In the years preceding the Turkish conquest, Christoupolis was threatened by the Serb kral Ste-

phen **Dušan** and its territory was ravaged by irregular bands of Ottoman Turks. In 1391 the city was demolished by the pagan conqueror and the residents sought safety in flight. Neapolis was converted into a barracks and its defences were strengthened (1425). The temporary occupation of the city by Venetian forces did not deflect the course of history. The city continued its life in the centuries of subjection to the Ottoman Turks under its new name, Kavala, which is recorded for the first time in a document of the second half of the 15th century A.D. It was now, however, nothing more than a staging post for changing horses, a waste land, though one of strategic importance.

The situation seems to have changed, after 1526, when the Turks settled a population of Jews in the area, which they transported from the cities of Hungary. This kernel was surrounded by both Greeks and Turks.

Within a few decades the new city was pul-

461. The aqueduct of Kavala, built at the time of the sultan Süleyman the Magnificent (1520-1566), replaced an older Byzantine one.

sating with life. The fortress at the end of the peninsula (the modern district of Panayia) proved too small to hold all the inhabitants, who gradually occupied the surrounding area as well. The face of the landscape was changed by large-scale works designed to meet the increasing needs of the population: it was now, in the reign of sultan Süleyman I the Magnificent (1520-1566), that the new defensive enceinte enclosing the harbour as well as the city was built, that the imposing Aqueduct, known as Kamares, was erected, and that the mosque Ibrahim Pasha Dzamisi was founded.

In about 1550 the city had a large inn and a great number of cisterns, and resembled an island, surrounded on all sides as it was by the sea. In the second half of the century the harbour was used for the exporting of wheat, and also as an anchorage for the - not always welcome - pirate ships bringing prisoners for the slave market. In 1667 when Kavala was visited by the

Turkish chronicler Evliya Çelebi, the city had 500 two-storey, stone houses, arranged in five neighbourhoods, and there were two inns and a large number of warehouses outside the harbour gate. The fortress was the residence of the *frourarchos* (garrison-commander) and also the site of the gunpowder magazine. In the district below the fort, five mosques with leaded domes, belonging to the Sultan, proclaimed the voice of Allah.

As time went on, the city, standing as it did at the transition between West and East, became a port of call for an increasing number of travellers: priests, consuls of the great powers of the day, and amateur archaeologists and historians. Here was stored the merchandise of Smyrna and Egypt and the products of Thasos, and here, too,

362

the cannon-balls made at the famous town of Pravi (Eleutheropoulis) were loaded for the dockyards in Constantinople.

From the middle of the 18th century, thanks to the French commercial establishment founded in the city and the appointment of a French consul, Kavala entered into close commercial relations with Marseilles, to which it channelled cotton from Orphanio, rice from Drama, oil from Thasos and tobacco from the surrounding area. During the period of the Russo-Turkish war (1768-1774) squadrons of the Russian fleet seem to have plundered the stores of wheat before moving on to Euboia. They also cut down 17,000 trees on neighbouring Thasos for the timber needed to repair and construct ships. Just before the Greek revolution of 1821, the city numbered about 3,000 inhabitants, the number of houses had almost doubled, and the activity in the harbour gave Kavala the air of an international transit centre.

The liberation of southern Greece from the Turkish yoke and the creation of an independent state (1832) revived the hopes of the subject Macedonians and guided their activities. After 1850 the population of Kavala reveals an amaz-

ing vigour and activity, similar to that of the modern city, with new churches (St. Ioannis the Baptist) imposing tobacco warehouses, educational institutions, hospitals, community gymnasia and, finally, fine *archontika* (mansions) both municipal (the Great Club, and the girls' school) and private, all of them interesting examples of a variety of architectural influences. Just a few years earlier (1817), the house of Mehmet Ali had been constructed inside the fortress on the site of the temple of Parthenos, and the impressive *Imaret,* a complex housing the Ottoman church-school *(Mendreses)* and poor-house, had been built on the walls on the west side of the city.

In the last years of the 19th century, the Greek population of almost 10,000 held the entire trade of the city in its hands, and had produced important men of letters and scholars. At the dawn of the 20th century the city was ready to meet its destiny, which would lead it into the bosom of Greece after centuries of slavery (27 June 1913). Before this, however, it would experience the violence, the oppression and the malice of the Bulgarian army, which captured it in October of 1912 during a phase of the Turkish Balkan war.

462

463

462. The family house of Mehmet Ali in Kavala.

463. Old house in the district of Panayia in Kavala.

464. Old mansion (archontiko) in Kavala.

464

THE ARCHAEOLOGICAL MUSEUM

465

The Kavala Museum, which opened its doors at the end of 1964, houses antiquities from the excavations conducted by the Archaeological Service at Amphipolis, Oisyme, Neapolis (Kavala), Stryme, Dikili Tas and elsewhere. It includes reliefs and funerary stelai from Gazoros, Paradisos near the Nestos (Topeiros?), Drama, Aidonochori (ancient Tragilos), and Nea Kerdylia. There are special rooms for the displays of finds from excavations at the city and cemetery of Amphipolis (grave offerings from Macedonian tombs, jewellery, figurines, vases, funerary stelai), and from the sanctuary of Parthenos at Kavala itself (decrees with relief scenes, vases from the 7th to 6th centuries B.C., table supports, figurines and architectural members from the ionic temple of Parthenos - beginning of the 5th century B.C.). Other exhibits on the ground floor include prehistoric pottery from the settlements of Laphrouda, Amphipolis, Dimitra, Galepsos, Photoleivos, and architectural reliefs, statues and mosaics from Classical and Roman times from Aidonochori and Amphipolis.

466

The upper storey of the museum is devoted to the colonies of the Archaic and Classical period founded by the southern Greeks on the coasts of the northern Aegean and on sites deep in the hinterland. It plays host to grave-offerings from tombs at Oisyme, Galepsos, Dikaea, and Abdera. It also houses silver and bronze vases, figurines and coins from tombs in the tumulus at Nikisiani (late 4th century B.C.), chance finds from various sites in the counties of Kavala, Serrhai and Drama dating from all periods (vases, statuettes, funerary casks etc.). The composition on the inside of a poros sarcophagus, dating from about 300 B.C., is an interesting example of painting from Aidonochori echoing the achievements of Lower Macedonia.

465. Clay hand-made kantharoid vase with incised and punched decoration, from the prehistoric settlement at Stathmos Aggistas near Serrhai. Late Bronze Age. Kavala, Archaeological Museum.

466. Cycladic clay amphora from ancient Oisyme. 630-620 B.C. Kavala, Archaeological Museum.

467

468

467. Detail of a scene
of a band of Dionysiac
revellers from a red-
figure krater. End of the
5th century B.C.
Kavala, Archaeological
Museum.

468. Two clay figurines
of standing women,
from a tomb at
Amphipolis. Second half
of the 4th century B.C.
Kavala, Archaeological
Museum.

469. Bronze situla from tomb Γ (Gamma) in the tumulus at Nikisiani, near Kavala. End of the 4th century B.C. Kavala, Archaeological Museum.

470. Silver kalyx from tomb A in the tumulus at Nikisiani, near Kavala. End of the 4th century B.C. Kavala, Archaeological Museum.

470

471

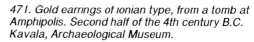

471. Gold earrings of Ionian type, from a tomb at Amphipolis. Second half of the 4th century B.C. Kavala, Archaeological Museum.

472. Gold finger ring with an inlaid, semi-precious stone, from a tomb at Amphipolis. 2nd century B.C. Kavala, Archaeological Museum.

473. Gold earrings with lion's head finials from a tomb at Amphipolis. End of the 4th-beginning of the 3rd centuries B.C. Kavala, Archaeological Museum.

472

473

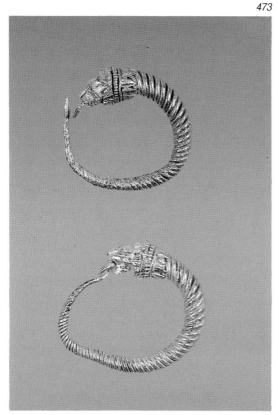

474

474. *Gold necklace attachment of fine gold sheet with a repoussé depiction of a Macedonian shield, from the "Macedonian" tomb at Philippoi. 2nd century B.C. Kavala, Archaeological Museum.*

475. *Gold wreath of oak leaves, from the "Macedonian" tomb at Philippoi. 2nd century B.C. Kavala, Archaeological Museum.*

475

476. *Funerary stele of an ephebe from Amphipolis. End of the 5th century B.C. Kavala, Archaeological Museum.*

477. *Painted funerary stele from Amphipolis. Middle of the 3rd century B.C. Kavala, Archaeological Museum.*

476

477

478. Clay plaque with comic masks, from Amphipolis.
Beginning of the 3rd century B.C. Kavala,
Archaeological Museum.

478

372

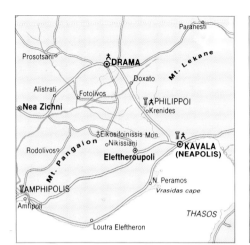

PHILIPPOI
and its region

479

HISTORICAL REVIEW

Philippoi was described by the Greek historian Appian as the gate between Europe and Asia. The city was built by Philip II (356 B.C.) on the site of the colony of Krenides, founded on the fertile land of Daton by inhabitants of Thasos under the leadership of Kallistratos, an exiled Athenian politician. The city swiftly developed into a centre for the exploitation of the rich gold-mines of mount Pangaion. The draining of the marshes enclosed by the three mountains, Orbelos, Symbolon and Pangaion, was a massive wealth generating work that resulted in the improvement of the climate and more effective land-use. The prosperity of the city is indicated also by its impressive coinage of gold staters and bronze pieces. The city was independent in the Hellenistic period and is thereafter lost in the oblivion imposed by the silence of the historical sources and the lack of excavational evidence. Perched on a steep rock, contemplating its past, Philippoi appears with the passage of time to have lost much of its population and was transformed into a township of no particular importance. It is described by Strabo as a "small residence". History, however, was to remember Philippoi, and indeed accorded it a privileged position, for the outcome of the bloody confrontation in October 42 B.C. to the west of the city between Brutus and Cassius on the one hand and Mark Antony and Octavian on the other

479. General view of the ancient city of Philippoi and the plain.

480. Plan of the archaeological site of Philippoi.

rocks of the acropolis, the new religion of Christianity, whose roots were laid in A.D. 49/50 by saint Paul, the Apostle of the Nations, found its place in the city and was given expression through imposing basilicas and baptisteries.

Latin was gradually displaced and from the 3rd century A.D. Greek relived the days of its former glory. Now the seat of an archbishop, who had 5-7 bishoprics in his jurisdiction, Philippoi saw the barbarian hordes threatening its walls and setting fire to its suburbs from as early as the middle of the 5th century A.D. The raids of the Goths were followed by those of the Slavs in the 7th and 8th centuries A.D. and later still - in the 9th century A.D. -by the more destructive incursions of the Bulgarians. In their efforts to strengthen the defences of the city between A.D. 963 and 969, the Byzantines constructed the defensive walls and erected towers on the acropolis. The Arab geographer Idrisi, who visited the city in the middle of the 12th century A.D., describes the lively commercial activity and makes specific mention of viticulture. The Via Egnatia, the main route connecting Dyrrhachion with Constantinople, which ran through the middle of the city, led to Philippoi being visited by Baldowin of Flanders, the Frankish ruler of Constantinople, now held by the Latins, by Ioannis III Vatatzes, the emperor of Nicaea in the 14th century A.D., by Andronikos II Palaiologos and by Ioannis Kantakouzenos.

The last to appear on the scene were the Turks (after A.D. 1387). In time the city was abandoned. The marshes strangled the plain, the inhabitants left and the only thing that remained to roam in the region was the name of Philippoi. The archaeologist's spade recovered the site from obscurity and restored to it the cultural dimension accumulated there by the twenty centuries of its history.

THE CITY AND ITS MONUMENTS

Ancient Times

The conical hill in the foothills of Mount Orbelos, on which stands the acropolis of Philippoi, gazes at "gold-bearing" Pangaion at the opposite end of the plain. At the foot of the hill, the once bustling city is still enclosed in those parts of the total length of about 3,500 metres of defence wall - ancient Greek and Byzantine - that have been spared, albeit in lamentable ruins, by time, the destroyer of all.

The original plan of the defensive complex

hand major consequences for the ancient world and tolled the knell of the republican constitution of Rome. Within a few years Octavian, the famous Augustus, turned the page of the Imperial period.

The character of the city was transformed with the advent of the new era. Immediately after the battle, Mark Antony settled the veterans of the Roman legions at Philippoi as the first colonists and in 30 B.C. Octavian sent Italians there to whom he granted land. From 27 B.C. onwards the name of the city was colonia *Augusta Iulia Philippensis.* The costly buildings, the imposing Forum with its two temples, the bath-houses, the large aqueduct, the statues and the honorific monuments adorning Philippoi, especially from the second half of the 2nd century A.D., gave the city a cosmopolitan character that was further enhanced by its location astride the Via Egnatia.

Alongside the local Thracian and ancient Greek elements whose religious beliefs were made manifest in primitive reliefs carved on the

481

481. The Agora (Forum) of Philippoi.

goes back to the founder of the settlement, Philip II. It is almost rectangular in plan, oriented north-south, and has at least three gates that have been confirmed by excavation and are known by their conventional names: the Neapolis (Kavala) Gate, the Krenides Gate, and the Marsh Gate. The city is "divided" diagonally into two unequal parts by the Via Egnatia: the north, upper section which appears to have been sparsely populated in antiquity, and the south section that housed the public buildings of the colony. The Forum (Agora) of Philippoi, the north side of which is oriented parallel to the great road linking Dyrrachion with Byzantion, consisted of a rectangular paved square measuring 100 m. x 50 m., the sides of which were bounded by stoas and buildings so that the monumental complex measured a total of 148 metres in length and 70 in width.

In the middle of the north side is preserved the tribunal, flanked on either side by a small building, today very badly damaged, and a fountain, both fountains being built at the expense of the *agoranomos* Lucius Decimius Bassus. The north-west corner of the Forum was occupied by a temple dedicated to the emperor Antoninus Pius, which has a cella and a pronaos (23.12 m. x 13.03 m.); the architectural remains and the finds from the excavation lead to the conclusion that the building had two corinthian columns *in antis* on the facade, a floor paved with slabs of marble, walls coated with plaster and a pediment with acroteria in the form of Victories in the corners and one in the form of Athena at the top.

A row of rooms to the south of the temple - rooms that formed the west side of the Agora (Forum) - seem to have been intended for the administrative authorities of the colony. This is attested by the apsidal building at roughly the centre of the complex, which is probably to be identified with the Curia, by the truncated statue of Abundance, and the "standards", that is a marble table with five hemispherical hollows of various sizes representing the official standards of weights and liquids.

The 100 m. long stoa on the south side of the Forum, which has two long rectangular areas at the back divided into smaller rooms, may perhaps have been the commercial and industrial sector of the city. The east wing, in contrast, was intended to house Logios Hermes (the god of learning) for the public library has been identified here. A corinthian-style building in the south-east corner, opposite the temple of Antoninus Pius, the interior of which is decorated with marble and which had a pronaos and a cella, and with acroteria in the form of Victories carved in the round, was dedicated to the empress Faustina and the Genius of the colony.

To the south-east of the Forum stood its counterpart, the Roman commercial agora, a complex which, like the palaestra destroyed by the Christians, faced onto a monumental paved street (9 m. wide) and which was destroyed almost completely by the Byzantines so that a basilica could be erected on its site. The voices of the small retailers may no longer be heard calling out their wares, and the wheels of the carts may no longer rut the paved streets that enclosed it on east and west, but the games of the idlers incised in the floor of the hexastyle colonnade of the stoa on the facade of the complex have survived to testify to human destiny, stubbornly resistant to time that erases all.

The full architectural design of the palaestra can hardly be recognised today, since its superstructure was quarried by the Byzantines for material to build the neighbouring basilica. It was a rectangular structure, measuring 78 m. x 58 m., with a central courtyard that communicated via three entrances with the street running along the outside of the north side, and via two more, one each in the south-west and south-east corners, with the section of the city to the south. Little remains today of the small amphitheatre in the centre of the east wing, which originally had seven rows of seats, and almost nothing at all of the rooms to the right and left of it. By contrast, the south-east section is better preserved on account of the slope in the terrain; the area of the toilets is more impressive in its conception (14 m. x 5.50 m.), with walls preserved to a height of 3 m. One of the most impressive halls in the west wing is the central room, which is spacious, paved, and has a monumental entrance facing onto the courtyard.

About 150 m. to the south-west of the palaestra, a structure of the second half of the 2nd century A.D., rise the ruins of the Roman baths, a building measuring 55 m. x 42 m. with an interior courtyard, in the centre of which there is a circular basin with steps. Built about A.D. 250 on the site of an earlier temple dedicated to the worship of Hercules, Libera and Liber (Dionysos), the public baths had rooms for rest and relaxation (halls on the east wing) with mosaic floors, apartments with hot and cold baths, dressing rooms, and hypocausts (west wing). The building was destroyed by a fire -perhaps at the end of the 3rd century A.D. - though it was repaired in the middle of the 4th century A.D., before being finally abandoned and allowed to fall into ruins.

On the low slopes of the hill of the acropolis, to the north of the Via Egnatia and the Forum, was a rectangular terrace 40 m. long and 11 m. wide, oriented north-west to south-east, on which the sanctuary of the Egyptian gods once occupied a dominating position. Five contiguous rooms connected by a shared rear wall - five small temples - were intended, as attested by inscriptions, for the worship of Isis, Serapis, Horus, Harpokrates and probably also Telesphoros.

On the same slopes, at the site of the ancient quarries, a number of small sanctuaries were erected during the 2nd to 3rd centuries A.D., dedicated to Silvanus, Hermes, Bacchus, Herakles, and Artemis-Bendis. A considerable sum of money was expended by the pious official Publius Hostilius Philadelphus to defray the cost of tiling the roof, paving the floor and carving an access staircase.

The theatre of Philippoi, one of the largest in the ancient world, was originally constructed at the time of the founder of the city, Philip II. This may be deduced from the study of sections of the retaining walls of the *cavea* and the *parodoi*.

The modern form of the theatre, however, derives mainly from repairs of the second half of the 2nd century A.D., when theatrical productions were giving way to bloody gladiatorial combats between men and animals, and men and men. In the interests of the easy spectacle, the first rows of seats were removed, the diameter of the orchestra was increased from 21.60 m. to 24.80 m., protective parapets were added, new rows of seats were constructed on the highest diazoma on semi-circular supports, the parodoi were roofed with vaults and the stage-building was erected, with a double colonnade and niches for statues. An underground tunnel was later constructed beneath the orchestra so that the animals could be led in without danger to the public.

The artistic decoration of the theatre at this phase was confined to the carving - on the pilasters at the entrance from the west *parodos* to the orchestra - of three clumsy relief figures depicting Victory, Nemesis and Ares. We are now already in the middle of the 3rd century A.D. and

482

pagan antiquity, wearied by controversy, is beginning to hand on the baton to the following period of spiritual and psychological struggle: at the beginning of the 6th century A.D., the glory of the Son of Man would find at Philippoi, a brilliant house in marbled basilicas, and the speech of saint Paul the Apostle would echo triumphantly in richly painted heavens.

Christian Times

The imposing basilica next to the Forum - also known as Basilica B - is called Direkler (= columns) by the early travellers and also by the scholars who have studied the monument; the name was given in awe by the Ottoman occupation to four powerful pillars that were the only

482. Elegantly decorated column capital from basilica B at Philippoi.

483. The Octagon at Philippoi.

483

ones visible of the building before the commencement of excavations.

The church has no courtyard - despite the fact that the ground had been prepared for its erection - and has overall dimensions of 62 m. x 47 m. It belongs to the type of basilica with a dome at the east (once seated on the four pillars whose bulk now dominates the horizon) covering the sanctuary and the space in front of it. The spacious nave, 31 m. broad, was divided by two parallel colonnades, each consisting of six columns, into three aisles, the middle one of which was vaulted. The aisles communicated with the narthex through three arched entrances. To the right and left of the sanctuary apse, which had a synthronon in it, were added the "phiale" at the north-east - a square room measuring 6.90 m. x 5.60 m. - and the diakonikon at the south-east, to meet the needs of the congregation and the clergy. Both these rooms had apses at the east and communicated with the nave and, as may be concluded from the fragments of their decoration, originally had marble revetment on the walls and marble-paved floors. Study of the architectural remains leads to the conclusion that this grandiose building of about the middle of the 6th century A.D. also had a gynaikonites above the side aisles and the narthex.

The Octagon of Philippoi, located in the first insula to the east of the Forum (Agora), was the cathedral of the city. It was built on an earlier bipartite rectangular building with interior dimensions of 25.30 m. x 9.90 m., which has been identified with a chapel dedicated by the bishop Porphyrios (middle of the 4th century A.D.) to saint Paul the Apostle. Constructed at the beginning of the 5th century A.D., the Octagon survived until about the beginning of 7th century A.D., surrounded by the annexes that were indispensable at the Early Christian period: the tripartite baptistery, the font, the prothesis and the diakonikon. The exterior had the form of a cube, while the interior had eight sides with a colonnade running all around them, and the building was surmounted by a dome, and had the sanctuary apse projecting at the east.

Research has brought to light a Hellenistic funerary heroon (2nd century B.C.), incorporated into the octagonal church; the surviving remains of this building consist of a subterranean, vaulted, funerary chamber and part of a crepidoma with three steps, on which rested the honorific building in the shape of a temple. It is believed that the dead man Euephenes Exekestou (inscription on the pediment over the unplundered tomb, who has been identified with a known person of the same name, an initiate into the Kabeirian mysteries on Samothrace), must have occupied an important position in the society of Philippoi to have been buried in the centre of the city.

The Episkopeion, a large rectangular building on the site of an earlier Roman structure, occupies the insula to the east of the Octagon, which has four wings of rooms set around a central courtyard, and has a second storey on two of the sides (south and west). The store-rooms and rooms for the preparation of food, and also those devoted to the production of wine, have been located in the semi-basement, while the residence and reception rooms, with wall-paintings and sculptural decoration, were on the upper storey.

A monumental staircase on the terrace to the north of the Forum on the opposite side of the modern national highway, leads to a peristyle courtyard and thence to the four-sided atrium of a three-aisled Basilica (A) with a font-spring incorporated into the architecture of its west side. The church is of hellenistic type, once had a timbered roof and is dated to the end of the 5th century A.D.; it has a narthex with a staircase at its north end leading up to the loft, a paved floor, a pulpit, an enkainion and a built synthronon. The later chapel, in the south-west corner of the atrium, was built after the destruction of the church, over a roman cistern, which is traditionally identified with the "prison of saint Paul".

Basilica C, a 6th century A.D. building in the enclosure of the Archaeological Museum of Philippoi, was discovered during work on the erection of this building. It is three-aisled with a narthex and a transverse aisle, rich sculptural decoration, chapels and other ancillary rooms, and served in part as a cemetery, after it had been destroyed by earthquake in the beginning of the 7th century A.D.

In the centre of the eastern cemetery at Philippoi - a predominantly Christian cemetery, in contrast with the western one, in the area of Lydia, which probably goes back to pagan times - the archaeologist's spade has brought to light a monumental three-aisled cemetery basilica ("extra muros"), dating from the second half of the 4th century A.D., which underwent significant modification during the 6th century A.D.

484. Basilica B (in the Forum) at Philippoi.

THE ARCHAEOLOGICAL MUSEUM

485

The Museum of Philippoi, inside the archaeo-logical site, is a building dating from the beginning of the 1960s, which houses chiefly finds from the excavations at the colony and also from a number of sites in the surrounding area (e.g. prehistoric vases from the Neolithic settlements at Dikili Tas and Sitagroi). Inscriptions of late Classical times (including the reply of Alexander the Great to the ambassadors of Philippoi) and from the Roman and early Byzantine periods. Fragments of free-standing sculptures mainly from the Roman period, portraits of emperors, and members of the royal family and private individuals from the 1st to the beginning of the 3rd centuries A.D., architectural members from public buildings, and basilicas.

485. Clay hand-made vase from the prehistoric settlement at Dikili Tas. Middle Neolithic period. Philippoi, Archaeological Museum.

486. Clay bowl from the prehistoric settlement at Dikili Tas, Late Neolithic period. Philippoi, Archaeological Museum.

487. Portrait of Lucius Gaius Caesar. Philippoi, Archaeological Museum.

486

382

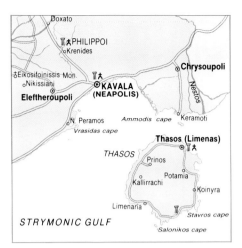
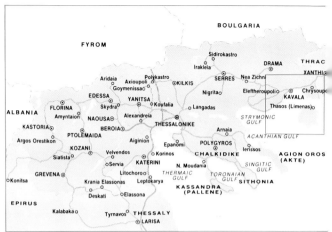

THASOS

HISTORICAL REVIEW

A mere eight kilometres from the mainland opposite, at the head of the Aegean, Thasos rises like a foam-girt pebble clad in the green of its pines and the pure white of its marble. The presence of humans here is attested from the Stone Age, though the island first appeared on the scene of history at the beginning of the 7th century B.C., when colonists from Paros, led by Telesikles, father of the poet Archilochos, responded to an oracle from the Pythia at Delphi and occupied the northern part of Aeria, as Thasos was called by some at that time. The seams of gold on the island, however, which, together with the excellent wine, were an inexhaustible source of wealth for the Thasians, did not fail to attract the attention of Phoenicians, those experienced merchants of the Mediterranean. Herodotus relates that well before the Parians settled here, the energetic and expansive Semites discovered the precious mines on the east slope of Mount Phanos (Koinyra) and began to exploit them; he also tells us that the Phoenicians were the first to give the island its present name.

The early, difficult years experienced by the colonists on the inhospitable Thracian coast opposite, which cost so many lives and sacrifices before their possessions were consolidated on the passes leading to the interior and before trading-posts were finally established at the natural roadsteads (Galepsos, Oisyme, Neapolis), were followed by creative periods of progress. The new state, standing on a privileged site on

488. *View of the harbour of Thasos from the castle. The ruins of the ancient city can be seen in the centre.*

the edge of a fertile plane, below the massif of Profitis Ilias (1108 m.) and before a sheltered harbour, swiftly grew in size, entered into relations with the rest of the Greek world and produced some outstanding works of art. At the end of the Archaic period it was already enclosed by defence walls 4,000 m. long, built of marble and schist, with gates adorned with fine reliefs.

The times of adversity experienced by Thasos as a subject of the Persian Empire from 491 B.C. onwards belonged to the past after the brilliant victories won by the Greeks at Salamis (480 B.C.) and Sestos (478 B.C.). The new state of affairs created in Greece, however, with the leading role played by Athens, whose personal interests were concealed, not particularly effectively, behind the shield of the Delian Confederacy, was not to the advantage of Thasos; the island quickly saw precious bases being lost to her in the area of gold-bearing Pangaion (Ennea Hodoi) and found herself cut off from strategic sites (foundation of Amphipolis). Furthermore, intolerable terms were imposed on the island in reprisal for its secession (465 B.C.) from the Confederacy, conditions that converted it into a second-class state, completely dependent upon Athens, deprived of its mines and commercial centres, and with its defensive walls demolished.

The revolt of the Four Hundred in 411 B.C. snatched Thasos from the iron embrace of Athens, only to plunge the island into a deadly confrontation between pro-Spartan oligarchs and pro-Athenian democrats, from which the small community only gained respite at the beginning of the 4th century B.C. The reconciliation gave the island a new, more flexible administrative framework, and endowed the city with a new town plan, in which the Agora and all the public buildings found their place. In 360 B.C. Krenides was founded to ensure a more effective exploitation of the mines of mount Pangaion and the Maronites were driven back from Stryme.

The Macedonian spear left Thasos theoretically independent (356 B.C.), though deprived of its sources of revenue on the Thracian coast, where the newly founded city of Philippoi played an important role in the coinage issues of the Macedonian kingdom.

With the Roman republic particularly favourable towards the island, and the Empire lavishly showering honours and privileges upon it, Thasos advanced towards the Middle Ages of late antiquity, facing the raids of the Vandals (A.D. 467-68) and the successive incursions of the Slavs (7th- 9th centuries A.D.). It watched the

Arabs neutralise the Byzantine fleet in its waters in A.D. 829. And it saw Leon of Tripolis, in A.D. 904, prepare the siege machines with which he would capture Thessalonike. From the Franks of Boniface (1204) to Michael VIII Palaiologos (1259-1282), from Zaccarias of Genoa (1307), to the Turkish pirate Belekomes and the brothers Ioannis and Alexios (1357), the island passed, in 1414, as a gift from Manuel II Palaiologos, into the hands of Jacob Gattilusi of Genoa, who was already lord of Lesbos, and down to A.D. 1449 experienced thirty years of prosperity and cultural regeneration: these were its final years of prosperity, however, since in that year the island was abandoned to Turkish rule. The vicissitudes of Thasos, however, did not stop at this point. It was captured by the Venetians (A.D. 1457), repossessed by the Turks (A.D. 1459), to be abandoned completely, since the majority of the inhabitants were transported to Constantinople on the orders of the sultan Mohammed II, and reverted again to Venetian occupation, until in 1479 it was finally incorporated into the Ottoman Empire.

The island became the private *timar* of kapoudan pasha, and came under the administration of the bey of Kavala. The natural wealth of the island quickly lead to the colonisation of Theologos and Megalo Kazaveti. In A.D. 1707, seven to eight thousand inhabitants brought their lord about 30,000 liras from the exploitation of timber, wax and oil.

It was not only the travellers who described and were dazzled by the wealth of Thasos, however. The pirates who were a stain on the Aegean at the beginning of the 18th century were attracted by the descriptions, and made sudden attacks, compelling the population, as at other coastal sites to withdraw into the interior and into inaccessible areas. During the Russo-Turkish War of the 1770s, which revived the hopes of the Thasians, the island supplied the Christian fleet with timber for ship-building. However, oppression, piracy, the intolerable subjection to the local *kodjabashides,* and the drain of revenues when the island returned to Turkish administration swiftly reduced the inhabitants to a wretched condition. When the French consul Cousinéry visited Thasos at the end of the 18th century he found only 2,500 people.

From 1813 to 1902, a firman issued by the sultan made Thasos the property of the vizier of Egypt Mehmet Ali, a ruler who was particularly friendly towards the inhabitants of the island since, himself descended from Kavala, he had spent his childhood with a family from Thasos. The turbulent 19th century, with the Greek War of Independence of 1821 dominating in its third decade, the Crimean War looming over the middle of it, and the major events in Central Europe (unification of states) setting their mark on its final decades, ended on Thasos in a period of economic decline and social disturbance, leading to the intervention of the *Sublime Porte* and the return of the island to Turkish administration. The new state of affairs created in the Balkans, however, with the Greek kingdom victoriously extending its borders towards the north, led admiral P. Koundouriotis to free Thasos on the 17th of July 1912 and return it to the motherland.

THE CITY AND ITS MONUMENTS

A fan opened towards the Thracian coast, Thasos. The ancient city of Thasos, with the ruins of its public and private buildings rising amongst the houses of the modern village of Limena. Between the headland of Pachy to the west, and the rocks of Evraiokastro to the east, at the edge of a verdant plain bounded - and also protected - by two acropoleis with castles on them, the city of Telesikles with its well-built defence walls, offers a green enchanting, windswept welcome to the traveller. With the scent of the pine and the brine of the sea.

1. The Agora

The Agora complex stands the centre of the city, not far from the closed harbour with which it was connected by a wide street; it is rectangular

489. Map of Thasos.

489

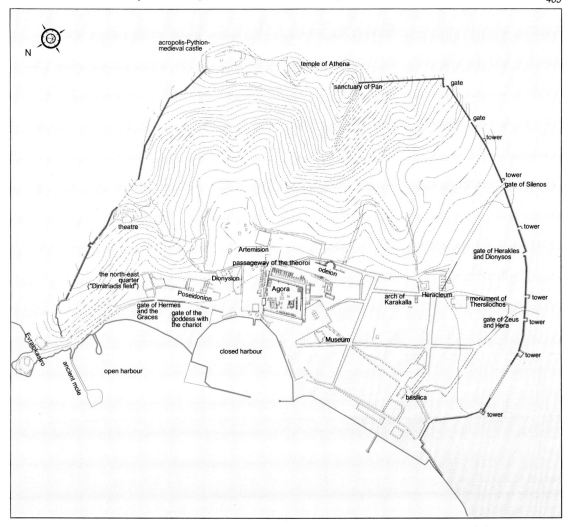

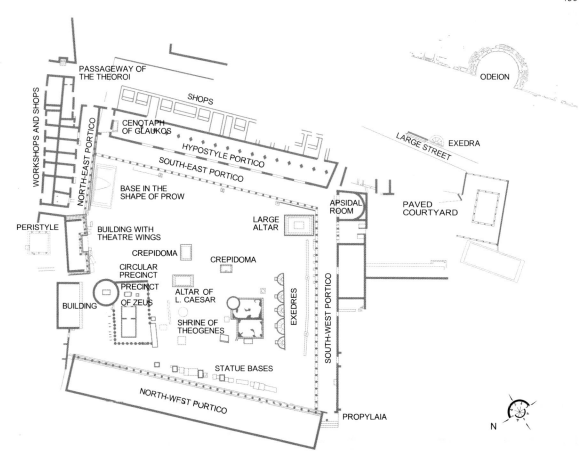

490. Plan of the Agora of Thasos.

491. View of the Agora.

in plan and enclosed on three sides (the east, south and west) by stoas, while the north side is bounded by a row of cult and administrative buildings (4th-3rd centuries B.C.). The centuries, which in their passage have each left their individual stamp, gradually endowed this hub of the social-administrative and religious life of the state with elegant buildings, a spacious courtyard, exedras, temples, sanctuaries, honorific bases, statues, funerary monuments to heroised mortals, and temene, dating from the 4th century B.C. down to Roman times.

Here, in the Agora of the city, the grateful inhabitants of Thasos erected a cenotaph in honour of Glaukos, son of Leptines, who founded the city, along with Archilochos and other Parians. Here the wealthy Theodektes defrayed the cost of the erection of warehouses (2nd century B.C.), a monument in the form of the prow of a ship was erected for some victory in a sea battle (2nd century B.C.) and Theogenes son of Timoxenos, the Thasian athlete and hero of the Olympic and other games, was glorified with a sanctuary (next to

the circular building of the Theogeneion was found a marble cylindrical "treasury", that is, an offering-box, for the contributions of the faithful). The Thasian brothers Dionysodoros and Hestiaios, who maintained commercial relations with Samothrace, Lampsakos and Rhodes, and through their prestige influenced the Roman officials at Thessalonike, were immortalised here (1st century B.C.) with bronze statues. And since the new morals that came from the west demanded new customs, statues of the various emperors vied from the 1st century A.D. onwards with the vainglorious inscriptions on the pedestals on which they were erected. "Order", however, in the area of the Agora was imposed by the presence in the north-west corner of the courtyard, of the temenos of Zeus Agoraios which had

388

492. The cenotaph of
Glaukos, founder of
Thasos.

493. Inscription from
the cenotaph of
Glaukos, friend of the
poet Archilochos, found
in the Agora of Thasos.

493

a small single-room temple *in antis* and an altar in front of the entrance (original phase 4th century B.C.).

2. The Passageway of the Theoroi, the Dionysion, the Artemision, the Poseidonion

To the north-east of the Agora is a monumental passageway bounded by two parallel marble walls decorated in antiquity with late archaic severe-style relief slabs (470 B.C.), now in the Louvre, bearing scenes of Apollon, the Nymphs and Hermes (the passageway is known as "the Passageway of the Theoroi"). From it an ancient road led to the Dionysion, passing on the right a large communal well (5.70 m. x 1.80 m.) and, on an artificial terrace further to the east, the sanctuary of Artemis (the honorary statues from the 3rd-1st centuries B.C. that adorned the sacred precinct, are now in the Museum of Constantinople). About 100 m. from the "Passageway of the Theoroi", the temenos of Dionysos - it was described as the Dionysion by Hippokrates (end of the 5th century B.C.), who spent three years on the island - has a triangular plan and two entrances, though not all the buildings of which it consisted have yet been uncovered. A better-preserved structure is the prostyle building in the shape of the Greek letter Π standing on a crepidoma - a choregic monument - which had a semi-circular base on the inside of the north, short side, on which stood statues of Dionysos (in the centre in larger than life size), Tragedy, Comedy, Dithyramb and Nocturnus (the surviving statues are on display in the local Museum). Of a similar choregic monument nearby, also dating from the 3rd century B.C., a headless Muse wearing a peplos, a statue of the God of wine wearing a himation and *thymele* are all that survives. Not far from the Dionysion, a temenos, the shape of a trapezium in plan, and with propylaea, a stoa, and *oeci* on the south, west and north sides and sacrificial altars in the central courtyard, was dedicated in the 4th century B.C. to Poseidon, Lord of the Sea, by Xenophanes, son of Myllos. Aphrodite (or Amphitrite) Pelagia and Epilimenia Hera, both patron goddesses of merchants and sailors, were worshipped together with Poseidon in this temenos.

3. The north-east Quarter

In the region between the closed harbour and Evraiokastro, which is known conventionally as

494. Head of Dionysos from the larger than life size statue erected on a choregic monument in the precinct of the god. Beginning of the 3rd century B.C. Thasos, Archaeological Museum.

"Dimitriadis' field" are preserved the remains of settlements covering a period of approximately ten centuries. Here, excavation is removing the successive ruins, layers and deposits, in order to trace through time the history of a particularly interesting urban quarter of ancient Thasos, reconstruct the building phases, recreate its gradual extension towards the shore, and study the daily life and occupations of the inhabitants from the 8th century B.C. to the 5th century A.D. While the visitor, silent in the face of time, listens to the waves as they break in the embrace of the open harbour and foam on the rocks on which stands the chapel of the Holy Apostles -a brilliant white jewel at the summit of the peninsula, set amongst the remains of a 5th - 6th century A.D. basilica, of early Christian graves and other Christian buildings, that stood upon some ancient sanctuary, dedicated to Zeus, Athena, Artemis, the Nymphs and Kore.

4. The Theatre

Nestling in a natural hollow facing west, the theatre of Thasos has its *cavea* resting on the north-east defence wall. The modifications (to both the *orchestra* and the *skene*) imposed by the 1st and 2nd centuries A.D., when the building was used for gladiatorial combats, have not entirely obliterated the form of the theatre at the beginning of the 3rd century B.C., the date at which the doric *skene* was erected (the *proskenion* was dedicated to Dionysos by Sysistratos son of Kodes). The seats in the *cavea*, however, belong to the Roman period, and on some of them can still be seen the inscribed names of individuals or families who had reserved seats.

It may be regarded as certain that the theatre seen by Hippokrates at the end of the 5th century B.C. was also constructed on this site.

5. The south-west Quarter

In the first century A.D., Tiberius Claudius Kadmos commissioned the sculptor Limendas to erect statues of his family on an exedra to the south-west of the Agora, on the large paved road that was also the main axis of the city from north-east to south-west.

In this quarter of the city, which is known conventionally as the "Roman quarter", Hadrian's sojourn, so beneficial to the Greeks, bestowed a fine courtyard paved with marble and surrounded by an ionic peristyle, and further to the east, an elegant odeion (facade: 52 m. - diameter of orchestra: 12.90 m.).

Further to the south, the pious inhabitants took care as early as the 5th century B.C. to erect a special temenos in honour of the greatest god of the island and patron of Thasos -Herakles: monumental propylaea led to the sacrificial altar, which was set in a single-room, peripteral temple, inside which was a cult statue and *oeci* - rooms for the priesthood or lodgings for the worshippers.

6. The defence Wall and the Acropoleis

From the beginning of the 5th century B.C. a horseshoe-shaped defence wall, built of isodomic masonry with square towers, encircled the inhabited area of the city in the narrow strip by the sea, and also the slopes of the foothills of Profitis Ilias, which were roughly twice the area and seem always to have been difficult of access and uninhabited. Though sections of the west and

496

east wall have been plundered, the enceinte is of exceptional interest in having gates at intervals adorned with fine reliefs, the scenes on which have given rise to the conventional names for the gates: the Gate of the Goddess with the chariot (probably Hermes leading the chariot of Artemis), The Gate of Hermes and the Graces - on the north side by the shore, the Gate of Silenos (end of the 6th century B.C.), and the Gate of Herakles and Dionysos (beginning of the 5th century B.C.), the Gate of Zeus and Hera - on the south and south-west sides.

At the highest point of its circuit the defence wall forms two acropoleis within which are enclosed two sanctuaries - the sanctuary of Pythian Apollo and that of Athena, both of them badly damaged by the defence works planned here first by the Byzantines and then by the Gattilusi (15th century A.D.).

495. The ancient theatre.

496. Relief of Silenus with a kantharos, from the gate in the city wall named after him. End of the 6th century B.C.

497. Inscription of the Gattilusi in the Community of Kastro on Thasos, 15th century A.D.

497

THE ARCHAEOLOGICAL MUSEUM

The Museum of Thasos, a building of 1934, is at present awaiting the completion of the annex which, as an extension of the original kernel, will house more conveniently the objects acquired from time to time - mainly finds from excavations on the site; even in its present form, however, it is one of the richest museums of northern Greece in terms of the importance of its exhibits, and one of those archaeological establishments that of themselves offer a highly interesting panorama of Greek art from the years of the "archaic smile". Column capitals and funerary stelai with volutes and palmettes in the ionic style of Paros, cornices with lotus-flowers and architectural members carved with doric severity keep company with clay simas and antefixes with fresh reliefs depicting human beings, animals and demons. Youths bearing rams and korai, representations of Silenos, hermaic stelai, depictions of Pegasos. Young men in the style of Scopas, gods and heroised mortals. Statues - personifications of Comedy and Tragedy, theatrical masks, Muses, and sea goddesses. Portraits of philosophers and Roman generals and emperors. Early Christian peacocks. And vases, decorative ivories, coins, weights, inscriptions, witnesses to time. Witnesses to the progress made by the island. From the years of the quest for man's destiny to the period of the redemption of the soul.

498. Clay hand-made amphora from the prehistoric settlement at Kastri, on Thasos. Neolithic period. Thasos, Archaeological Museum.

499. Ivory lion's head from the decoration of a piece of furniture, from the Artemisium. 6th century B.C. Thasos, Archaeological Museum.

500. Clay plate from the sanctuary of Artemis on Thasos. 660 B.C. Thasos, Archaeological Museum.

501. Fragment of a clay sima from the Archaic Prytaneion (Town Hall) of Thasos. 540-525 B.C. Thasos, Archaeological Museum.

498

499

500

501

503

504

502. Youth carrying a ram from the Pythion on Thasos. Ca. 600 B.C. Thasos, Archaeological Museum.

503. Fragment of a clay female bust, from the sanctuary of Artemis. Second half of the 6th century B.C. Thasos, Archaeological Museum.

504. Fragment of a clay antefix with a relief scene of Bellerophon astride Pegasos, probably from an Archaic temple in the Herakleion on Thasos. 540-500 B.C. Thasos, Archaeological Museum.

506

505. Male scopadic head (middle of the 4th century B.C.), from the propylaia of the Agora. Thasos, Archaeological Museum.

506. Archaistic head from a hermaic stele, from the Agora. Thasos, Archaeological Museum.

507. Head and torso of a statue of Hadrian, from the Agora, ca. A.D. 130. Thasos, Archaeological Museum.

505

507

508. *Statuette of Aphrodite on a dolphin, from Thasos. 3rd century B.C. Thasos, Archaeological museum.*

08

509. Marble head of Alexander the Great from a
building in the form of a temple on Thasos. Roman
copy of a Hellenistic original. Thasos,
Archaeological Museum.

WEST (UPPER) MACEDONIA

West (Upper) Macedonia was the cradle of the Macedonian Nation. It was from here (the area of Argos Orestikon), according to one version, that the forefathers of the Argead kings set forth in their descent to the plains of the rivers Haliakmon, Loudias and the lower Axios. The region is essentially isolated from the world around, with the mountain ranges of Pindos and Barnous to the west, the Chasian, Cambounian and Pierian mountains to the south, Bermion and Boras to the east, and the mountain massif of Dautica, Babuna and Dren to the north, leaving only small corridors of communication.

Inhabited by related Macedonian tribes (the Orestai, the Lynkestai, the Elimeiotai, the Tymphaioi and the Pelagones), and divided into small kingdoms, it was annexed to the state of Lower Macedonia by Philip II and thereafter followed its fortunes. After the battle of Pydna (168 B.C.) and the division of Macedonia into four districts "merides", Upper Macedonia formed the fourth "meris", with the exception of Orestis, to which the Romans had granted independence.

Surface finds have been discovered dating from the Palaeolithic period (a pseudo-levallois blade in the region of Siatista-Paliokastro) and there are Neolithic settlements on the banks of the Haliakmon, next to the old bridge on the national highway from Kozani to Athens (now at the bottom of the artificial lake created by the Polyphytos dam) and around the drained marsh of Saringiol (Akrini, Ayios Demetrios, Koilada, Drepano and Mavrodendri). Mycenaean pottery has been found in the tumulus known as "Vasilara Rachi tou Velvendou" and at Ano Kome near Kozani, and there are Late Bronze Age remains at Rymnio, Aiane, Ayios Panteleimon Ostrovou (Pateli) and Armenochori near Florina, and wattle-and-daub lake settlements at Dispelio near Kastoria; grave offerings and traces of habitation dating from the Late Iron Age have been discovered at Spelaio near Grevena, Axiochori near Boion and in the Koilada of Kozani. The region entered the historical period self-sufficient and at the same time singularly isolated.

The imported black- and red-figure vases at Farangi and Pyrgoi, bronze statuettes, clay figurines, gold jewellery, funerary inscriptions incised on venerable monuments, bowls and a variety of objects from cemeteries and settlements dating from the 6th to the 4th centuries B.C. at Aiane, Ano Kome and Perivoli near Grevena, the "Macedonian" tombs at Spilia in Eordaia and at Liknades near Boion, and the flourishing residences of the late Classical and Hellenistic periods (Petres near Florina) are all indications that, thanks to the road that preceded the Via Egnatia, Upper Macedonia received the artistic messages of the South, combining them with the local restlessness in the cultural sphere, and that it felt the reverberations of the miracle of Alexander's campaign to the East.

A mountainous land devoted to stock raising, a land of large lakes - Ostrovou, Cheimaditis, the Great and Small Prespa, and Petres - Upper Macedonia had no large cities (with the exception of Herakleia Lynkestis, modern Monastir/Bitola) but only small towns and rural settlements, which in many cases survived to the end of the Roman Empire - settlements without a name and those whose name is known, towns whose site has been established by excavation and others for which it has yet to be located: Aiane, Elimeia, Graia, the state of the Oblostioi, Bevi, Batynna, Lyke, Argos Orestikon etc. Official inscriptions (Letter of Philip V to Koilada), statues (Kalamitsi), relief stelai (Sydendron, Skopos), architectural remains (Polyneri), votive inscriptions (Perdikkas, Akrini, Ano Kome, Ptolemais and Voskochori), manumissions (Exochi), honorary altars (Kozani, Kaisareia, Kastoria, Velvendos, and Ayios Achillios), funerary monuments (Ethniko, Kato Kleines, Nestorion) still search in the plains, in regions by the rivers and in inaccessible areas for the birthplace of their owners.

A rough, other-worldly land, where the process of disintegration of the tribal structures was retarded and the spread of urban institutions significantly delayed, it preserved its archaic character for several centuries retaining in this way some of the primitive elements of macedonian civilization.

This closed geographic unit with its autonomous kingdoms (down to the time of Philip II) and its "koina" (leagues) with tribal characteristics that survived until the Roman period (the Koinon of the Elimeiotai, the Koinon of the Lynkestai and the Koinon of the Orestai) furnished the army of Alexander the Great with brilliant generals and experienced warriors (Ptolemy and Perdikkas) and was the first area to be plundered by the Romans when, in 199 B.C., they invaded the Macedonia of Philip V. Here, too, were played out some of the military engagements that preceded the final confrontation between Julius Caesar and Pompey at Pharsalos in Thessaly (48 B.C.). The conversion of Macedonia into a *provincia inermis* (unarmed province) from the time of Augustus, and the later shift of the frontiers of the Roman Empire to the northern Balkans plunged the region into the routine of daily life; left behind in the antechamber of events, it simply watched the centuries pass by, using the Via Egnatia, never pausing to rest. It awaited the stirring events of the 3rd century A.D. With the reforms of Diocletian and Constantine the Great, Elimeia and Orestis were attached to the new province of Thessaly. According to the *Notitia Dignitatum,* Upper Macedonia at the end of the 4th century A.D. was divided between the "dioceses" of Thessaly, Macedonia and New Epirus, and according to the "Synekdemos" of Hierokles, a text of A.D. 527 that reflects the situation of A.D. 460, this westernmost part of Macedonia was distributed between the administrative units of "Macedonia A", "Macedonia B", and "Thessaly".

Lying on the route from north to south, West (Upper)Macedonia did not escape the plundering attentions of the Goths, the Ostrogoths and the Slavs. In 479 the first of these captured Herakleia Lynkestis and put it to the torch. The Ostrogoths who followed in 482 razed it to the ground. Sklavenoi, Bulgarians and Kutrigurs sowed terror throughout the whole of the 6th century A.D., as they made for Thessaly, ravaging the countryside and burning cities and villages. Cities like Stoboi, Vargila, Herakleia had to wait for Justinian I before they recovered the lost brilliance of their basilicas and wealthy residences. And it was only at this period that passes and vital sites were clad in their crenellated castles. As part of a grand design, Keleteron, Serbia and Caesareia prepared for the following centuries, for the future barbarians and the ambitious conquerors of the North. For the centuries that would bring the Bulgarians of Samuel, the Normans of Roger, and the Franks of the Fourth Crusade.

A small part of West Macedonia was attached to the so-called "Despotate" of Epirus, a second (and largest) part to the jurisdiction of the Frankish kingdom of Thessalonike, and the third fell into the hands of the Bulgarians, before Upper Macedonia returned to the embrace of the regenerated Byzantine Empire after 1261, having suffered badly from the continuous turmoil and plundering. The future held no better promise however, for the armed confrontation in the bosom of the imperial dynasty (Andronikos II and III Palaiologoi, Ioannis V Palaiologos, Ioannis Kantakouzenos) on the one hand and the expansionist designs of the Serbian state on the other led to the capture of prisoners and high-sounding "liberations". Ochrid, Kastoria and Prilep passed from one camp to the other. From one occupation to another. The 14th century A.D. beheld the beginning of the end with blind eyes. Dazzled by passing victories, the still-born fireworks of ephemeral situations, and dizzied by the pursuit of glory, it left its rear exposed to the Ottomans, who in 1354 set foot on the continent of Europe. Serbs, Bulgarians, Albanians and Byzantines prepared the chains of captivity, in 1385 for Monastir (Bitola), after 1389, probably, for Kastoria and Ochrid and in 1393 for Serbia. No-one was there to stop them.

The Yürük Turks who settled in A.D. 1390 in the areas of Kozani and Ptolemais brought with them forced conversions to Islam. Amidst the whirlwind of conquest, the populations of the plains fled to the semi-mountainous or inaccessible areas with the Christianity of their forbears hidden away in their troubled souls. Villages were abandoned and memories died a slow death amongst the ruins. Tradition has it that this period of uprooting and displacement saw the foundation of Kleisoura, Voyatsiko and Selitsa, and that these were years in which settlements like Siatista and Kozani were strengthened, since their strong positions and the opportunities they afforded for a new way of life offered a longed-for security to the persecuted. The situation deteriorated further with the decline of the Ottoman Empire, which was evident as early as the end of the 16th and beginning of the 17th centuries A.D.: to the oppression by the Turkish authorities were added plundering raids by bands of Albanians and arbitrary acts of cruelty by a number of pashas. As elsewhere, however, after the initial shock and the painful realignments of the early years, the intolerable burden of slavery soon gave birth to champions of freedom and the faith, and mobilised the seed of that genius which the Greek nation hides - an inexhaustible store - in the bowels of its history. On the revered bodies of the new martyrs of the nation, Hosios Nikanor founded the monastery of Zavorda, and Hosios

Dionysios erected churches. Inventive craftsmen from the villages of Kastoria took heart and issued forth, taking their trowels and skills to the plains and villages to furnish wood-carved housing for the wealthy merchants of Nymphaion, Ochrid, Siatista, Kozani and Kastoria: merchants whose caravans filled the market places of Austro-Hungary and Constantinople, of Italy (via Dyrrhachion), of Moldo-Wallachia with wool, cotton, hides, tobacco and wheat; merchants who decorated the luxurious rooms of their *archontika* (mansions) with coloured wall-paintings, with dreams and wondrous visions. On the victims of acts of indescribable bestiality by irregulars or even by the official representatives of authority, and with the Russo-Turkish War of 1768-1774 promising a freedom that was not to be, the old Ziakas at Grevena, and the much-sung *klepht,* D. Totskas and his children revived the ancient glories of Thermopylae, and Kosmas Aitolos, Evgenios Voulgaris and the priest-monk Paraskevas of Amphilochia rekindled the teachings of Plato and Aristotle in young hearts. Together with West Macedonian emigrés in the lands of free Europe who from afar bestowed upon their fatherland whatever they could spare from their hard-earned incomes, they instilled into the suffering people endurance, stubborn obduracy and belief in a regeneration. Clergy and laymen, in the Century of Enlightenment, methodically prepared to enjoy the freedom of which they were in fact to be deprived of for at least a hundred years by the coarse rule there of Ali Pasha of Ioannina, by international political developments and by the interests of the great powers, and the death rattle of the once mighty Ottoman Empire. On the soil of West Macedonia, freedom, bathed in blood, accompanied the Greek armies of the Balkan Wars of 1912-13, holding by the hand the sadly lost Pavlos Melas († 1904), the Archbishop of Kastoria Germanos Karavangelis, Athanasios Brouphas († 1896), the chieftain from Boion, the warrior chief Kotas and a host of other unnamed combatants of Pindos and Grammos, the free besieged caught between the hammer of Slav expansionism and the anvil of the Ottoman yoke.

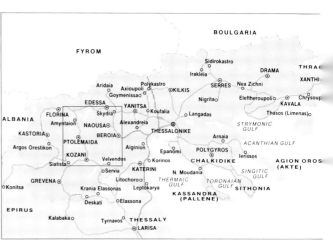

KOZANI
and its region

510

HISTORICAL REVIEW

In the 18th to 19th centuries A.D. Kozani was a dynamic commercial and industrial centre, with "grandiose two-storey houses", adorning the four districts of Saint Athanasios, Saint Demetrios, the Saints Anargyroi and Saint Georgios, very little of which has survived post-war town-planning and programmes of urban renewal to stand tall amongst the tasteless standardised apartment blocks.

Created in the 14th to 15th centuries A.D. by transfers of population from Epirus and neighbouring Servia, the small township to the south of the Koilada of Kailaria which had the character of a closed self-sufficient settlement, standing formerly close to dense forests, received further influxes of population from the Agrapha villages (1612) and other parts of Thessaly down to the 18th century, that transformed it into an important commercial and cultural centre with notable activity in the areas of tanning, weaving, wax-making, bronze-work and furs, which spread the wings of profit and progress mainly to Hungary and other countries of free Europe. Under cover of the protection granted it by the favour of the sultan's mother.

Merchants and craftsmen, emigrés and wealthy bourgeois endowed 18th-century Kozani with cobbled streets, fountains, churches, bridges and *archontika,* like those of Diapha-Paschalides, G. Lassanis, Gr. Vourkas (A.D.

510. *General view of Kozani.*

1748), Vourkas-Katsikas and of E. Vamvakas. In 1813 they gifted to it the "good life" by building, in the enclosure of the church of Saint Nikolaos, the House of Improvement that became known throughout West Macedonia - that is the library formed by donations of books from archbishop Meletios (1734-1753), Euphronios Raphael Popovits a son of Kozani who was a professor in Vienna, and others, which is still today a beacon of knowledge for those who comb the archives searching for the memories and commands of the Nation.

The valuable dedications in venerable houses of worship (the candelabra in the church of Saint Nikolaos, a work of 1744 and the gift of Karakazanis, who lived in exile in Hungary, the sacerdotal vessels and the bronze chandeliers are mentioned here as a token example), and the concern shown for the erection or renewal of churches and public welfare buildings attest here too, as in countless examples in other Macedonian towns, to that constant interest of the Greek in beautifying and glorifying his own native town. Examples of benefaction and concern for one's birthplace.

THE ARCHONTIKA (MANSIONS)

The archontiko of Gr. Vourkas

The residence of Gr. Vourkas, one of the best preserved archontika in Kozani, built in 1748, fortunately did not share the fate of the twin structure to the west, which was demolished in 1971. It was purchased by the Greek state and is now used as the headquarters of the staff charged with protecting the monuments of the region.

A two-storey building with a small paved courtyard on the north side, and formerly standing in the middle of a large private estate, the archontiko of Gr. Vourkas is a typical example of Kozani mansions in the middle of the 18th century A.D.: on the ground floor was a spacious paved area *(mesia)* into which one emerged from the main entrance, and from which a wooden staircase led up to the first floor (the staircase was closed by a trap-door, or *glavani),* on which were the summer reception rooms *(mousaphir onta),* equipped with built-in cupboards *(mousandres),* divans *(minderia)* and hearths, a *doxato* (a raised platform for the orchestra), bedrooms, cel-

511. *The Folklore Museum of Kozani.*

512. *Mousandra (cupboard) in the kalos ontas (sitting room) of the mansion of Gr. Vourkas at Kozani.*

513. *Panelled doors in the mansion of Gr. Vourkas at Kozani.*

lars, and sitting rooms *(kaloi ontades),* enclosed balconies *(sachnisia)* and fanlights with plaster decoration, the gaps in which were closed by coloured glass, allowed the inhabitants to gaze on the river Haliakmon below and bathed the interior - lavishly decorated with floral and other geometric compositions - with warm light. On the ground floor, the courtyard with the hearth *(bouchari),* the coffee room *(kafe onta)* with its braziers *(mangalia)* and the storeroom *(magazes)* were a focus for the activity of the owner and his family during the endless winter months. Barrels *(vaenia)* of wine, storage jars for cereals and liquids, rooms for food and agricultural produce were all kept in the vaulted basement. The security of the property was guaranteed by a stone, saddle-vaulted enclosure two metres high, with a strong wooden, nail-studded outer door.

THE ARCHAEOLOGICAL MUSEUM

The archaeological collection of the county of Kozani has been housed since 1989 in a neoclassical building in Dimokratias street known as the "Katsikas House", which was presented to the Municipality of Kozani by the Panayotides family. It consists of portable finds brought to light by, mainly, rescue excavations, in various parts of ancient Eordaia, Elimeia and south Orestis, which were handed over by citizens who were lovers of antiquity or saved from disappearing forever by conscientious employees of the state. Vases from the Prehistoric to the Roman periods, weapons, jewellery, inscriptions, sculptures, funerary stelai, clay figurines and coins. The four rooms of the residence-museum house a variety of finds in tasteful wall-cases and freestanding showcases, enabling the visitor to browse through the history of the region, its artistic achievements and the activity of its craftsmen and artists, to follow the movement of its commercial and industrial products, and to verify for himself the high standard of living enjoyed by the inhabitants of Upper Macedonia - this mountainous area of northwest Greece with its large plains, great rivers and harsh ranges of hills. We may admire the metal vases, in silver and bronze, from the Classical cemetery of Kozani and from tombs at Apidea Boiou, Metamorphosis, Saint Paraskeve, Anarrachi and Saint Christophoros. Helmets and offensive weapons, in bronze and iron, from Phrourio and Elati. Jewellery from Tsotyli, Axiokastro, Spilia, Ano Komi, Bouphari and Apidea - all superb examples of ancient gold-working and miniature metal-working from the Iron Age to the Roman period. Creations of the potters wheel from the Prehistoric settlements around the Yellow Lake (Sari Giol), now drained, from Late Helladic tombs at Ano Kome and tombs of the Mycenaean period at Servia, from Protogeometric settlements on the banks of the river Haliakmon, and from Early Iron Age cist graves at Koilada. Red-figure vases from Metamorphosis and Pharangi, and the Classical cemetery in Philippou street, Kozani and at Apidea, and Hellenistic and Roman pottery from Eratyra, Tsotyli and Platania. Inscriptions, reliefs and sculptures worked in the round from Koilada, Perdikkas, Liknades, Elati and Exochi, which attest to the worship of chthonic and heavenly deities, immortalise the memory of beloved ones, preserve political institutions and, most importantly of all, bear witness to the unbroken presence of the Greek language and Greek civilization in this sensitive region of front-line Hellenism.

514

514. Silver inscribed bowl from the cemetery on Philippou Street in Kozani. Beginning of the 5th century B.C. Kozani, Archaeological Museum.

THE HISTORICAL-FOLKLORE MUSEUM

Founded by the Association of Letters and Arts of the county of Kozani, the Historical-Folklore Museum and the Museum of Natural History of Kozani, housed in a multi-storey building erected in 1987 in P. Charisi street in the style of a Macedonian mansion, comprises collections of facsimiles and original specimens from the eco-system of the region (fossils, stuffed animals, birds and insects), reconstructions of the interiors of traditional houses, and both outdoor and indoor work-places, objects-tools of everyday rural and city life from other, more human and more sensitive periods. In the upper storeys and the basement unfold scenes, long-forgotten in our days, of gold-smiths' workshops, mobile photographic studios, pottery-workshops, marble cutters' workshops, shoe makers' and tailors' shops; costumes adorned with silver parade by, together with precious dowries, mirrors of the popular soul and popular art, guarded in wood-carved chests; and the wisdom, ability and inexhaustible inventiveness of the West Macedonians from the time of the Ottoman occupation down to the first post-war years are lovingly and carefully displayed. Before de-Hellenisation and the division of memory into building plots.

The Museum of the Macedonian Struggle, founded by the Society of Letters and Arts of the County of Kozani in 1992, is situated about 30 km to the south-west of Kozani, near the village of Chromio.

515. *Ontas (room) of the George Sakellariou mansion at Kozani. Second half of the 17th century. Kozani, Folklore Museum.*

515

516

517

516. Thracian korones (crowns). Kozani, Folklore Museum.

517. Dowry chest, 1777. Kozani, Folklore Museum.

518. Tepelikia (ornamental kerchief pins). Kozani, Folklore Museum.

518

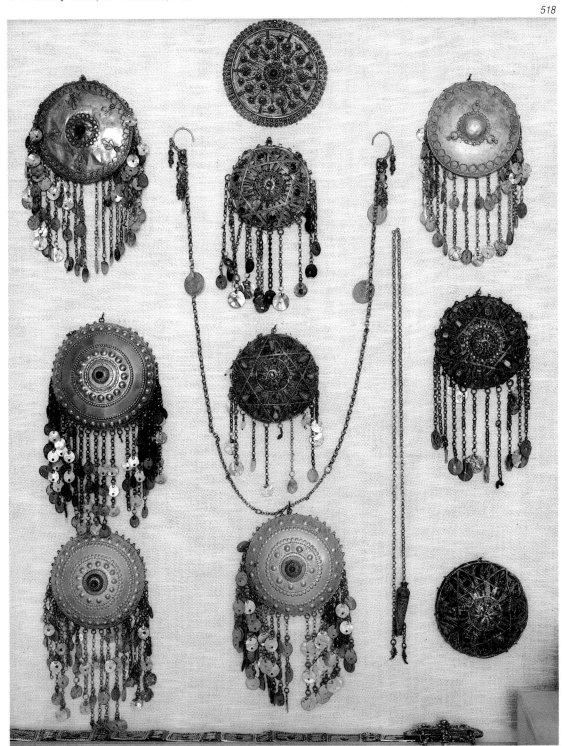

410

AIANE
and its region

519

HISTORICAL REVIEW

The existence of the town of Aiane in Elimeia is attested by both literary (Stephanus of Byzantium, the Palatine Anthology) and epigraphic evidence. According to the mythological tradition, Aiane was founded by Aianos, son of Elymos, a Tyrrhenian. With a prehistoric (Mycenaean period, Early Iron Age) Archaic and Classical past, the region around the modern village of the same name, which has yielded both portable and nonportable remains, evolved mainly in the Hellenistic period and the years after the Roman Conquest.

Archaeological discoveries of recent years locate the ancient settlement of Aiane on the hill of Megali Rachi roughly half-way along the road to Kaisareia, and place its cemeteries at Tskaria and Leivadia, to the east and north of the settlement respectively. Isolated finds have been discovered from time to time, however, at the sites of Rachi Tseika, Rachi Kommenoi, in the area of the modern community, at Megali Rachi etc., attesting to the existence of satellite rural settlements and tombs, which are dated from the time of the Early Bronze Age to late antiquity. Although it seems premature to arrive at any firm conclusions, since investigation is still at the stage of searching for secure reference points, it seems fairly certain that life at Aiane came to an

519. The acropolis of ancient Aiane.

end some time in the 1st century B.C. and that the city was then transferred to neighbouring Paliokastro near Kaisareia.

This new administrative centre of the region, the "city of the Caesars" as it is called by an early Christian inscription, was the seat of the bishopric of Kaisareia in the early Byzantine period. Protected by a stout defensive enceinte, the foundation of Valentinian II and Valens (A.D. 364-367) - most probably - played a leading role under Justinian I, as a bastion in the defence of the Byzantine Empire against the barbarian hordes of the North, a role secured to it by its privileged position on the banks of the river Haliakmon, opposite the pass of Sarandaporos to Thessaly.

The rapid change in the political scene, however, resulting from the emergence of the Bulgarian danger, moved the line of resistance to neighbouring Servia, stripping Kaisareia of the honours showered on it by the past. Basil II the Bulgar Slayer, indeed, possibly out of fear that the raids would be repeated, ordained the demolition of the fortresses of Elimeia - those at Servia, Soskos and certainly that at Kaisareia. Before the subjection of the region - and the whole of Macedonia - to the Ottomans, Aiane/Kaisareia saw the Normans in A.D. 1185, on their way to the second city of the Byzantine Empire, experienced Latin rule as part of the Frankish Kingdom of Thessalonike, on the borders of the "Despotate" of Epirus, and was captured by the Serbian armies of Stephen Dušan (1355). Early in the 15th century it was plunged into the middle ages of the Ottoman occupation.

With an unmixed Greek population, Kalliane - Kali Aiane, according to popular etymology - resisted the fate of slavery with its belief in the ability of Christianity to endure; it founded the churches of the Archangel Michael and of Saint Nikolaos (1548 and 1552) and continued to honour the grace of the Virgin in a Komnenian building at the centre of the settlement, and the glory of Saint Demetrios (11th to 12th century A.D.) at a distance of two kilometres to the west.

During the years of preparation for the national uprising (18th century) the rich villages on the north banks of the river Haliakmon, caught between the hammer of the *klephts* and the anvil of the Muslim-Albanians, fell prey to terror and anarchy.

Reduced to a wretched condition, Kalliane offered itself to the Macedonian struggle, offered its priests and its inhabitants, and welcomed the Greek armies of liberation in December 1912.

THE ARCHAEOLOGICAL SITE

THE CITY

Ancient Aiane, which was in all probability unwalled, spread over the hill of Megali Rachi, one and a half kilometres to the north-east of the modern village of the same name, on a series of terraces formed by the rocky terrain next to the deep ravine of Chandaka, overlooking the bed of the river Haliakmon. Controlling all four points of the horizon, and with rich sources of drinking water, it has all the hallmarks of a township-fortress-observation post, and also of a point of reference for the villas and isolated installations scattered throughout the region (Rachi Tseika, Kouri, Lakka Papazisi, Ano Komi etc.).The remains have been discovered so far of three buildings, probably of a public character, standing on the various plateaux of the hill. The architectural remains that have escaped plundering by the inhabitants of the region and the other portable finds give an indication of the monumental character of these structures and date the earliest building phases to the beginning of the 5th century B.C.

Two of these buildings stand on the eastern plateaux and include rooms with stoas; one is perhaps to be identified with the residence of the ruler of the region and the other with the cult wing of the complex, where the sanctuary of Themis is possibly to be sought. The third building is on the crest of the south hill, and also has large dimensions and a roughly square plan, with a large circular cistern at the centre.

Around the highest terrace, on which has been located the administrative-religious centre, private residences with several buildings phases standing on plateaux set at different levels, reveal the vast number of different architectural types to which the inhabitants of Aiane had recourse in order to tame the sloping terrain: the house conventionally called "the house of the pi-

520. Bronze statuette of a peplophoros kore. Middle of the 5th century B.C. Aiane, Archaeological Collection.

521. Clay figurine of Cybele from a house at ancient Aiane. First half of the 2nd century B.C. Aiane, Archaeological Collection.

522. Bronze vase from the bottom of the cistern of a public building on the hill of ancient Aiane. 2nd century B.C. Aiane, Archaeological Collection.

520

521

522

523. The stele of Aiane is one of a series of Macedonian funerary stelai dating from the 4th century B.C. These were produced by local craftsmen influenced by Attic models, and are characterised by their provincial clumsiness and freshness. This stele depicts a Macedonian family: the dead man, seated and wearing a chlamys and kausia (Macedonian hat), two women with a child in front of him, and another man behind him. 4th century B.C. Paris, Musée du Louvre.

thoi" to the north, the lower courses of which are of rubble masonry and the upper of sun-dried bricks, probably had a wooden structure on the first storey. The "house of the staircases", on the southern plateau, standing at the foot of the rock against which it is also supported, has several levels that communicate with each other by means of stone staircases. Part of the ground floor was given over to storage-rooms that contained pithoi, a hearth and vases and objects of household function, though some figurines of the goddess Cybele were also discovered in them. Finally, the "house of the loom-weights" to the south-east with a vast number of loom-weights. The settlement had workshops producing figurines and metal-working workshops and maintained cultural contacts with the rest of the world down to the period at which it was abandoned. Throughout its life, however, it remained a provincial town, in the hinterland of a farming and stock-raising country. A town that was organised, it seems, on the model of the Greek cities of the south (agoranomos etc.). The ruins of its houses, public buildings, and temples of Herakles Kynagidas, Hermes Agoraios and Zeus Hyp-

524

525

524. Piece of silver sheet in the shape of an ivy leaf with gilding on the upper surface, from the north cemetery of ancient Aiane. First half of the 4th century B.C. Aiane, Archaeological Collection.

525. Gold roundels with impressed representations of Macedonian stars, from the north cemetery of ancient Aiane. First half of the 4th century B.C. Aiane, Archaeological Collection.

sistos supplied the early building material for neighbouring Palaiokastron near Kaisareia, to which the administrative centre was transferred at the beginning of the Imperial period. Two honorific bases, one for the emperor Antoninus Pius (A.D. 138-161) and the other for the emperor Marcus Aurelius (A.D. 161-180) suggest that this new site was the headquarters of the Koinon of the Elimeiotes, the centre of the political and religious organisation of villages and towns of Elimeia.

THE CEMETERIES

The cemeteries of Aiane have been located both around the hill of the city and on distant sites, sometimes in clusters of graves, and sometimes taking the form of isolated monuments. They date from the Late Bronze Age down to the Late Hellenistic period.

The cemetery of Archaic and Classical times, at the site of Leivadia to the north of the settlement, consists of twelve built chamber tombs and other smaller cist and pit graves, in some cases set in funerary enclosures. The majority of them were plundered in antiquity, but several of their precious grave offerings escaped the pillaging: clay figurines, vases in the black- and red-

figure style, cut-out plaques of bone, silver and gold jewellery or mouthpieces, metal vessels, glass aryballoi, spear-points, helmets, necklaces, earrings etc. Both the architecture of the funerary structures, and the type of grave offerings and burial customs place Aiane of the Archaic and Classical periods in the same cultural group as contemporary cemeteries in Macedonia.

The following period (4th -1st centuries B.C.) is represented by the cemetery at Tskaria, about one kilometre to the east of the ancient city. The 80 pit graves, some plundered and some badly damaged by ploughing, which were simply dug into the soft limestone of the region, contained bronze vases, local clay pottery, weapons, bow fibulae, strigils etc. and belonged to the "koine" of the late Classical-Hellenistic periods as formulated in Macedonia. The Hellenistic cemetery of Aiane was probably the source of the funerary stelai dating from the 2nd and 1st centuries B.C., some carved with reliefs others plain, that now adorn the local collection - the majority of them proof of a love of antiquity on the part of the inhabitants, who handed them in years before the beginning of the systematic investigation of the site.

THE ARCHAEOLOGICAL COLLECTION

It is to the love of antiquity of the inhabitants and the zeal and enthusiasm of the charismatic local teacher in the period following the civil war, that the Collection of Aiane owes its soul. The archaeological collection has been housed since 1969 on the ground floor of the Community administrative Offices, together with the folk souvenirs of the Greek modern history. Countless finds handed in by pupils and conscientious citizens, along with grave offerings from tombs and portable objects from buildings brought to light by recent archaeological investigations, prehistoric pottery, archaic statues, hellenistic funerary stelai, figurines, Roman inscriptions, coins from all periods, weapons, jewellery, and vases from the Classical period and later, founded at Aiane, Rymnio, Kteni and Kaisareia - all make this a brilliant collection from Elimeia, a corner of the macedonian north that was unknown or scarcely known a few years ago. The collection will soon be given the home it deserves in a new building.

526. Clay stand. 15th-14th centuries B.C. Aiane, Archaeological Collection.

527. Head of a clay figurine from an Archaic tomb. Second half of the 6th century B.C. Aiane, Archaeological Collection.

526

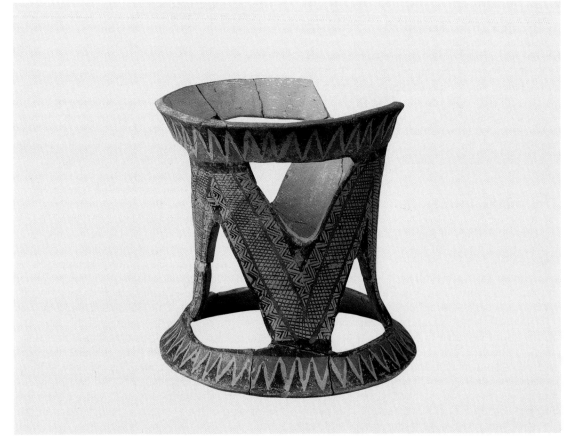

418

528. *Clay female figurine. Middle of the 6th century B.C. Aiane, Archaeological Collection.*

529. *Red-figure lekythos by the Bowdoin painter (?). 470-460 B.C. Aiane, Archaeological Collection.*

528

529

530. Bronze bow fibulae, from a tomb in the east cemetery. First half of the 4th century B.C. Aiane, Archaeological Collection.

531. Bronze strigil; the handle has a stamp with the name of the owner or maker: ΑΔΑΜΑΣ- Adamas. From a tomb in the east cemetery. 4th century B.C. Aiane, Archaeological Collection.

532. Bronze oinochoe, from a tomb in the east cemetery. Second half of the 4th century B.C. Aiane, Archaeological Collection.

531

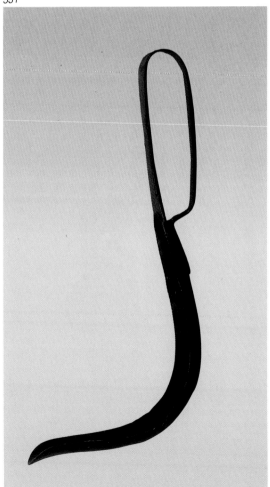

532

533. Gold funerary mouthpiece. Second half of the 6th century B.C.. Aiane, Archaeological Collection.

534. Gold band earrings. Aiane, Archaeological Collection.

535. Gold bead in the form of an amphora. Aiane, Archaeological Collection.

536-537. Gold pin and necklace with gold beads in the form of amphoras. Aiane, Archaeological Collection.

536

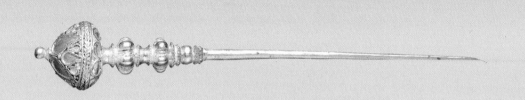

537

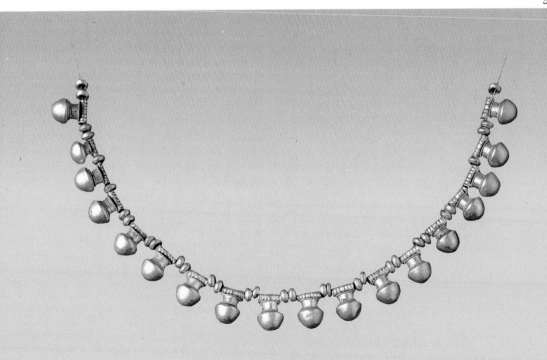

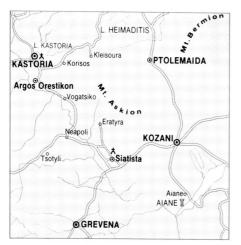

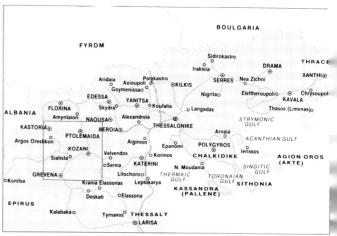

SIATISTA
and its region

538

HISTORICAL REVIEW

Siatista was founded, probably at the beginning of the 15th century A.D., by Christians from the plains fleeing before the Turks, who were then expanding into northern Greece, and lies at a height of 930 m. above sea level at the heart of an inhospitable landscape, hostile to man, formed of the monotonous grey curves of mountain peaks and bare mountain sides. The inhabitants brought with them, behind the uncertainty and instability of the times, their high morale, the genius of the nation, Greek speech and an indomitable spirit. And above all, amazing drive and energy.

The town consists of two settlements, the lower Geraneia and the upper Chora, in which evolved a distinctive urban centre with an architectural style distinguished both by its modern features and by its faithfulness to tradition; this development was based on the prosperity stemming from the occupation of the progressive inhabitants of Siatista with furs, weaving and viticulture, and the development of strong commercial contacts not only with Epirus but also, in the course of time, with Western Europe (Venice, Budapest, Vienna) and Russia.

Thanks to the financial contributions from well-to-do emigrés, the economic prosperity of wealthy merchants, and the skill of craftsmen from Konitsa and other villages of the Pindos range, roads were paved *(kalderimia),* water-supply and drainage networks were planned, and two-storey houses with tiled roofs were erected *(archontika),* with enclosed balconies

538. View of Siatista with Mount Askion (Siniatsiko) in the background.

(sachnisia), fanlights of multi-coloured glass, store-rooms on the ground floor, and sunny verandas (liakota) and reception rooms (kaloi ontades) adorned with coloured wood-carved ceilings and painted wooden panelling on the walls. From about 1710 to the end of the century, the brilliant 18th century of the Greek enlightenment, Siatista was adorned with wonderful examples of urban architecture: the archontika of Poulko (1752-59), Kanatsoulis (1746-1757?), Manousis (1746?), Nerantzopoulos (1754-1755) and many others.

THE ARCHONTIKA (MANSIONS)

The archontika of Poulko in Geraneia, those of Manousis and Nerantzopoulos in Chora, restored in the traditional style, and the property of the Kanatsouli family (1746-1757?), which have been expropriated by the state and are open to visitors, are characteristic examples of the architecture of Siatista from the period when this wealthy town was at its zenith. Behind strong, well-built enclosures and within paved courtyards, these two-storey mansions raise their tower-like bodies, stone-clad and impregnable, the timber framework visible in their plastered outer walls, with barred windows and heavy, nail-studded doors on the ground floor, and airy enclosed balconies (sachnisia) on the first floor with

539. The mansion of Nerantzopoulos in the district of Chora, Siatista.

540. Lunette with coloured glass from the mansion of Nerantzopoulos.

541. Part of the wall-painting from the winter ontas (room), with the main scene depicting Aphrodite. From the Kanatsoulis mansion in the district of Chora, Siatista.

542. Part of a wall-painting from the Keratzis mansion in the district of Chora, Siatista.

lace-like coloured lunettes and sensitive paintings.

As well as gardens, out-door ovens, kitchens, stables, chicken-coops, wells, pavilions and store-rooms, they had timbered courtyard on the ground floor (mesies), sunny balconies on the mezzanine (diliaka), sitting rooms on the first floor (ontades) with painted walls and brightly coloured cupboards (mesandres), panelled ceilings, and hearths with relief plaster surrounds.

A world of surprising other-worldliness. Amidst its solitude and memories of the past, a world still human. A world of men. Nurtured on the tradition of the hellenism of Byzantium and of the West-European spirit of the period. The small world, the great world of the Macedonians under Turkish rule.

541

542

426

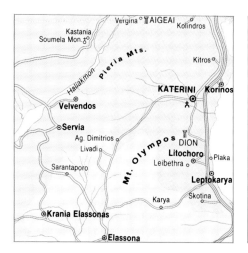

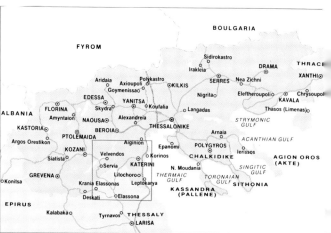

SERVIA
and its region

543

HISTORICAL REVIEW

The fortress of Servia, a conical hill with strong walls dominating the narrow pass of Sarandaporos that communicates between the middle reaches of the river Haliakmon and Thessaly, is now mute, its memories climbing the inaccessible slopes of the Pierian mountains, as it contemplates its turbulent past shrouded in abandonment. At the time of Evliya Çelebi, the main-village, also called Servia, at the foot of the hill had six districts of Muslims and eight with a mixture of Greeks and Jews, with well-constructed stone houses, and mulberry trees and vines in the gardens. It had twelve mosques, a tekke (muslim monastery), a bath-house and shops. It had an advanced silk industry and produced bathing-wraps that were famous throughout the entire Ottoman Empire.

The region has traces of habitation from the prehistoric period - Vasilara, Rachi, Velvendos, Avles Goules - and also from the historical period (the "state of the Oblostioi", known from an inscription of A.D. 200, was probably located somewhere near here), though it rose to prominence mainly in Byzantine times. It was here that Heraklios (610-641) first settled the Serbs, from whom the place took its name according to one theory; here too, Basil II the Bylgar Slayer exiled tzar of the Bulgarians Samuel (A.D. 1001) and later, in 1223, Theodore Komnenos Doukas An-

543. Part of the fortress of Servia, with the Polyphytos dam in the background.

gelos despot of Epirus established a bishop here, having detached the city from the Frankish kingdom of Thessalonike. In 1256 Servia came under the rule of Theodore II Laskares emperor of Nicaea, in 1341 it passed into under the jurisdiction of Stephen Dušan, and in 1350 it became a possession of Ioannis Kantakouzenos.

The pass had strategic significance from as early as antiquity, since it controlled the crossing into southern Greece; from the very first moment of the Turkish conquest, it attracted the interest of the new regulators of the political situation in the Balkan peninsula: the first occupation of the pass in 1393 was followed a few years later by its definitive capture which laid the foundations of Ottoman domination in the area. No mosques have been located inside the enclosure of the medieval settlement, however and none of the six christian churches inside the fortress - Saint Konstantinos, Zoodochos Pigi, Saint Nikolaos, Saint Solomoni, Saint Ioannis the Baptist and the Katechoumenoi - was converted into a mosque, attesting to the harmonious coexistence of the two communities.

Times were difficult, however, and the anarchy born of the Venetian-Turkish confrontation (1684-1699) led organised bands of robbers to unspeakable acts of violence against the inhabitants, especially those of the semi-mountainous areas like Servia. Despite this adversity, however, and despite pressure on the part of the Turkish authorities, attempts to force conversion to Islam, and the exploitation of the tax-farmers down to the middle of the 18th century, the activity of the local inhabitants continued unabated and the trade-fair *(bazar)* of Servia acquired a reputation far beyond the narrow boundaries of the surrounding plain. This was the period in which Kosmas Aitolos was sowing the seeds of knowledge and of national consciousness, in which the urban class was searching for its identity, Christianity for its faith and Hellenism for its roots. The period of the terrorism of Ali Pasha of Ioannina, of the *armatoles* and of insurrection. Of *klephts* and sacrifices.

THE MONUMENTS

THE WALLS

The fortress of Servia has a plan completely irregular in shape, dictated by the irregular configuration of the steep rock on which it was built, and is divided into three uneven parts: the acropolis, the last refuge in case of capture, at the extreme and highest point, the upper city, and the lower city, with a dividing wall between them. Despite the difficulties and the lack of adequate information, it has been suggested that the defence wall was constructed in the years A.D. 1216-1257, when Servia was occupied by the despots of Epirus, while repairs and rebuilding work are assigned to the decade A.D. 1341-1350, a period of Serbian occupation.

THE CHURCHES

Of the six churches preserved inside the enclosure of the lower city, the only evidence for the existence of three of them are the formless ruins.

The imposing, three-aisled basilica (after A.D. 1001), the most eminent church of Servia, possible honoured the name of Saint Demetrios - its present name (Katechoumenoi or Saranda Portes) is undoubtedly a creation of the scholarly tradition.

The church of Saints Theodoroi, a patriarchal monastery, is an aisleless basilica in type, with a pitched wooden roof, dating from the second half of the 11th century A.D., and is enclosed within a four-sided roofed room with an attached cistern.

Nestling to the north-east of the basilica on a platform especially cut into the rock, the aisleless chapel of Saint Ioannis the Baptist, a building of the 14th century A.D., was repaired and extended during the course of its life. Its badly damaged wall-paintings for long helplessly contemplated the sky of Elimeia, before the Archaeological Service protected them with a newly constructed roof.

544. View of the acropolis of Servia from the east.

545. The south-east side of the 11th century three-aisled basilica in the lower city of Servia.

544

545

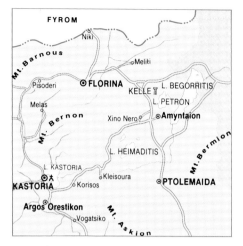

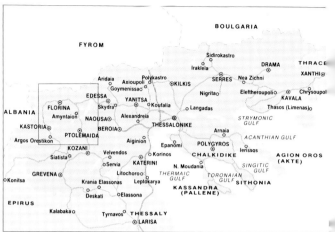

PETRES (KELLE?)
and its region

546

HISTORICAL REVIEW

Flourishing mainly in the interval between the end of the 3rd to the middle of the 1st centuries B.C., the settlement on the hill (at the north extreme of Eordaia) 1.5 kilometres to the northwest of the community of Petres and about 42 kilometres south-west of Florina is a typical example of an Upper Macedonian village, with an economy based on farming and stock-raising. Although the identification of the site with that of Kelle known from medieval portolanos is attractive, the archaeologist's spade has yet to discover epigraphic confirmation of this. Portable finds have demonstrated its importance, however, located as it was a short distance from the Via Egnatia, next to the Petres lake, which was once larger than at present and at the head of the fertile plain of Amyntaion, from which it was possible to cross into Lynkestis.

Interest in the systematic investigation of the site was unjustifiably late in manifesting itself. It was not until 1982 that the Archaeological Service attempted for the first time (an endeavour that has been repeated since at regular intervals) to add a historical dimension to the isolated finds occasionally brought to light by chance - votive inscriptions, manumissions and funerary inscriptions, statues, mile-stones and other objects, now in the Museum of Florina.

THE ANCIENT SETTLEMENT

Built behind a stout defence wall with courses of poros blocks, the settlement on the "Gratista"

546. *The hill of Gratista at Petres with the ruins of the ancient city (Kelle?).*

hill has a free urban development exploiting as best it could the contours of the hill. The residences are organised in groups of three or four houses, sharing a common outer wall and climbing the terraces on the south, east and west slopes, from which they control a wide radius of the surrounding area. The houses of Petres were two-storey structures with no courtyard but with basement rooms for storing wet and dry foodstuffs or for use as workshops, and they contribute to a better understanding of the hellenistic house by adding their own particular version to the general type.

In contrast with the rubble masonry of the ground-floor walls, which also serve as supports for the entire structure, the upper storeys were built of lighter material (timber-frames). These were intended as residential rooms, and their interiors were decorated with very high quality

plaster in a variety of colour combinations. The settlement was criss-crossed by a system of horizontal - parallel to the contours - streets about 2.50 m. wide, with other narrower streets (1.50 m. wide) at right-angles to them. A system of clay pipes, parallel with the streets, and ending in fountains and wells, ensured that the settlement had a continuous supply of drinking water.

With its dual nature as a farming centre - thanks to the fertile plain - and a commercial entrepôt - thanks to the Via Egnatia and its predecessor - the settlement at Petres in Eordaia enjoyed great economic prosperity and a high standard of living, as can be concluded from its confirmed commercial and cultural contacts with cities in Lower and East Macedonia and also with the West. The settlement had local workshops for pottery, figurine-production, metal-working and probably also sculpture. At the same time, the vast number of farm tools reveals that the inhabitants also engaged in farming activities.

About the middle of the 1st century B.C., the hellenistic city was abandoned and the population transferred to the site of the modern village of Petres, where settlement phases from Roman times have been attested.

547. Ruins of the ancient city (Kelle?) on the hill of Gratista at Petres. The plain of Amyntaion can be seen in the background, with part of the lake of Petres at the top left.

547

THE ARCHAEOLOGICAL MUSEUM OF FLORINA

548

The Archaeological Museum of Florina is housed in a 1965 two-storey building opposite the railway station. It contains prehistoric vessels and objects of daily use from Servia near Kozani and other settlements of Lynkestis (Armenochori); inscribed roof-tiles from the Hellenistic period from houses at ancient Lyke, which was excavated in the west part of the islet of Ayios Achillios (Orestis); vases and other objects from the ancient settlement at Petres (Eordaia); vases from the Hellenistic city on the hill of Ayios Panteleimon in Florina, votive stelae with relief scenes, funerary stelae from Kato Kleines, Ethniko, Vevi, Skopos, Achlada, and Pyle; honorary inscriptions from Saint Achillios; mile-stones from the Via Egnatia from Petres (Eordaia); statues of Artemis and mortals heroised after death; along with wall-paintings detached from the church of Saint Achillios.

548. Clay black-figure krater from a local workshop. The belly of the vase has a relief zone decorated with scenes from the Sack of Troy, with the inscriptions ΙΛΙΟΝ (Ilium), ΝΕΟΠΤΟΛΕΜΟΣ (Neoptolemos) and [ΣΤΡ]ΑΤΙΩΤΑΙ (soldiers). Second half of the 2nd century B.C. Florina, Archaeological Museum.

549. Clay black-glaze skyphos from a local workshop with relief decoration of long, broad petals around a central medallion with a rosette. End of the 2nd-beginning of the 1st centuries B.C. Florina, Archaeological Museum.

549

550

552

550. Torso of a headless marble statue of Artemis from Petres. Roman period. Florina, Archaeological Museum.

551. Inscribed marble funerary stele of the family of Dabreios, from Petres. 2nd century B.C. Florina, Archaeological Museum.

552. Marble votive stele with procession of arrephoroi, 2nd century A.D. Florina, Archaeological Museum.

553. Marble parapet slab from an iconostasis, from the church of Saint Achillios. 11th century. Florina, Archaeological Museum.

554. Detached wall-painting from the church of Saint Achillios, depicting the archangel Michael. 12th century. Florina, Archaeological Museum.

555. Sanctuary doors with a scene of the Annunciation from the church of Saint Athanasios at Ayios Germanos, Prespa. 1527/8. Florina, Archaeological Museum.

553

554

555

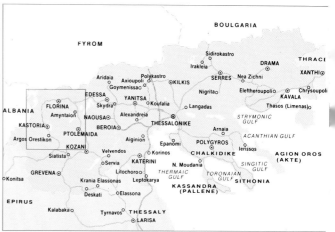

KASTORIA
and its region

556

HISTORICAL REVIEW

The Kastoria of Justinian I, built precisely on the same site as the modern city and known as Kastron in the middle Byzantine sources, has preserved little of its ancient Greek and Roman past: the numerous portable finds, two or three inscriptions and a number of architectural members are the only testimony from Keletron - the Celetrum of Livy - the city of Orestis whose fluctuating destiny is still today mirrored in the dark waters of the lake of the same name by which it is enclosed. Almost all the remains from the past (defence walls, churches) belong to the Byzantine and post-Byzantine periods. This fortress by the lake was visited (199 B.C.) by the Romans under the consul Sulpicius, was destroyed by Alaric's Visigoths (A.D. 385) or, according to others, by Theoderic the leader of the Ostrogoths (A.D. 480), and captured by a ruse in A.D. 918 by the Bulgarian tzar Symeon. In 1018, after the dissolution of the short-lived Bylgarian state of Samuel, Basil II Bulgar Slayer established his general Eustathios Daphnomilis here with an army to supervise the surrounding region and the passes. Standing on the routes from north to south and from west to east, Kastoria was captured, after the defeat of Alexios I Komnenos at Dyrrhachion, by the Normans of Bohemund, son of Guiscard (A.D. 1081), came under the control of the "De-

556. Panoramic view of Kastoria.

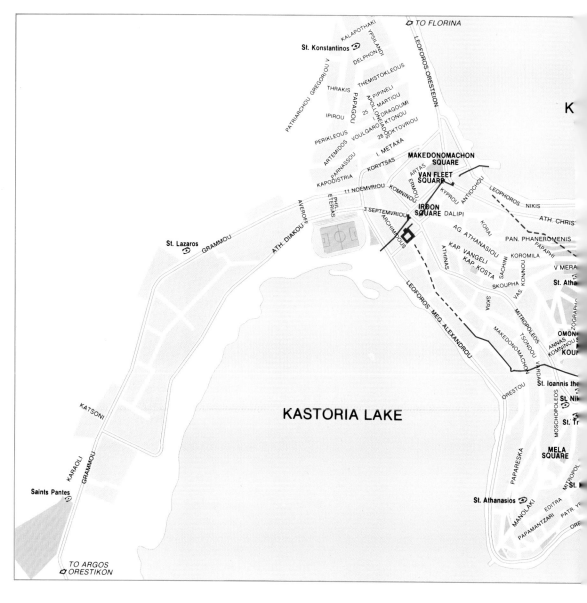

557. Plan of Kastoria showing the byzantine monuments.

spotate" of Epirus (before A.D. 1220), was annexed to the empire of Nicaea (A.D. 1252, 1259) and, after A.D. 1261, formed an integral part of the revived Byzantine Empire. From A.D. 1334 to 1341, the city was victim of the uncertainty and fluidity prevalent in Macedonia on the morrow of the civil war between the Palaiologoi, and was caught between the conquering designs of the Serb kral Stephen Dušan and the attempts of Andronikos III Palaiologos to preserve the territory he had won. The reign of Ioannis Kantakouzenos (middle of the 14th century A.D.), and later, was similarly a period of changes of master. Sometime shortly before A.D. 1387, when the final bastions were capitulating one after the other to the

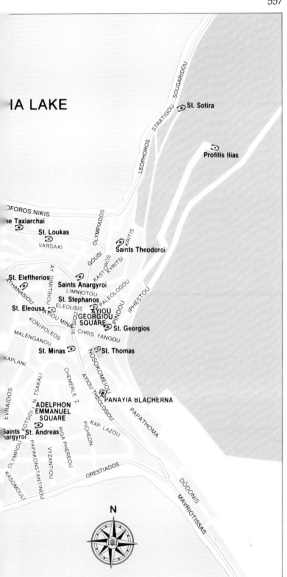

slavery of the inhabitants was soothed by the balsam poured on their souls by hosios Dionysos and later by Kosmas Aitolos, the pagan yoke was alleviated by their occupation with profit-making professions (fur trade, specialisation in the sector of building etc.), and obscurantism and intolerance were mitigated by the flourishing of letters, by contacts with free Europe and by migration. The seat of a *kaymakam,* Kastoria had a school from as early as 1614, maintained by Kastorianoi in Constantinople, the teachers in which included, at various times, G. Palladas (later the patriarch of Alexandria from A.D. 1688 to 1710), Methodios Anthrakitis, Anastasios Vasilopoulos and others. It is clear from references in Evliya Çelebi and in Chatzis Kalphas (17th century A.D.) that Kastoria was the *hass* of the sultana Fatma and that it formed a *kazas* worth 150 aspra, with 110 villages in its territory. Also that there were 20 districts - 16 Greek, 3 Turkish and 1 Jewish - outside the fortress, with about 2,500 houses, around 100 shops and narrow streets. An elegant description of the city has been left by Pouqueville at the beginning of the 19th century A.D., and Colonel Leake recorded his recollections of his visit, also adding information about the antiquities of Kastoria and the occupations of the inhabitants. Until as late as the 19th century, the migrants from Kastoria who grew wealthy in Vienna, Odessos and Constantinople and the interior of the empire, built lavishly decorated *archontika* (mansions) and adorned their churches with wood-carved iconostaseis, pulpits and candelabra: P. Emmanuel, Papaterpos, Nantzis and Tsiatsapas.

At the turn of the 18th to the 19th centuries, the rich and commercially powerful "Hellenoupolis" of the north, as it was called by the German geographer L. Schultze Jena at the beginning of the 20th century, breathed in the principles of the French Revolution and, like its expatriated children, dreamed the visions of Rhigas Pheraios. Having become an initiate, it in turn initiated the warriors of the uprising. It offered its own martyrs, laymen and clerics alike, on the altar of the Great Idea. From behind its moral defences, it resisted pressure, and offered a refuge to warriors and money for the common cause.

Pinned down, however, at a transit point of the armies, it was unable to make any practical contribution during the uprising on Olympos and Vermion (A.D. 1822). It resisted Slav expansionism, however, and avoided the embrace of the Bulgarian exarchate, created after the Crimean War. Its weapons were Greek letters -which in-

crescent of the East (the Ottomans) and the hand of God was withdrawn from Thessalonike, the great Evrenos bey captured Kastoria, too, with Turkish soldiers. It had for some time been in the hands of the Albanian tyrants Stoyias and Theodore Mouzakis.

The Turkish conquest closed a chapter for the city of the beavers, the city of the "hundred churches", the "very rich" Kastoria of the Arab traveller Idrisi (12th century A.D.), a brilliant chapter illustrated by brilliant wall-paintings, by the tall, slender structures of venerable churches, with their cloisonné masonry, a chapter heavy with memories of glory and prosperity.

In the difficult centuries that followed, the

variably conquered the barbarians - and it planted trees of knowledge in schools (the brilliant educator Anastasios Picheon); its weapons were the Orthodox faith - which invariably overcame unbelievers - and it armed the hearts of its priests (the revered figure of the archbishop of Kastoria, Germanos Karavangelis). It covered the sadly lost Pavlos Melas (1904) with its soil shortly before the final confrontation. With the collapse of Turkish authority - the result of co-operation by the Balkan states against the *Sublime Porte* - it was liberated by the Greek armies (1912). The blood of the chieftain Kotas, the ink of the man of letters Athanasios Christopoulos, the lancet of Constantinos Michael and of Thomas Mendakasis, all pledged to the regeneration of the nation, could now be proud of their contribution.

THE MONUMENTS

THE WALLS

The few surviving ruins of the defence wall, in combination with the study of earlier photographs, texts and maps, show that the fortification of Kastoria was preserved almost unchanged from the time of Justinian I, with only a few additions here and there. The fortification is elliptical/rectangular in shape with a section closing off the neck of the peninsula on which the city was (and is) built, and its two parallel arms run along the banks of the lake, embrace the acropolis and enclosing at the tower of Koumbelidiki.

THE BYZANTINE CHURCHES

The development of Byzantine painting from the 10th to the 18th century A.D. can be studied almost without break in the churches of Kastoria. These churches are all built in roughly the same style, being three-aisled or aisleless basilicas vaulted or with pitched roofs, and usually with the central aisle raised and cloisonné masonry on the exterior to which decorative brick-work was added, and were private churches erected

558. Part of Justinian's defence wall, preserved in the market place of Kastoria.

558

by distinguished exiled officials of the court at Constantinople. They frequently also contained the tombs of their donors.

The Anargyroi

The church of the Anargyroi, in the type of a three-aisled basilica with the central aisle, elevated to a different level, and the narthex at the west, is dated by the earlier layers of wall-paintings to the beginning of the 10th century A.D. Later interventions date from the 12th century A.D. Amongst the finest examples of the painted decoration of the church may be counted the "Lamentation" on the north wall - a composition that was a precursor of the western theme of the Pieta.

Saint Stephanos

A three-aisled basilica with a narthex, an elevated central aisle and a womens' gallery *(gynaikonites)* on a sort of second floor, the church of Saint Stephanos is dated to the transition from the 9th to the 10th centuries A.D. by the - severely damaged - compositions in the first layer of wall-paintings, and received a series of modifications in later centuries (12th to 13th centuries).

Taxiarches Metropoleos

Dedicated to the Archangel Michael, this three-aisled church is one of the earliest examples of its kind from the 10th century A.D. The later wall-paintings of the monument, however, date from the years of the occupation of the city by the Serb kral Stephen Dušan (A.D. 1359/1360); these compositions are clearly Byzantine and typical of the artistic currents of the period.

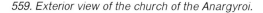

559. Exterior view of the church of the Anargyroi.

560. Exterior view of the church of Saint Stephanos.

561. Exterior view of the church of the Taxiarches Metropoleos.

Saint Nikolaos Kasnitzes

The simple aisleless church of Saint Nikolaos - known also as Kasnitzes, after its builder, who was presumably also called Nikolaos, like the patron saint of the church - has some outstanding wall-paintings and is an important point of reference for 12th century Byzantine painting.

562

563

Panayia Koumbelidiki

The church of the Panayia, known also as the "Koumbelidiki" from the unusually tall dome at the centre (*koumbes* = dome in Turkish) - the only example in the ecclesiastical architecture of Kastoria - is a small tricoch church in which can be traced the development of Byzantine painting during the 13th century A.D. The wall-paintings executed on the outer west wall date from the 15th century A.D., while those in the exonarthex are works of the 17th century A.D.

Panayia Mavriotissa

The katholikon of the monastery of the Panayia Mavriotissa, in an idyllic location at the edge of the lake of Kastoria, just outside the city, is a structure of the 12th century A.D. that illustrates the principles of monasticism through the austerity of its wall-paintings, the metaphysical content of subjects in the compositions and the dark colours.

Saint Ioannis the Theologian

The parietal decoration of the church of Saint Ioannis the Threologian, close by the Panayia Mavriotissa, is typical of the wall-paintings of the middle of the 16th century A.D. (1552), which continued the local tradition in the post-Byzantine period, and introduces the visitor to the chapter of ecclesiastical painting under the Ottoman occupation.

562. Exterior view of the church of Saint Nikolaos Kasnitzes.

563. Exterior view of the church of the Panayia Koumbelidiki.

564. The archangel Gabriel kneeling before the Virgin (part of the Platytera). 12th century wall-painting from the aisleless church of Saint Nikolaos Kasnitzes.

565. "Christ commanding the winds", wall-painting from the chapel of Saint Ioannis the Theologian in the Mavriotissa Monastery.

566. The Dormition of the Virgin. Wall-painting from the church of Saint Nikolaos Kasnitzes.

564

565

566

THE ARCHONTIKA (MANSIONS)

The wealthy mansions of Kastoria - the *ar-chontarikia* - stand firm on the local rock in a stepped arrangement, gazing from on high over the lake. Eminent two- and three-storey structures, built in rows (terraces) or as individual buildings, with gardens behind stone fences, some of them abandoned to the indifference of time, others to the lack of compassion and ignorance of men, and others - fortunately - to the care of the state and individual citizens, they are all incontrovertible witnesses to the wealth that flowed into the city of the beavers from its inhabitants' preoccupation with fur-making.

Built in the type of the Macedonian/Balkan house, the archontika of the Emmanuel brothers (who fought the struggle alongside Rhigas Pheraios), of Moralis-Tsiatsapas (1754), Vasdekas (1728) Pavlis-Menozias-Aivazis, Kyr Giannakis-Nantzis (1796), Sapountzis, Bassaras and others, all exhibit the basic architectural and decorative elements characteristic of the buildings like them at Siatista, Kozani, Beroia, Ochrid, Valsa, Perlepes and elsewhere, adapted to the needs of the site and the customs of the local inhabitants: an interior courtyard with open and semi-open ancillary rooms, a solid stone-built ground floor and mezzanine, a first and second floor with a plastered *tsatmas* (mud mortar), barred windows, enclosed balconies *(sachnisia)*, timbered rooms with coloured fanlights, cupboards *(mousandres)*, hearths, *doxata* (raised platforms), beds and lavishly adorned ceilings.

Formerly in harmonious dialogue with the environment, introspective but loquacious, the *archontika* of Kastoria are today speechless, with the yearnings of the lake in every fissure, stubbornly resisting the expropriation of memory. Countering oblivion with their aged bodies. Against the cold wind of a "progress" of suspect aspirations they bring to bear the warmth of history and humanity.

567

567. The mansion of the Emmanuel brothers.

568. The kalos ontas (sitting room) of the mansion of Nerantzis Aivazis.

569. Ontas (room) at Kastoria.

570. The mansion of Nerantzis Aivazis, now the home of the Folklore Museum.

571a. Detail of the decoration of the kalos ontas (reception room) on the first floor of the Aivazis mansion at Kastoria.

571b. Detail of the decoration of the kalos ontas (reception room) on the first floor of the Aivazis mansion at Kastoria.

572. Wall-painting with a view of Constantinople in the kalos ontas (sitting room) of the mansion of Nerantzis Aivazis.

571α

571β

572

THE BYZANTINE MUSEUM

573

In a prominent, privileged location , the newly built Museum of Kastoria is devoted to Byzantine art, with its finds -exclusively icons of high quality - accompanying the numerous religious architectural monuments scattered throughout the length and breadth of the city of Kastoria. A gallery is planned for the prehistoric (Dispelio), Classical-Hellenistic and Roman (funerary stelai from Archangelos, near Ayia Anna in Nestorio, and Pentavryso) antiquities from Orestis.

575

574

573. *The Virgin Hodegetria (front of a two-sided icon). 16th century B.C. Kastoria, Byzantine Museum.*

574. *The Akra Tapeinosis (back of the same two-sided icon). Beginning of the 15th century. Kastoria, Byzantine Museum.*

575. *The prophet Elijah, a typical work of the late Komnenian period. 1180-1200. Kastoria, Byzantine Museum.*

576. *The Dormition of the Virgin. Third quarter of the 14th century. Kastoria, Byzantine Museum.*

576

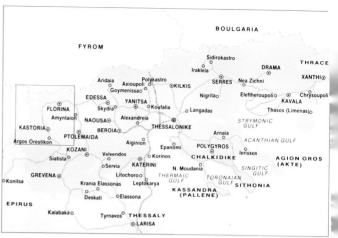

THE PRESPES LAKES
and their region

577

HISTORICAL REVIEW - ANCIENT AND CHRISTIAN MONUMENTS

The setting and the rising of the sun in this westernmost corner of Upper Macedonia are reflected eerily in the leaden waters of Great *(Megali)* and Lesser *(Mikri)* Prespa, through the reeds and aquatic plants that strangle the banks and conceal the flat-bottomed boats of the few inhabitants of the region - hermits living on the fringes of earthly alignments, of the borders today separating the three nations Albania, the former Yugoslavia and Greece.

The area is accessible only through three passes-defiles (one at Pisoderi, the second at Krystallopigi and the third to Monastir/Bitola) suffers a severe isolation, by the massifs of Barnous and Bernos, has the allure of a virgin nature bequeathed to it by the forgetfulness of men.

The region of Prespes, part of Orestis, possessed of interesting finds from prehistoric times and from the Early Iron Age, the remains of settlements from the Late Hellenistic period (possibly the town of Lyke on the small island of Ayios Achillios, which is identified by an inscription), and above all a dozen ecclesiastical foundations dating from the 11th to the 19th centuries A.D., some grandiose and monumental in scale standing on eminent plateaux, and others smaller, humble and other worldly, clinging like stone dove-cotes to the rocks on the banks of rivers, walks in the shadow of time with time in its hands.

577. View of the Prespa region

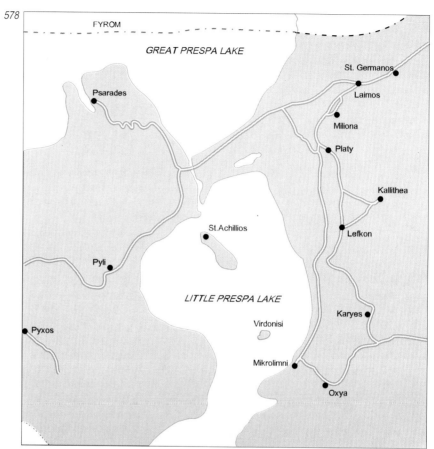

578. Map of the Prespa region.

579. The basilica of Saint Achillios, interior.

Churches of Orthodox Christianity, yellowing pages from a book of Byzantine and post-Byzantine art and architecture, from the period when the region was under the sway of the Bulgarian tzar Samuel (end of the 10th-beginning of the 11th centuries A.D.: basilica of Saint Achillios, in which the tomb of this king lies), when the Byzantine troops of Basil II the Burgar Slayer were proclaiming the glory of the empire, fortifying the land along the lakes with powerful forts, from the time of Michael VIII Palaiologos and his son Andronikos II (scete of the Transfiguration on Great Prespa, 13th century A.D., Saint Nikolaos at Pyli, 13th-14th centuries A.D.), from the period when the family of the Dragasedes (Palaiologoi), which supplied the last emperor of Byzantium, Constantine XI, a martyr equal in rank to the apostles, dominated the valley (scete of the Panayia Eleousa on Great Prespa, beginning of the 15th century A.D.) down to their subjection to the Turks and liberation in 1912 (Saint Georgios on the small island of Ayios Achillios, end of the 15th century A.D., scete of the Small Ascension on Great Prespa, 15th century A.D., scete of the Presentation in the Temple at Laimos, 15th to 16th centuries A.D., Monastery of the Panayia Porphyra, first phase A.D. 1524, church of Saint Nikolaos at Platy, 1591, church of Saint Athanasios at Ayios Germanos, 1816, church of the Ascension at Karyes, 1883, church of Saint Paraskeve at Pyxos, 1899, church of Saint Athanasios at Mikrolimni, 1908).

The setting and the rising of the moon in this westernmost corner of Upper Macedonia have for centuries now painted the deep waters of *Megali* and *Mikri* Prespa with the same smoky-silver brush, have painted with a nostalgic longing for the past all the grass-covered walls left behind by time in his passage, all the wall-paintings preserved by the durability of their materials. The setting and rising which in this land have forgotten their age.

580

581

582

580. The church of Saint Porphyra on the island of Ayios Achillios.

581. The church of Saint Paraskeve in the village of Pyxos.

582. The church of Saint Athanasios in the village of Mikrolimni.

583. Saint Spyridon. 19th century wall-painting from the church of Saint Athanasios in the village of Oxya.

584. Saint Vikentios. Wall-painting dating from 1743 from the church of Saint Germanos.

585. The Last Supper. Wall-painting dating from 1591, from the church of Saint Nikolaos (Saint Soteira) at Platy.

586. The Dormition of the Virgin. Wall-painting dating from 1410, from the small church of the Panayia Eleousa.

586

BIBLIOGRAPHY

Hammond, N. G. L., *A History of Macedonia I* (Oxford, 1972).
Hammond, N. G. L., Griffith, G. T., *A History of Macedonia II* (Oxford, 1979).
Hammond, N. G. L., Walbank, F. W., *A History of Macedonia III* (Oxford, 1988).
Papazoglou, F., *Les villes de Macédoine à l' époque romaine*, BCH Suppl. XVI, 1988.
Lazaridis, D., *Φίλιπποι – Ρωμαϊκή Αποικία (Αρχαίες ελληνικές πόλεις 20, 1973)*.
Kalleris, J. N., *Les Anciens Macédoniens I* (Athens, 1954), *II* (Athens, 1976).
Vacalopoulos, A., *Ιστορία της Μακεδονίας 1354-1833* (Thessalonike, 1969).
Theocharidis, G., *Ιστορία της Μακεδονίας κατά τους Μέσους Χρόνους 285-1354* (Thessalonike, 1980).
Will, E., Mossé, C., Goulowsky, P., *Le monde Grec et l' Orient, II* (Le IVe siècle et l' époque hellénistique) (Paris, 1985²).
Dimitriadis, V., *Τοπογραφία της Θεσσαλονίκης κατά την εποχή της Τουρκοκρατίας (1430-1912)* (Thessalonike, 1983).
G. Chionidis, *Ιστορία της Βέροιας (της πόλεως και της περιοχής)* (Beroia 1960).

Aslanis, I., *Η Προϊστορία της Μακεδονίας. Ι. Η Νεολιθική Εποχή* (Athens, 1992).
Grammenos, D., *Νεολιθικές Έρευνες στην Κεντρική και Ανατολική Μακεδονία* (Athens, 1991).
ΚΕΡΝΟΣ, Τιμητικός τόμος για τον καθ. Γ. Μπακαλάκη (Thessalonike, 1972).
Ancient Macedonia I (1970). II (1977). III (1983). IV (1986). V (1993).
Ancient Macedonia (Catalogue of an Exhibition in Australia/Melbourne, Brisbane, Sydney) (Athens, 1988).
Egnatia 1, 1989. *2*, 1990.
Το Αρχαιολογικό Έργο στη Μακεδονία και Θράκη 1 (1988). 2 (1991). 3 (1992). 4 (1993). 5 (1994).
Treasures of Ancient Macedonia (Catalogue of an Exhibition in the Archaeological Museum of Thessalonike), (Athens, 1979).
Ιστορία του Ελληνικού Έθνους (Ekdotike Athenon).
Alexander the Great. History and Legend in Art (Catalogue of an Exhibition in the Archaeological Museum of Thessalonike) (Athens, 1980).
Μνήμη Δ. Λαζαρίδη. Πόλις και Χώρα στην Αρχαία Μακεδονία και Θράκη (Athens, 1990).
La Civilisation Grecque. Macédoine Royaume d' Alexandre le Grand (Catalogue of an Exhibition in Canada) (Athens, 1993).

ΜΑΚΕΔΟΝΙΑ. 4000 years of Greek History and Civilization (Athens, 1982).
Macedonia from the Mycenaean Period to Alexander the Great (Catalogue of an Exhibition in the Archaeological Museum of Thessalonike and in Bologna) (Athens, 1988).
Macedonia and Greece in Late Classical and Early Hellenistic Times, Studies in the History of Art 10, 1982.
Thessalonike. From the Prehistoric period to Christian Times (Guide to an Exhibition in the Archaeological Museum of Thessalonike) (Athens, 1986).

Οι Αρχαιολόγοι μιλούν για την Πιερία 1 (1985). 2 (1986). 3 (1990).
Sindos. Exhibition Catalogue (Athens, 1985).
The Search for Alexander. An Exhibition (Washington, 1980).
Treasures of Ancient Macedonia (Athens, 1979).
Macedonia from Philip II to the Roman Conquest (Ekdotike Athenon, Athens, 1993).

ΑΜΗΤΟΣ. Τιμητικός τόμος για τον καθηγητή Μ. Ανδρόνικο (Thessalonike, 1987).
Θεσσαλονίκη. Ιστορία και Τέχνη (Έκθεση Λευκού Πύργου) (Thessalonike, 1986).
Η Θεσσαλονίκη και τα Μνημεία της (Thessalonike, 1985).
Hoepfner, W., Schwandner, L., *Haus und Stadt im Klassischen Griechenland* (Munich, 1986).

Miller, St. G., *The Tomb of Lyson and Kallikles* (Mainz, 1992).
Miller, St. G., *Hellenistic Macedonian Architecture. Its Style and Painted Ornamentation* (Bryn Mawr, 1971).
Gossel, B., *Makedonische Kammergräber*, (Berlin, 1980).
Rhomiopoulou, K., *A New Monumental Chamber Tomb with Paintings of the Hellenistic Period Near Lefkadia*, West Macedonia, AAA VI, 1973, 87-92.
Drougou, St., Touratsoglou, I., *Ελληνιστικοί Λαξευτοί Τάφοι Βεροίας* (Athens, 1980).
Andronikos, M., *Βεργίνα: οι βασιλικοί τάφοι και οι άλλες αρχαιότητες* (Athens, 1984).
Andronikos, M., *Βεργίνα Ι. Το Νεκροταφείον των τύμβων* (Athens, 1969).
Lilimbaki-Akamati, M., *Λαξευτοί θαλαμωτοί τάφοι της Πέλλας* (Thessalonike, 1987).
Petsas, Ph. M., *Ο τάφος των Λευκαδίων* (Athens, 1966).
Rhomaios, K. A., *Ο Μακεδονικός Τάφος της Βεργίνας* (Athens, 1951).
Saatsoglou-Paliadeli, Ch., *Τα επιτάφια μνημεία από τη Μεγάλη Τούμπα της Βεργίνας* (Thessalonike, 1984).
Touratsoglou, I., *Λευκάδια* (Οδηγοί ΚΕΡΑΜΟΣ) (Athens, 1973).
Lazaridis, D., Rhomiopoulou, K., Touratsoglou, I., *Ο Τύμβος της Νικήσιανης* (Athens, 1992).
Vokotopoulou, I., *Οι Ταφικοί Τύμβοι της Αίνειας* (Athens, 1990).

Brixhe, C., Panayotou, A., *L' atticisation de la Macédoine: l' une des sources de la Koiné*, Verbum 11, 1988, 245-260.
Panayotou, A., *Des dialectes à la Koiné: l' exemple de la Chalcidique*, ΠΟΙΚΙΛΑ (ΜΕΛΕΤΗΜΑΤΑ 10) (Athens, 1990, 191-228).

Gaebler, H., *Die antiken Münzen Nord-Griechenlands III²*. Die antiken Münzen von Makedonia und Paionia, (Berlin, 1936).
Le Rider, G., *Le monnayage d' argent et d' or de Philippe II* (Paris, 1977).
Price, M. J., *The Coinage in the Name of Alexander the Great and Philip Arrhidaeus*, (London, 1991).
Touratsoglou, I., *Die Münzstatte von Thessaloniki in der römischen Kaiserzeit 32/31 v. Chr.-268 n. Chr.* (Berlin, 1988).

Kremmydi, S., *Η Νομισματοκοπία της Ρωμαϊκής Αποικίας του Δίου* (Thessalonike, 1993).

Edson, Ch., *Inscriptiones Graecae IX, 2.1* (Thessalonicae et viciniae), (Berlin, 1972).

Rizakis, Th., Touratsoglou, I., *Επιγραφές Άνω Μακεδονίας* (Athens, 1985).

Akamati, M., Veleni, P., *Νομός Φλώρινας, από τα Προϊστορικά στα Ρωμαϊκά Χρόνια* (Greek Ministry of Culture, 1987).

Karamitrou-Mentessidi, G., *Αιανή Κοζάνης, Αρχαιολογικός Οδηγός* (Thessalonike, 1989).

Karamitrou-Mentessidi, G., *Κοζάνη, Πόλη Ελιμιώτιδος, Αρχαιολογικός Οδηγός* (Thessalonike, 1993).

Lazaridis, D., *Νεάπολις, Χριστούπολις, Καβάλα. Οδηγός Μουσείου Καβάλας* (Athens, 1989).

Makaronas, Ch., I., Giouri, E., *Οι οικίες Αρπαγής της Ελένης και Διονύσου της Πέλλας* (Athens, 1989).

Pandermalis, D., *ΔΙΟΝ, Αρχαιολογικό Μουσείο και Αρχαιολογικός Χώρος*.

Siambanopoulos, K., *Ιστορικό-Λαογραφικό Μουσείο Κοζάνης* (Society of Letters and Arts of the County of Kozani), (Kozani, 1992).

Chrysostomou, P., *Τα Γιαννιτσά και η περιοχή τους*, (XVII Ephorate of Prehistoric and Classical Antiquities, 1992).

Tsigaridas, E., *Μονή Λατόμου (Όσιος Δαβίδ)* (Thessalonike, 1987).

Tsitouridou, A., *Η Παναγία των Χαλκέων* (Thessalonike, 1985).

Makaronas, Ch., *Η "Καμάρα", Το θριαμβικό τόξο του Γαλερίου στη Θεσσαλονίκη* (Thessalonike, 1969).

Bakirtzis, Ch., *Η βασιλική του Αγίου Δημητρίου* (Thessalonike, 1986).

Mavropoulou-Tsioumi, Chr., *The Church of St. Nicholas Orphanos*, (Thessalonike, 1986).

Gounaris, G., *The Walls of Thessaloniki* (Thessalonike, 1982).

Pazaras, Th., *Η Ροτόντα του Αγίου Γεωργίου στη Θεσσαλονίκη* (Thessalonike, 1985).

Zikos, N., *Αμφίπολις. Παλαιοχριστιανική και βυζαντινή Αμφίπολις* (Athens, 1989).

Mavropoulou-Tsioumi, Chr., *Μονή Βλατάδων* (Thessalonike, 1987).

Nikonanos, N., *Οι Άγιοι Απόστολοι Θεσσαλονίκης* (Thessalonike, 1986).

Evyenidou, D., Kanonidis, I., Papazotos, T., *The Monuments of Prespa*, (Athens, 1991).

Tsigaridas, E., *Christian Halkidiki* (Ministry of Culture, 10th Ephorate of Byzantine Antiquities, 1992).

Vera Bitrakova Grozdanova, *Monuments de l' époque hellénistique dans la R. S. de Macédoine,* (Skopje, 1987).

Guide de Thasos (Ecole Française d'Athènes) (1967).

Οδηγός Θάσου (Γαλλική Αρχαιολογική Σχολή Αθηνών) (1974).

Lazaridis, D., *Οι Φίλιπποι* (Thessalonike, 1956).

Xyngopoulos, A., *Έρευναι εις τα βυζαντινά μνημεία των Σερρών* (Thessalonike, 1965).

Xyngopoulos, A., *Τα μνημεία των Σερβίων* (Athens, 1957).

A. B. Tataki, "Ancient Beroia Prosopography and Society", *Ποικίλα (Μελετήματα 8)* (Athens, 1988).

ACKNOWLEDGEMENTS

Ekdotike Athenon wishes to thank all those who have assisted in the preparation of this Guide. In particular, thanks are due to the Ephorates of Prehistorical, Classical and Byzantine Antiquities of Macedonia and to the Philosophical School of the University of Thessalonike, who have supplied information, permits to photograph monuments and objects on display in Macedonian Museums, and to publish drawings and plans of archaeological sites and restored monuments, and whose general assistance has been invaluable. Ekdotike Athenon also thanks the Numismatic Museum of Athens, the Numismatic Collection of the Credit Bank, Athens, and the Archaeological Receipts and Expropriations Fund, for making slides available.

We are also grateful to the Museums, Collections and photographers outside Greece who have co-operated on the illustration of the Guide by providing additional slides, in particular:

– Staatiche Museen Preußischer Kulturbesitz-Münzkabinett, Berlin.
  © bpk, Foto Rosa Mai: fig. 429.
– Musée du Louvre, Paris. © Photo R.M.N.: fig. 107, 108, 109, 320.
– Staatliche Antikensammlungen und Glyptothek, München. Foto
  Chr. Koppermann: fig. 203.
– Dumbarton Oaks, Trustees of Harvard University, Washington D.C.
  © 1994: fig. 97.
– Artephot, Paris. Photo A. Held: fig. 56.

FYROM

L. DO

Skra
Eidomeni
Evzoni

Mt. Boras
Foustani
ALMOPIA
Axioupoli
Polykastro
Aridaia
Mt. Paikon
Goymenissa
Gyna

Apsalos
Europos

Axios

EDESSA
YANITSA
Koufalia
Skydra
PELLA

L. MEGALE PRESPA
Niki

Psarades
Meliti

Mt. Barnous
L. BEGORRITIS
Lefkadia
Krya Vrysi
L. MIKRE PRESPA
Pisoderi
FLORINA
KELLE
L. PETRON
MIEZA
NAOUSA
Chariessa
Alexandreia

Melas
3 Pigadia
Xino Nero
Amyntaion

ALBANIA
Krystallopigi

Mt. Bernon
L. HEIMADITIS
Seli
Mt. Bermion
BEROIA

KASTORIA
L. KASTORIA
Kleisoura
Meliki

Korisos
PTOLEMAIDA
Vergina
AIGEAI
Kolindros
Aiginion

Argos Orestikon
Kastania
Soumela Mon.
Touzla
Nea M

Nestorio
Vogatsiko

Mt. Askion
Methone

Mt. Grammos
Eratyra
Pieria Mts.
Kitros
PYDNA

Mt. Boion
Neapoli
KOZANI
Haliakmon
KATERINI
Korinos

Eptachori
Tsotyli
Siatista
Velvendos

Pyrsogianni
Ag. Dimitrios
DION

Pentalofos
Aiane
Servia
Livadi
Litochoro
Plaka

Mt. Smolikas
AIANE
Mt. Olympos
Leibethra
Leptokarya

Konitsa
GREVENA
Sarantaporo
Karya
Skotina
Platamonas

Haliakmon

ZAGORIA
Deskati
Krania Elassonas

Elassona

Peneios
Ampelakia

EPIRUS
Kalabaka
Tyrnavos

THESSALY
LARISA

TH

459

BOULGARIA

Exochi
Skaloti

Promachonas
Kato Nevrokopi
Volakas

Mt. Kerkine
N. Petritsi
SINTIKE
Mt. Vrontou
Vrontou
Mt. Falakron
Paranesti

Poroia
Mt. Menoikion
THRACE

Sidirokastro
Prosotsani
DRAMA

L. KERKINE
Irakleia
Doxato
Mt. Lekane
XANTHI

Efkarpia
SERRES
Em. Pappas
Alistrati
Fotolivos
PHILIPPOI

Strymoniko
Nea Zichni
Krenides
Chrysoupoli

KILKIS
Gazoros
Strymon
Eikosifoinissis Mon.
KAVALA
(NEAPOLIS)

Lachanas
Rodolivos
Nikissiani
Mt. Pangaion
Eleftheroupoli

Vertiskos
Nigrita
N. Peramos
Ammodis cape
Keramoti

Asseros
Mt. Bertiskos
Sochos
AMPHIPOLIS
Vrasidas cape

Langadas
Mt. Kerdylion
N. Kerdylia
Amfipoli
THASOS
Thasos (Limenas)

Lete
(Derveni)
Arethousa
Asprovalta
Loutra Eleftheron
Prinos

L. KORONEIA
Stavros
STRYMONIC GULF
Potamia

ONIKE
Mt. Kissos
(Chortiatis)
L. BOLBE
Rentina
Kallirrachi
Koinyra

Therme
N. Apollonia
KALINDOIA
N. Madytos
Olympias
Marmari cape
Limenaria

Mikra
Zangliveri
Mt. Cholomon
STAGEIRA
Stratonike
Salonikos cape
Stavros cape

Peraia
Souroti
Galatista
Stageira
Stratoni
ACANTHIAN GULF

nomi
ANTHEMOUS
Vavdos
Arnaia
Arapis cape

Petralona
Cave
POLYGYROS
Ierissos
Ag. Theodoroi cape
ESPHIGMENOU

nis cape
Nea Roda
Ouranoupoli
CHILANDARI

Nea Kallikrateia
Nea Triglia
OLYNTHOS
Ormylia
Arkouda cape
Arkoudi cape
ZOGRAFOU
VATOPEDI

CHALKIDIKE
Ag. Nikolaos
AMMOULIANE
Konstamonitou
PANTOKRATOROS

N. Moudania
Agios Mamas
Nikitas
DIAPOROS
DOCHEIARIOU
XENOPHONTOS
Karyes
STAVRONIKITA
KOUTLOUMOUSIOU

Nea Potidaia
TORONAIAN
Vourvourou
SINGITIC
AG. PANTELEIMONOS
XEROPOTAMOU
IVERON
KARAKALOU

AIC GULF
POTIDAIA
(KASSANDREIA)
Nea Fokaia
GULF
GULF
Dafni
SIMONOPETRA
PHILOTHEOU

Pyrgos cape
ARHYTIS
Afytos
Neos Marmaras
Rigas cape
Sarti
GREGORIOU
AG. DIONYSIOU
GREAT LAVRAS

KASSANDRA
(PALLENE)
Kallithea
SITHONIA
Sykias cape
S. PAUL'S
Akrathos cape

MENDE
Porto Carras
Sykia
Pinnes cape (Nymphaion)
AGION OROS (AKTE)

Poseidi
Pefkohori
TORONE
Kalamitsi

Kassandras cape
SKIONE
Koufos
Drepano cape (Ampelos)

Paliouri

Paliouri cape
(Kanastraion)

ΥΠΟΥΡΓΕΙΟ ΠΟΛΙΤΙΣΜΟΥ

Ε

567 52820

ΤΑΜΕΙΟ ΑΡΧΑΙΟΛΟΓΙΚΩΝ ΠΟΡΩΝ

ΤΑΠ